# Jubilee Kumar

Seema Sonik Alimchand has been a flight attendant, a voice professional, a presenter and copywriter for television, radio and other media. The daughter of noted music composer Master Sonik of the Sonik-Omi duo, Seema developed an interest in the Indian film industry from an early age. She is the author, presenter and producer of the popular album *100 Years of Hindi Film Music*, and the author of the biographies of superstars Rajinikanth (*The Warrior Within*) and Dara Singh (*Deedara aka Dara Singh*). Her forthcoming works include a historical novel, *Monsoon Earth*, a series for young adults and two theatrical productions.

**Praise for the book**

'An engrossing work which reveals the man behind a superstar whose films often reflected the social trends of a country that had just begun to find its voice.' – *Telegraph*

'Works both to introduce Rajendra Kumar to those who did not know him and to represent him in a new light for even his most ardent fans.' – *Cinestaan*

'More than worth a read as it recreates the aura and charm of a time when an unlikely star became the biggest box office phenomenon but never really made a big deal of it.' – *Firstpost*

'A telling account of Rajendra Kumar's coming to grip over his waning career, the progression brought about by age, the dwindling crowd of admirers and the problem of reinventing himself.' – *Tribune*

# Jubilee Kumar

*The Life and Times of a Superstar*

SEEMA SONIK ALIMCHAND

hachette INDIA

First published in hardback in India in 2020 by Hachette India
(Registered name: Hachette Book Publishing India Pvt. Ltd)
An Hachette UK company
www.hachetteindia.com

This edition published in 2021

SRD



All images except for those specifically credited to their sources are courtesy the personal collection of the Estate of Rajendra Kumar Tuli. For images from *Mayapuri* magazine, special thanks to P.K. Bajaj and Aman Bajaj for their support.



Hardback edition ISBN 978-93-88322-39-3
Paperback edition ISBN 978-93-91028-14-5
Ebook edition ISBN 978-93-88322-40-9

Hachette Book Publishing India Pvt. Ltd
4th/5th Floors, Corporate Centre,
Plot No. 94, Sector 44, Gurugram 122003, India

Typeset in Minion Pro 11/15
by InoSoft Systems, Noida

Printed and bound in India
by Manipal Technologies Limited, Manipal

MIX
Paper from responsible sources
FSC™ C043100

In loving memory of our father,
the legendary Rajendra Kumar

*Kumar Gaurav*
*Dimple Kumar Patel*
*Kaajal (Tulsi) Chellaram*

*Farishtey se behtar hai insaan ban na,*
*Magar is mein lagti hai mehnat zyaada.*

It's better to be a human being than an angel,
Though it requires one to work harder.

– *Ilana Iqbal*

# Contents

# Author's Note

*Jubilee Kumar* is based on the real-life events of the legendary actor Rajendra Kumar as related to me by the actor's family. It brings together their memories of his life's events, their collection of news and interviews, their photographs, and the information they shared with me in the form of video recordings and interviews with other film personalities. I have depicted all of the above to the best of my ability, and attempted to retain the inspirational flavour and moving aspects of a great life. A few details have been changed, some events have been compressed, and some scenes and dialogues have been created for dramatic and narrative purposes. The memory has its own story to tell, but I have done my best to make it tell a truthful one.

For the opportunity to write the jubilee star's biography, I stay eternally grateful to the following people for sharing their time, memories and experiences, all of which have deeply enriched the book – Shukla Kumar Tuli, Kumar Gaurav Tuli, Dimple Kumar Patel, Kaajal (Tulsi) Chellaram, Kamla Bhandari, Virendra Tuli, Vikram Tuli, Manoj Kumar, Asha Parekh, Salim Khan, Prem Sagar, Randhir Kapoor and David Dhawan.

# Foreword

The desire to put together and publish a book about my father grew out of a need to fill the void of the twenty years I had to live through after losing him to cancer.

I have missed his presence every day since, because he touched my life and that of many others in significant ways.

His handsome features, gentlemanly manner and engaging personality (he wasn't my superhero for nothing!), along with his sincerity, his passion for hard work and his ability to emote on screen, made him a legend of Indian cinema in the 1960s and 1970s.

Born into an affluent family in what is now Pakistan, my father enjoyed an idyllic and luxurious childhood, which came to a brutal end with the partition of India. Forced to flee across the newly drawn border into a life of deprivation in Delhi, he endured several hardships before an opportunity took him to Bombay (now Mumbai) and the film world, for which he had nurtured a passion all along. Unfazed by repeated rejection, my father overcame the many obstacles that were thrown his way, determined to let nothing come between him and his goal. With time, he went from being an assistant director to a star performer in films and earned the fond nickname that his audience and the industry would bestow on him – Jubilee Kumar.

In his personal life, as in his professional one, he was known for his integrity and for being a devoted husband, a loving father, and a caring son and sibling. In fact, many felt that it was his sincerity as a human being that came through on screen as well, helping him to portray the roles of lover, husband, son and brother with utmost conviction.

Despite his fame and significant contribution to India's film industry, many young people today have never heard of the jubilee star called Rajendra Kumar. Sadly enough, my own children, who are now in their twenties, have little idea of the larger-than-life personality their grandfather was and the important place he made for himself in the hearts of his many fans and admirers.

It is, therefore, from a deep sense of duty and love that I authorized the writing of this book. If the reader is able to come away from it with their spirits elevated and inspired even a little by how my father transformed his ordinary life to one of stupendous success through sheer grit and ambition, then I will know I haven't failed him as a chronicler of his life and, most importantly, as a loving daughter keen on keeping her father's memory alive.

***Dimple Rajendra Patel***

# 1

# A Narrow Escape

On an overcast August morning in 1940, the Tulis of Sialkot's Sankhatra (San-Khatra) village had left for Amarnath, travelling to Kashmir and onwards to the base camp in Pahalgam that was swarming, as pilgrimage spots invariably do, with thousands of seers, holy men, pilgrims and touts. Having reached the camp, Lakshmichand Tuli made the necessary arrangements for ponies and coolies to escort him, his wife Vidyawati and their thirteen-year-old son Rajendra up the treacherous mountain path to the shrine, before retiring for the night.

The following day, the family was awake long before sunrise. By 3 a.m., amid the chanting of Vedic hymns and the blowing of conch shells, they too had joined the congregation of devotees embarking on the tough 47 kilometre long trek into the mountains.

The actual climb began, however, once they'd crossed Chandanwari. It was freezing cold. Gloves were brought out and slipped on and winter jackets zipped up as the Tulis began the ascent. They were led by a musical band which set a rhythmic pace by beating drums as an accompaniment to the odes being sung to Lord Shiva.

The pilgrims undertaking this arduous journey – an experience of a lifetime for many of them – were further energized by their unified voices as they chanted mantras and clapped their hands to mark the beat. Occasionally, the cry of '*Bumm, bumm, bhole!*' would rend the air as the group made its way up the frozen route. At regular intervals, they would halt and cups of hot tea made the rounds, as did the food the devotees shared with each other. United in their spiritual fervour, a sense of oneness engulfed them as they snaked their way up the precariously steep trail.

Perched atop his hired pony like a prince, Rajendra Kumar Tuli gazed in fascination at the spectacular beauty of the landscape that unfolded before his eyes as his mount moved ahead at a steady trot, flanked on one side by the mountains and on the other by craggy valleys. The boy's parents walked alongside.

With darkness descending swiftly, the group of exhausted but exhilarated pilgrims broke journey for a night's halt at the Sheshnag camp, delighted with the piping hot meal of rajma chawal, aloo gobi and parathas that was served to them. They'd been trekking for more than fifteen hours. No wonder, then, that soon after dinner they were only too glad to huddle up inside the colourful tents that served as their accommodation for the night and go to sleep.

But barely had Rajendra shut his eyes than his mother shook him awake.

'I just went to sleep, Ma!' he mumbled in protest, rubbing his eyes, but then realized that all around him their fellow devotees were shaking out their mattresses and folding them up neatly.

Stretching, he stepped out into the pre-dawn darkness. *Is it morning or night*, he wondered, looking up at the sky from where a radiant silver full moon beamed down at him.

An hour later, the devotees were setting out again for the next leg of their journey.

They reached their destination at 3 p.m., following a mid-noon halt at the Panjtarni camp.

Surrounded by ice-capped mountains, the glacial Amarnath Cave where the shrine was located was engulfed in snow. Although the sun had risen by then and was shining brightly down on them, it was bitterly cold. But not enough, it seemed, to deter the devotees from taking the mandatory bath before queueing up for the darshan to pay obeisance to the stalagmite that symbolized the Shivalinga.

Not long afterwards, it was night-time again. Lying asleep beside his mother, Rajendra was awakened for a moment by what he thought was the sound of thunder. Too exhausted to investigate this further, he snuggled deeper into his comforter and fell asleep.

A surreal surprise awaited him when he woke up the next morning. Stray snowflakes drifted down from a dark sky, lasting for mere seconds before they melted. Almost as soon as they had petered out, a coppery sliver of sunlight arched its way across the mountains. But by the time the pilgrims were ready for the descent, clouds had begun to gather in the sky, with sparse rays of hazy sunlight peeping through them.

Braving the risk of an unseasonal blizzard sweeping across the terrain, the pilgrims set out on their return journey. Fortunately, the rains held off for most of the trek back to Pahalgam, but as they neared base camp, the temperature suddenly plunged to below zero and an ominous darkness descended on the trekkers. In the very next instant, a moisture-saturated cloud burst open, pelting them with icy rain. This gradually gave way to heavy snowfall. Huge hailstones seemed to shoot out from the skies, striking and instantly killing many, resulting in a panic-driven stampede. To add to the pandemonium, boulders broke off the mountains and came rolling down onto the devotees, turning the pilgrimage into a terrifying encounter with death. Many pilgrims slipped, fell and collapsed. Many others were trampled upon.

More than 250 people died on the road from Amarnath that day.

As rains continued to lash the mountains, despair overwhelmed the survivors. Several families were forced to leave behind the bodies of accompanying relatives who had slipped on the rock-strewn path and fallen to their deaths below.

Shielded by his resilient father, who hurried him to the base camp along with the other traumatized survivors, Rajendra had managed to escape the wrath of nature. His mother, however, couldn't be found anywhere. A distraught Lakshmichand decided to first settle his son in a safe place before going out to look for his missing wife. As one of the few pilgrims who had money on him, Lakshmichand forked out what was then a princely sum of ₹50 for a small tent with barely enough space to accommodate two people. But at least it was equipped with a coal stove. Lakshmichand sighed wearily, settling the sobbing boy close to the warmth of the stove.

'Stop crying!' he scolded. 'I am going to look for your Ma. You stay right here, do you hear me? Don't venture out. I'll be back soon.'

Outside, chaos reigned. Many of the canvas tents had collapsed under the weight of the snow and rain, leaving the devotees shivering under their wet blankets. The cruel cold had taken a severe toll on the hapless pilgrims; burst blood vessels had sent many into shock and several of the men and women had died of exhaustion and exposure. All through the night, Lakshmichand searched frantically for his wife, but to no avail.

Dawn was breaking when he returned to the tent, defeated and dejected, to find his son still lying on the damp floor, sobbing disconsolately. Squatting on the ground beside him, he drew the boy into his arms and said, 'I'm sorry, son, I could not find your mother.'

Rajendra's heart sank and he stared up at his father, his large brown eyes brimming with tears.

'No!' he cried out. 'Not my Ma!'

A deep yearning to climb into his mother's lap overwhelmed him, but she was gone forever, with the many others who had perished on that ill-fated night.

By mid morning, when the blizzard had finally died down, Lakshmichand set out for the railway station, his son's hand held firmly in his. Lost in thought, the two trudged on and had just about covered a mile when one of the Kashmiri horsemen who had escorted them uphill came running after them.

'Master, please come quickly!' he said urgently. 'Your wife is in bad shape.'

On hearing his words, father and son turned around at once and made a hurried, desperate trek back to Sheshnag, where Lakshmichand found his wife shivering in the cold and delirious with grief, because she believed she had lost both her husband and her child.

'Ma!' Rajendra shrieked, racing the last few steps to leap into her open arms, clinging to her and refusing to let go.

Many years later, reminiscing about that horrifying event in their lives, film star Rajendra Kumar would say that it was 'one incident...that I can never forget; one that left a mark on my childish heart and mind. The year was 1940; I had accompanied my parents on the yatra of Amarnathji, a cave in Kashmir situated at a height of 14,000 feet.' Speaking further on the experience that had traumatized the entire family and left an indelible impression on his mind, the actor said, 'That meeting with my mother who I thought was no more is indescribable. I can't explain the joy of the moment. And she too had been weeping the entire night, as she had assumed that her husband and son were gone forever. Our meeting was like a rebirth. I learned from my experiences. These helped me in my film career too.'

# 2

# Boys Will Be Boys

I was born on 20 July 1927 into an affluent family of Sankhatra, Sialkot. I never knew what the term 'difficult times' meant. I had a luxurious lifestyle, but my childhood was a very normal one. I was the oldest of five children. My grandfather Chajhuram Tuli loved me a lot. He loved me so much that... I can't really define it. He would make me sleep beside him till I was twelve or thirteen years old. Grandfather led a disciplined life. He always had an early dinner and it was early to bed, early to rise. Being the son of the number-one man in town, I was very playful and naughty and even arrogant, at times. My pride often led me into fights with my friends, who would get hurt and bruised in the scuffle. It was then up to my poor mother to appease the angry parents with apologies and sweets for the children.

*Rajendra Kumar Tuli*

Rajendra raced home from school. He tossed his satchel onto the couch and bounded up the stairs, bursting into one of the first-floor rooms of their six-storey house. Chajhuram Tuli walked in from the veranda adjoining his spacious suite.

'Dadaji! You are back!'

With that exclamation, the strapping twelve-year-old leaped into his grandfather's strong arms.

Chajhuram Tuli was one of the wealthiest men in town. Among the first to procure a military contract in the Middle East during World War I, he had amassed a sizeable fortune. Most of the army canteens in Bahrain and a few other Gulf countries belonged to him. But he'd had to start young and virtually from scratch. His father had passed away when he was a mere child and he'd had to fend for himself by selling boiled *chana* to the labourers working on the railway-track construction site. Gradually, he had been contracted to supply clothes, jaggery, tobacco, salt and tea to the workers, and beer and hookahs to the soldiers being sent off to the battlefront during World War I. Along with Chajhuram was another young boy like him named Ghasita, who supplied mithai and other sweetmeats to the workers in the labour camps. While Ghasita would grow up to become Ghasitaram Halwai, Chajhuram became a top commissioning agent and was known as Chajhu Shah, the title of 'Shah' being awarded in those days to highly successful and influential village folk. Soon, riches began pouring in and by the time World War I ended, he had made a fortune.

With the war over, Chajhuram built a six-storey home for his family in Sankhatra, a small kasbah near Sialkot. Constructed at a cost of ₹1 lakh – an enormous sum in those days – the house had forty-two rooms and was one of its kind. Every floor in Chajhu Shah's grand mansion stood 20 feet high, the total height of the entire structure being equivalent to that of a twelve-storey building today. One of the rooms was stacked with wheat, another with rice, a third with bajra and so on, much like in a granary.

Sankhatra village had a mixed population, with around 55 per cent constituting Hindus. It was practically ruled by the Khatri clan, the Tuli Khatris being among Sialkot's richest and most influential people. Sankhatra was also known for its traders and many a trade fair was held there.

Once the Tuli family had settled in, Chajhuram set up a textile business, specializing in the Bosky fabric that became so popular with clients that he was able to expand his business by opening a second branch in Karachi. Subsequently, his son Lakshmichand, whose life of ease had hardly ever demanded even a day's work from him, was put in charge of the Sialkot trade – the textile business being right up his epicurean sleeve – while his father settled down in Karachi and managed the sale of the merchandise there. For two months every year, however, the father-and-son duo would exchange places, with Chajhuram taking over the business in Sialkot and his son handling the one in Karachi. This worked well for both men and for the two branches.

In March 1939, the tall and stately Chajhuram travelled from Karachi to his home in Sankhatra, as he had been doing for the past few years. But, as on every other visit, he could not help being dismayed by his son's extravagant lifestyle.

With a taste for the good things in life, Lakshmichand Tuli, popularly known as Lakha Shah, would entertain friends and business associates every evening in the outhouse of their vast home. Engulfed in the heady scent of jasmine flowers and perfumes imported from Arabia, his guests would enjoy his lavish hospitality, which included sumptuous meals, an endless flow of intoxicating drinks, shishas and the spectacle of courtesans singing and dancing for their pleasure.

Chajhuram Tuli, however, was a disciplinarian who even forbade the use of abusive language in his haveli. He neither smoked nor drank alcohol. He was also a strict vegetarian. Given his austere habits, his disapproval of the excesses in which his son and his friends were indulging was obvious. Whenever Chajhuram came home to Sankhatra from Karachi, he would attempt to deal with the situation firmly and bring about a change, but his efforts met with little success.

*If not my son, I can at least instil sound values in my grandchildren*, he told himself with resignation. So every evening after work, he'd freshen up, have his dinner and then retire to bed early, enthralling Rajendra with his wartime stories.

'You know, son, I admire the British for their discipline. Imagine, even their wars were fought in a systematic manner!'

'How so, Dadaji?' his grandson would ask.

'World War I was a disciplined war. It would commence at 9 a.m. daily, with the sounding of a bugle, and end at 5.30 p.m. sharp, with the blowing of a second bugle.'

'And then?'

'Then hordes of exhausted, perspiring and wounded soldiers would rush to the one place they'd waited for the whole day – my military canteen. Tossing guineas on the counter, they'd proceed to dunk their beer mugs into the drums of beer that I'd keep ready for them and drink to their heart's content.'

'I can picture the whole scene...but people fighting with people...' Rajendra mused aloud.

'Oh, yes! War happens, but with ethics in place. Those were tough times for many,' Chajhuram sighed.

'Tell me more, Dadaji,' the boy implored his grandfather.

'That's enough for today. Now go to sleep.'

'Okay! But promise me – another story tomorrow?'

'Promise,' Chajhuram mumbled, falling asleep instantly.

The weeks passed swiftly and his two months' stay in Sankhatra soon came to an end. On the eve of his departure for Karachi, Chajhuram had his dinner early and retired to his room by 8.30 p.m., with a fidgety Rajendra lying on the bed beside him, waiting for his grandfather to fall asleep.

'You are restless tonight,' Chajhuram observed. 'Don't you want to hear any stories?'

'No, Dadaji, you have to leave tomorrow. You sleep,' Rajendra insisted.

His grandfather shut his eyes and, within moments, was fast asleep.

Rajendra's concern over his grandfather getting adequate rest was, however, a ploy to conceal his real intention. He had, in fact, planned to catch the 10 o'clock show of a film with his friend Hardayal.

Earlier that afternoon, on their way back from school, Hardayal had pointed out the poster of the Punjabi film *Heer Syal* that had just released. The two friends had made up their minds right away to watch it that very night.

Now lying motionless beside his grandfather on the four-poster bed and feigning slumber, Rajendra was watchful and alert. As soon as he heard the old man's soft snores settle into a rhythmic pattern, the boy slithered out from his relaxed embrace and tiptoed to the wooden coat rack where his grandfather had hung up his white pyjamas. Rummaging through its pockets, Rajendra drew out a few coins, picked up his slippers and sneaked out of the house. The iron gate squeaked as he pulled it shut behind him and hurried off to the theatre.

Hardayal was waiting for him. Agog with excitement, the two then hastily purchased the tickets, their anticipation at its peak as they marched into the theatre.

Mission Movie had begun!

*Heer Syal*, the romantic fable starring Baby Noor Jehan, ended half an hour past midnight. The lights were out at home when Rajendra crept in. As surreptitiously as he had slipped out, he stole under the covers of his grandfather's bed, but sat up with a start when a voice muttered in the darkness, 'I've been waiting for you... Where did you run off to?'

'Dadaji!' the boy exclaimed in alarm. 'You're awake?'

'Answer my question first!' Chajhuram said sternly. 'Does your mother know of these nocturnal escapades of yours?'

'No, she doesn't,' his grandson stammered. 'But...'

'I know you went to watch a film.'

'Yes, cinema...'

'You moron!' Chajhuram thundered at his grandson. 'Instead of concentrating on your studies, you chant "cinema, cinema!" day in and day out! I'm warning you right now: mend your ways or some day you will turn into cinema!'

The old man had intended his words to be a reprimand, a message of caution. But, unbeknownst to him, they would become a prophecy for the future. Instead of curbing Rajendra's obsession with movies, his grandfather's warning merely served to fuel his yearning for this form of entertainment.

Rajendra Kumar's love for movies had been born when he was all of five in a cinema hall in Karachi where his father had taken him to watch a silent film. There in the theatre, the boy had sat in silence, enthralled by the wondrous phenomenon unfolding before him. In one corner, on a kind of lowered platform, sat a man with a tabla; in another was a musician with a harmonium. Both played their instruments in tandem, with the shadowy images enacting the drama on a fabric screen. It was a mesmerizing experience – the background score and songs, along with live sound effects produced by voice artistes that included ringing phones, train whistles, gunshots, thunder and lightning, hoofbeats, chirping birds and animal calls. Adding to the excitement were the cheers, whistles and hoots from the audience. Rajendra enjoyed the music and drama immensely. Watching three to four films a week then became a fixation of sorts, and his dreams began to contain just that one thing – cinema.

Though movies continued to serve as a catalyst and an outlet for his latent creative instincts, and his poet friend Hardayal shared his passion, Rajendra applied himself diligently to his studies.

One morning, as the two twelve-year-olds set off for their school, the madrasa, their schoolbags containing the mandatory wooden slate and Urdu textbook slung across their shoulders, Hardayal said to his friend, 'Maulvi Master is very strict. What if he finds out we bunked school yesterday?'

'Let him find out!' Rajendra challenged. 'With due respect to our teacher, no one can touch me.'

'Oh really!' his friend retorted. 'Have you forgotten the long cane he carries around school? And he definitely isn't afraid of putting it to use, regardless of a student's family status.'

'Hmm…' Rajendra mused. 'I wonder why our parents hand us over to our teachers with the permission to cane us so hard that the flesh comes off our bones. And so what if we bunk school occasionally? Both of us are the best students in class. We study hard, don't we?'

'Yes. And fight hard too,' Hardayal declared with a smirk, holding up his hands so that his friend could see the condition of his palms. 'My palms are still tingling from the punishment meted out to me last week for hitting that senior boy.'

'Oh, he deserved it,' Rajendra said, stoutly defending his friend. 'He started the fight.' He paused and said, 'Look, Hardayal, I have an idea. Whenever we get to know that Maulvi Master is angry with us, we don't attend class at all, okay? We just go watch a movie. It's that simple!'

Having come to a decision, Rajendra entered the classroom with Hardayal.

The school day progressed. After yet another brawl with his schoolmates, a muddied and bruised Rajendra, along with Hardayal, stood with his head bowed before Maulvi Ghulam Gauns Master. As the teacher's cane whipped back and forth, tanning their palms, they bore the pain silently.

From the very next day, both boys decided never to attend school again. It was their act of rebellion against the school's attempt to tame them into obedience. They'd leave their respective homes on time, as they did every morning, so that their families wouldn't notice any change in their routine. But, instead of going to school, the boys would spend the entire day in a park en route.

This continued for a week until the maulvi realized that both Rajendra and Hardayal had been absent from school for far too long. Something was certainly amiss. With growing suspicion, the teacher grilled the other students about the boys' whereabouts and many of them were only too happy to squeal.

Having heard their accounts, a furious maulvi stomped out of the classroom and rushed to the park. Eager to catch the boys red-handed, he found a spot where he would be concealed from view and began scanning the gardens. When he finally did catch sight of the two boys, however, his curiosity got the better of him and his anger dissipated. He inched forward stealthily, until he was close enough to overhear them. Hardayal was seated cross-legged on the grass, reciting Urdu verses that he had composed himself, laced though they were with the choicest of abuses. Rajendra strutted around, enacting the drama that the verses described, rendering the dialogues like a seasoned film actor.

'Rajendra! Hardayal!' the maulvi yelled, stepping out from behind the mango tree where he had been hiding.

Startled, the two boys jumped to their feet, ready to flee, but halted in their tracks when Maulvi Master warned, 'Stop! Don't you run away now!'

*We've been caught*, Rajendra thought with a sinking heart, eyeing the stick in the teacher's hand.

Strangely enough, the maulvi merely pointed to the ground with the cane, motioning the culprits to sit back down on the grass. The boys stared up at Maulvi Master towering over them.

'I had no idea that both of you were so gifted,' the maulvi began, his tone revealing no trace of sarcasm or anger, much to the surprise of his two errant students. 'Hardayal, excellent rhyming and wonderful use of the Urdu language, I must admit – but for those bad words! I believe you have it in you to evolve, some day, into an outstanding Urdu poet.' Turning to look at Rajendra, he predicted, 'And as for you, *barkhurdar*... I see an actor in you and I believe you will, some day, make a mark in cinema. But remember this: without excellence in education, success will not come to either of you easily. Devote yourself to your studies and watch your talents bloom.'

The maulvi's wise words made a profound impression on their young minds. Although films and mischief remained an integral part of their schooldays, the two friends applied themselves to their studies with greater perseverance. When the time came, both of them enrolled in Lahore's Hailey College of Commerce to complete their education.

# 3

# A World Turned Topsy-Turvy

Until then, I had been completely focussed on my education, although my love for movies hadn't diminished. With the advent of the talkies era, replete with dialogues, songs and dance, my thirst for movies increased. At the same time, I knew in my heart that films were a distant dream. The reality was the enterprising business run by my family. That is where my future lay. But then, in 1947, when I was studying in my second year at Hailey College in Lahore, the news of India's partition was broadcast. I still remember I was in a T-shirt and shorts – half-pants – Father in a pyjama–kurta and Mother in a Punjabi suit as we left our palatial home. I thought, *It is only a time bomb and nothing will happen; we will return home. If we could live under the Brits, why not under Muslim rule?* They were our brothers, after all. But a shock wave ran through the entire country.

*Rajendra Kumar Tuli*

At 4 p.m. on 3 June 1947, the then governor general and viceroy of India, Lord Louis Mountbatten, addressed the nation over the radio, announcing the historic plan for

India's independence from British rule and its partition into two nations. Following this declaration, the new State of Pakistan was born on 14 August 1947, and on 15 August India was declared an independent country, with Jawaharlal Nehru assuming the office of prime minister.

In the chaos that ensued thereafter, with the exodus of thousands of Muslims to Pakistan and the migration of countless Hindus to India, the distrust and hatred that had been simmering between the two communities for some time surfaced and violence broke out, escalating alarmingly, with little in the way of an organized police force to rein it in and maintain law and order. As the days passed, the number of migrants moving across the border from either side increased. Large numbers of Hindus, Sikhs and others left for east Punjab on the Indian side of the border – empty-handed, divested of their rights, their lands and their homes. Similarly, agitated Muslim refugees fled across the border to Pakistan. They arrived in the new land, the one they had chosen as their refuge, with tales of unspeakable atrocities and terror fanning the already raging fires of communal hatred. Migrants on both sides were angry and frustrated and thirsted for revenge.

Despite the turmoil in the rest of the country, in Rajendra Tuli's hometown, Hindus, Sikhs and Muslims had continued to live in harmony. But one morning a gathering of Sankhatra's Muslims warned the Tuli family to leave what was now Pakistani territory.

'We love and respect you like we do our own people,' they said, 'but the Muslim refugees pouring in from India are thirsting for blood. They cannot be trusted. Therefore, we're urging you to leave your home and move to India, before any harm comes to you. Our men will escort you out of town to safety. We would also advise you to not carry any valuables with you. It might endanger your lives.'

On 26 August 1947, exactly eleven days after India's independence, the dazed Tulis left their palatial home for the last time, destitute but for the clothes on their back. As Rajendra, his parents, his three younger brothers and two sisters began their journey towards the unknown, Lakshmichand Tuli couldn't help but turn around for one last look at his home. *What is happening is unreal, unbelievable*, he thought, before walking away into an uncertain future. At the back of his mind was the hope that they'd return home as soon as the furore had died down.

Dera Baba Nanak, the border town on the Indian side, was nearly 76 kilometres from Sialkot. There were thousands in the convoy that took to the mountains, moving from Pakistan on to the Dera Baba Nanak route.

As he walked along with his family, Rajendra could not erase the memory of his hometown receding from view. *And what about Dadaji*, he wondered, sorely missing his grandfather.

Reluctant to leave his homeland, Chajhuram Tuli had stayed back in Karachi. When urged to change his mind and join the exodus, he'd retorted, 'I am confident that this irrational violence, this fanaticism will cease and people will come to their senses soon!'

Now, here they were, without his grandfather. Rajendra drew a deep, shuddering breath as his eyes fell on his father, whose furrowed brow and bewildered gaze betrayed the stress of leading his family to safety and his foreboding of the horrors that might lie ahead of them. Lakshmichand had lost everything – his home, his livelihood. His years of hard work had come to naught. But the determination to survive the odds and not acknowledge defeat showed in his set jaw, although his steps seemed to falter occasionally as anxiety over the difficult and unpredictable future looming ahead seized him.

Facing an uncertain future, soaked to the skin, cold and hungry and terrified, their tears merging with the pouring rain, the Tulis, along with their fellow migrants, endured nature's fury for four days and nights as they trudged through fields and marshy terrain, through freezing, windswept mountain passes and flooded plains, across raging rivers and humid forests.

Many died of hunger, disease and exposure on the way, some felled by murderous attacks by their fellow humans from another community. *But we will make it*, Rajendra Kumar resolved, shifting the weight of his youngest brother, the two-year-old Ranjit, from one tired arm to the other.

*The sleep of the innocent*, he thought with a sigh, gazing down at the child in his arms and trudging on, but as they waded through another gushing stream, a tingling heaviness bore down on his young arms. Thankfully, the rain had stopped by then and the sun had reappeared, setting the sky ablaze. Hot and exhausted, the dispirited refugees decided to take a breather and settled down to rest on the banks of a river – the Ravi.

Rajendra Kumar perched on the edge of a rock, leaning into the waters to wet the hem of his shirt. He wiped his brother's face with the damp cloth, but the boy did not stir. He stared back at his older brother with a vacant, glassy expression.

'Ma!' Rajendra called out, his voice bordering on panic.

Hurrying over, his father shook the baby gently to rouse him and trickled drops of water into his open mouth to resuscitate him. But the child lay utterly still, unresponsive. And, moments later, his eyes closed.

'He has gone,' Rajendra's mother said in a tremulous whisper, tears welling up in her eyes. 'Lay him down in the river. It will take him to God's home.'

But Rajendra refused to obey his mother. 'No, Ma,' he said, 'I can feel his heartbeat. He is alive. As long as I can feel him breathing, I will not put him down in the river.'

'No, there is no breath, no heartbeat,' Lakshmichand declared, echoing his wife's words.

With a heavy heart, Rajendra placed his little brother under a large peepal tree on the insistence of his parents and covered him with a piece of cloth. Then the family resumed their trek, stepping down into the river and wading through its waters.

But halfway across the river, as they made their way to a newly liberated India, Rajendra was overcome by the urge to turn back; he had to rescue Ranjit. Driven by the thought of his baby brother lying abandoned in the wilderness, he made his way back to the spot where they'd left him. Then, cradling the seemingly dead child in his arms and holding him close to his chest, Rajendra ran back to the banks of the River Ravi and waded across it, stepping onto the soil of free India.

Thanks to his older brother's courage and initiative, Ranjit Tuli miraculously survived the ordeal of migration.

But even before the family could rejoice over the baby's revival and new lease of life, and the convoy could celebrate their escape to safety, a conflict of a different kind had broken out. Across the border, on the Indian side, food packets dropped by Indian Army planes were driving the starved and exhausted refugees into a frenzy. They pounced upon the relief provisions and fought each other off like street dogs to fill their aching bellies. Since the Tulis couldn't manage to get their hands on more than two such packets, each of them received hardly a few mouthfuls of food. Before they knew it, the choppers had exhausted the stock of provisions they were carrying and roared off.

Hunger still gnawing at their insides, the refugees resumed their journey. It was late in the evening when they finally arrived at the Dera Baba Nanak refugee camp. Here, they were provided by the State with temporary shelter in tents and food, clothing and medical aid.

As Rajendra Kumar sat fanning his little brother at the refugee camp to give him some relief from the unbearable heat and the buzzing flies, he couldn't help a hysterical chuckle escaping his parched lips. *The wheel of fortune has turned*, he mused to himself. *Rich and well-fed families like ours, driven out of their spacious homes, are now cooped up in miserable conditions, fighting with each other for food and water... Wah, India! Wah, Pakistan! Happy independence to us all!*

Two days later, the refugees boarded a bus to Amritsar.

The monsoon burst in all its fury as the dust-laden bus rattled on to Amritsar. Rivers roared, threatening to breach their banks. Fields were inundated and bridges collapsed.

Even in the interiors, the devastation, destruction and bloodshed had left a gaping wound in the heart of the holy city. A physically and emotionally depleted Rajendra Kumar gazed at it all with a heavy heart. Corpses of animals and human beings lay strewn across roads bathed in blood. Countless bloated bodies floated in pools of floodwater. The sight was gruesome and heart-rending.

'I had assumed the turmoil would be over soon, but look at the extent of the massacre that has taken place!' a well-to-do Punjabi man sighed. 'The divide is permanent, irrevocable. There's no going back.'

On hearing his words, a sense of doom gripped the already disheartened refugees who had just made the crossing.

Young Rajendra, however, was in no mood to accept the man's gloomy prognosis. *Utter rubbish*, he told himself. *Of course we will go back! Our beautiful home, our precious possessions, our lives cannot be snatched away by anyone so easily.* He rested his head against the bus window and smiled through half-closed eyes, recalling the privileged life he'd once led. *I travelled on my personal tonga to college... I remember how stylish and well dressed we were, and so were the girls... The evenings we spent with friends on Lahore's main street, at the club, the restaurants and the wonderful pubs we visited.* Barely awake now, he recalled his holiday with his cousin Shyam Behl in January that same year in the popular hill station of

Shimla. *We had planned to spend the summer months in the cool climes of Shimla where I'd received the thrashing of my life.* The memory made him chuckle.

All of eighteen, Rajendra Kumar had fallen in love with a girl at the hill station, but soon learnt that there was no future to their relationship. His broken heart had prompted him to jump off a cliff and end his life, much like the hero in *Jugnu*, the last movie he'd watched. So there he'd stood, on the edge of the precipice, ready to emulate his onscreen idol and take the leap, when a hand had grasped him and pulled him back. Shyam had, fortunately, been following him and had saved his life.

His cousin had first counselled him and then, to drive home the point, given Rajendra a sound thrashing. 'Never again will you think of suicide, you get that?' he had yelled.

Rajendra laughed aloud at the memory now – and, forget dying for love, all notion of romance had evaporated from his system. What a wonderful three months of fun and frolic it

*With Ramanand Sagar, his father Lakshmichand Tuli and Shyam Behl*

had been! They'd hoped that the tumult of this ominous event called 'partition' would die down by the time they returned home. How tragically wrong they had been!

Their holiday had come to a sudden end on the first of August 1947, when their parents asked them to return home immediately. Life for the Tulis was never the same again.

*And here I am today,* Rajendra thought, *stripped of everything; just a poor refugee, moving further away from home...simply hoping that we will return soon.*

A child's wail broke through the sultry air. Rajendra Kumar opened his weary eyes, abruptly coming back to the present. The jam-packed bus with its narrow aisle reeked of sweat, body odour, grease and diesel. *Disgusting!* He sighed and dozed off again, his head colliding with the rusted metal bars as the bus bounced painfully over rough roads, until it finally shuddered to a halt in the middle of the ravaged city. The groggy young man awoke with a start, feeling disoriented. They had arrived at yet another refugee camp, this one bordering the Golden Temple in Amritsar. Here, families that had once been wealthy were reduced to eating simple meals of daal and roti for their survival. Frequent outbreaks of cholera were common and medical assistance was scarce.

Sitting amidst the squalor of the refugee camp, Lakshmichand Tuli muttered to no one in particular, 'If only I had enough money to set up a small shop or some kind of work, then maybe...' He fell silent, sighing in despair.

Rajendra sat up suddenly. 'Pa,' he said, a smile lighting up his face, 'we actually might have some money. Why the hell didn't I remember this earlier? You know I had a bank account, right?'

'Yes, I do,' his father replied.

'Do you remember Dadaji scolding me for opening it? Both of you had said, "Silly angrezi trends! Why should we keep our money in others' homes?"'

'I know, son,' Lakshmichand admitted. 'And today we have lost it all. But I never believed in this banking system.'

'But Pa,' Rajendra persisted, 'listen to this: I had eighteen thousand rupees in my account and, by some twist of fate, I had shifted my account to Shimla in May this year, just before going on holiday.'

'What? Eighteen thousand rupees!' His father jumped up and embraced his oldest son. 'We can start our life again!' he said, enthused. 'We can do so much with the money! Oh, thank God! Thank you, God!'

The whole family rejoiced over this sudden windfall, dreaming of a fresh start, but the next morning's newspapers put an end to their hopes. The New India Bank where Rajendra had his account had been closed down. Once again, the Tulis' world came crashing down. Instead of the new beginning they had been dreaming of, the struggle to survive took precedence with renewed force. Thereafter, Rajendra would make daily attempts to reclaim his money, but in vain.

Six months passed in Amritsar and the Tulis' hand-to-mouth existence continued, until one day, in a fortuitous moment, the New Bank of India declared that it would repay 75 per cent of all deposits to its account holders, albeit in yearly instalments.

The very next day, riding on the bank's promise, Rajendra and his family boarded the train to Delhi, a natural choice for better job prospects.

The capital of independent India was a city overflowing with outsiders and half a million refugees at its doorstep. But it was not exactly a haven in waiting. Here too Rajendra's family was given shelter in a refugee camp within the grounds of a mosque near Delhi railway station. For the umpteenth time since he had been forced out of his home and the world he had known, Rajendra told himself, a wry smile on his face: *This is how nature plays with life. It's the irony of fate.*

Meanwhile, shorn of his dignity and pride, Lakshmichand Tuli set out on his daily rounds of the claims office, hoping for compensation for the vast property he had been forced to abandon in Sialkot. The mornings dragged on and ultimately ended in futility, merely heightening his feelings of desolation and hopelessness. The latter part of his day would be spent taking up whatever menial jobs came his way.

Thankfully, after a few months, his persistence bore fruit and the government agreed to compensate refugees with evacuee homes. Lakshmichand and his family were finally allotted their own two rooms in a shared accommodation in Delhi's Subzi Mandi area.

> Our new home in Subzi Mandi seemed quite big after the months we'd spent in tents. To imagine that from a six-storey building with seven rooms on each floor, with fifteen to twenty servants attending to each of those floors, and a separate room for each of us, we were now reduced to living in a two-room shared accommodation. Father, Mother, my brothers and sisters lived in the house under miserable conditions. Grandmother and Grandfather too came later. I didn't know where to go, what to do. Father, in the meanwhile, had become a cloth seller and my sister started stitching clothes. That used to hurt me very much, because I loved my sister and couldn't take it that she was doing such menial jobs for others. And to top it all, these people, who paid so little money, sometimes screamed at her in anger… But I was helpless. Also, I had never imagined myself serving somebody, till a day in early 1948–49, when my father's old friend came to meet him.
>
> *Rajendra Kumar Tuli*

A hand-to-mouth existence in miserable conditions was taking a toll on the young Rajendra. In addition to the scars he bore from the partition – the impact of bloodshed, near-death experiences and loss – he agonized over his father's plight. As he stood waiting in a queue at the employment exchange with thousands of youngsters like him, he sighed. *Every day I stand in queues and every day I return empty-handed*, he thought to himself. *I am the oldest in my family, but am unable to lighten my father's burden.* He reproached himself constantly as he shuffled along in the moving queue. At the end of the day, disheartened, yet again, he returned home, his eyes welling up as he heard the whirring of his sister's sewing machine.

Just a few days earlier, when his first bank instalment of ₹3,000 had arrived, his younger sister Kamla had suggested, 'Bhaiya, buy me a sewing machine. I can take orders to stitch clothes and supplement our income.'

The very idea that his sister would have to earn money to help the family had nearly crushed his spirit. But with no option in sight, he'd agreed to buy her the sewing machine. With the remaining money, his father had opened a small cloth stall in Sadar Bazar. This was the only business the Tulis were familiar with and knew how to run. With grit and determination, they set about rebuilding their lives, like millions of other migrants who had crossed over from Pakistan.

Time flew and the end of 1948 was upon them. One day, a friend of Lakshmichand's dropped in for a visit. Rajendra Kumar, a strapping, handsome twenty-one-year-old by then, greeted the man and touched his feet, a gesture of respect reserved for elders who reciprocated by bestowing their blessings.

'Tuli, your son is strong and good-looking. He should join the police force,' the visitor suggested.

'Hmm,' Rajendra's father responded. 'But we don't know a soul in Delhi. How do we get him in?'

'Don't worry,' the visitor reassured him. 'I know the IG (Inspector General) of Police here. I'll put in a word for your son.'

Having made that promise, the friend took his leave.

A month later, Rajendra was called for an interview. To his surprise, he was finally offered the job – the post of an assistant sub-inspector – in early 1949.

But then the wheels of fortune turned again. Just two days before he was to join his training in Punjab's Phillaur, his whole life changed when Raj Kumar, who had been a close friend of his in Sialkot, came to meet Rajendra at his home in Delhi.

'Partition really did us in,' he declared, seating himself across from his friend. 'We lived like kings there... And here...'

'It's all destiny,' Rajendra observed with a smile. 'But, tell me, Raj, what about you? Where do you live now?'

'In Bombay. I have my own advertising agency there,' his friend replied. 'But I often visit Delhi to meet my parents. And this time, when I heard that you were here, I had to come and see you.'

'Good that you did, because the day after tomorrow, I am to leave for training. I have a job in the police force, can you imagine? Me, a policeman! It just doesn't feel right.'

'Then come to Bombay with me,' Raj suggested eagerly. 'Join my company. As it is, I can't handle everything by myself. Together, we can make it a success.'

'Bombay!' Rajendra exclaimed, beaming with delight. 'The city of dreams! The city of cinema!'

His mind was already working furiously as he imagined his future opening up in the city of dreams.

So what does a blind man need? A pair of eyes! I had already been dreaming of Bombay. It was my long-cherished desire to be a cinema man. I could become an actor. So I simply agreed [to Raj's plan]. I said yes, but when I told my father, he didn't like it. However, he could do nothing to dissuade me. He knew of my love for cinema. He came to see me off at Delhi railway station. I had saved a gold ring from the possessions I'd brought over from Pakistan, which I sold in Chandni Chawk for sixty-three rupees. Thirteen I spent on a third-class train ticket and the balance of fifty rupees, I kept in my pocket. I touched my father's feet. He blessed me. 'Okay,' he said, 'if this is your ambition, I can't force you to do otherwise, because we do not have any business to offer you now. My only desire is that you should conduct yourself like a gentleman in the film industry. I've heard that Mr Prithviraj Kapoor is known as the perfect gentleman in cinema. Be like him.' I kept my promise to him my whole life.

*Rajendra Kumar Tuli*

# 4

# Dreams, Exploitation and Opportunity

The book of life turns [its] leaves; new leaves every day; this is how my life in films started.

*Rajendra Kumar Tuli*

Bombay was the financial and film capital of India. Migrants from Punjab, Calcutta (now Kolkata) and Madras (now Chennai) were employed in the various industries here.

When Rajendra Kumar arrived in the city, he first put up with his friend in a shared accommodation in Mumbra, a suburb of Thane district in Bombay. But within a few days of working with him, it appeared to him as if Raj himself were struggling to make a living, vying for print ads and small classifieds. *He has no business sense and cannot even make ends meet. So how can he pay me for my services*, Rajendra wondered. But he was happy to have made it to the city.

As time went by, however, things took a turn for the worse. Raj began treating him shabbily and refused to pay him his dues, so much so that a disillusioned and starving Rajendra tried to stave off hunger pangs by surviving on roasted gram and glasses of water. His instincts told him, however, that Raj did have enough money to clear his dues, because he himself was eating well, living a comfortable life and pampering his girlfriend too. But what was Rajendra to do? *I cannot let go of my money. Nor can I go back to Delhi a failure*, he told himself. *Maybe I should confront Raj...*

So, one fine day, a desperate Rajendra did just that. He demanded to be paid.

As usual, Raj tried to shrug him off. 'I have no money,' he declared.

But this time, the situation would have a different outcome. His friend's dismissive attitude and blatant lies, his utter lack of compunction in cheating Rajendra of his just dues had awakened the hitherto dormant pride, confidence and righteousness of the young scion of Sankhatra's once wealthy Tuli clan.

*Oh, no*, Rajendra told himself, fuming with indignation, squaring his shoulders for what lay ahead. *Not today. Today, I will get my dues.*

Grabbing Raj by the collar, Rajendra pushed his partner up against the wall and rummaged through his pockets.

'See!' he grinned victoriously, holding up a fistful of notes. 'Three hundred and fifty rupees in all!' he exclaimed, counting out the money. Pocketing three hundred rupees, he hurled the remaining fifty at Raj and said, 'Fifty is what I came to Bombay with and now you will take this fifty and return to Delhi.'

Dragging the now terrified Raj to the railway station, Rajendra bought him a ticket and ordered, 'Get on the train. And remember, I don't want to see you in Bombay ever again. You understand?'

That marked the end of the partnership. Rajendra, however, retained the small room he had rented and continued to live in Mumbra for a few more months. But soon he ran short of money and had to vacate that place as well. With nowhere to go, he took to sleeping on the footpath. He'd pay a bribe of ₹1 to the havildar – a local policeman who, in the line of duty, rounded up vagrants he came across on his beat – to look the other way and allow him to continue sleeping on the footpath. This went on for a couple of nights. Then a doctor friend of Rajendra's learnt of his plight and offered him a room in his Mumbra clinic.

Aside from food and shelter, his biggest worry was the matter of making a living. How would he go about it? The universe had the answer: films! That was his dream and his destiny.

With a new resolve, fired by the ambition of forging a career in the world of cinema, Rajendra Kumar began setting out every day in his bid to find ways of making his dream come true. He soon realized, however, that his shy demeanour and natural inhibitions were proving to be an impediment. Unable to summon up the courage to actually ask for work, he returned home, defeated, on most days.

Two weeks passed. By this time, his money had dwindled to almost nothing.

That's when a letter arrived unexpectedly from his cousin and best friend Shyam Behl, with whom Rajendra had often spent time in Shimla.

Shyam wrote: 'On one of my recent visits to Shimla, I met the noted film lyricist Rajinder Krishan. I spoke to him about you. Take this letter and go see him at Famous Studios. He has promised to help you.'

As Rajendra read through the contents, he was momentarily overwhelmed by a feeling of bittersweet nostalgia for his earlier life of ease and luxury. With a sigh, he folded the letter. In those good old days, he remembered meeting Rajinder Krishanji himself in Shimla. *I hope he recognizes me*, he mused. *I must get in touch with him.*

Early next morning, Rajendra Kumar dressed with care. His hair neatly combed back, his fair face glowing in anticipation of what might come of the meeting, he set out for Famous Studios on Cadell Road and met the noted lyricist, handing him the letter of recommendation that his cousin had written for him.

Rajinder Krishan was a kind man. He also saw the potential in the handsome young man standing before him and said, 'Don't worry. You can start by working with me. I'll try and get you a job as soon as I can.'

Henceforth, a purposeful Rajendra would set out every day from home on the long journey to Famous Studios. He had to take a train to Thane, from where he walked the remaining distance of 25 kilometres to reach the studios at four in the afternoon. Despite the arduous commute, his excitement at being a part of the film industry, even if in a small way, remained unabated.

Rajendra Kumar's career in films thus began with odd jobs that the lyricist assigned him.

Being educated and fluent in Urdu, I would 'fair' [make fair copies of] the [rough version of] dialogues written by Krishanji. Tea and dinner were taken care of. One day, Rajinder Krishanji said, 'You are such a simpleton. You neither smoke nor drink. How will you work in the film industry?' I asked, 'To become an actor, do I have to drink and smoke?' He said, 'No, but it is a style [trend], a social etiquette.' 'All right then,' I said, 'if it is necessary, I don't mind.' So my first drink was offered to me by Mr Rajinder Krishan in Eros Bar behind Eros Cinema. I had a small drink that day, an initiation into drinks. It somehow helped me to get over my inhibitions. Not that I became an alcoholic. And, yes, Rajinder Krishanji kept his word too. There was a new company called Verma Films. They were about to start a film called *Patanga* to be directed by H.S. Rawail.

*Rajendra Kumar Tuli*

In 1949, H.S. Rawail was all set to begin work on *Patanga*, starring Nigar Sultana and Shyam. Rajinder Krishan spoke to the film's producer and put in a word for the young Rajendra, who was subsequently employed as an assistant director (AD) on a remuneration of ₹50 per month. *Ah*, Rajendra thought to himself, thrilled at the prospect of working on a film, *the magic number again! Fifty!* He believed it was fated. And it certainly seemed so when for the film's very first shot, 'Rawail Sir', as he called the director, asked the handsome but gawky Rajendra Kumar to play a walk-on part. All he had to do was run across to the actor playing the role of a village landlord and inform him that a son had been born.

Rajendra soon settled down to work as a second assistant director, a position in which his education and writing skills came in handy. He primarily applied himself to producing fair copy of the movie's scenes and dialogues. *This is where I belong*, he said to himself, smiling happily as he busied himself in organizing things for the upcoming shoot.

Destiny too endorsed Rajendra's chosen path, it seemed, because after only a month at work, Rawail, pleased with the young man's skills and sense of commitment, raised his salary to ₹75 per month. Young Tuli was thrilled at the recognition of his worth and, although an increment also meant increased workload, he bustled around with renewed enthusiasm, working on continuity sheets, dialogue preparations and scene rehearsals with the actors – all of which proved to be a great learning experience for the twenty-one-year-old newcomer. Only one thing eluded him: he yearned to give the clap before the shot, a job reserved for the first assistant director Sadhu Singh. That didn't happen for a long time, but while he waited expectantly for that day, everybody on the film set was quite taken with him. While *Patanga*'s statuesque leading man, Shyam, had already begun calling Rajendra Kumar 'hero *beta*', the leading lady, Nigar Sultana, had grown very fond of the good-looking assistant director. *Maybe because of my neatness, my discipline, and my education,* Rajendra reasoned modestly to himself.

By the time *Patanga* was completed, Rajendra's salary had shot up to ₹125 per month.

> In 1949, we would be shooting for fifteen days a month; and for that [work] junior staff used to get two rupees as lunch money, apart from our salaries. That was a great bonus. Twelve annas we'd spend on a good lunch, twelve annas on dinner and eight annas on a Gold Flake [cigarette] packet. I had started smoking. The rest of it and my salary would be saved for good clothes and Hollywood movies that I loved to watch and then discuss with my friends. By this time, I had developed a taste for film direction too. The first shot of *Patanga*, where a young man runs to the zamindar's house [to deliver the news of a son's birth] was given to me by the director. When my name appeared in the credits of *Patanga*, I felt such a thrill, but my director never encouraged me to act. He would say, 'What! *You* cannot become an actor.' And I'd reply, 'Okay, fine. I will go into direction. I will become a big director one day.' 'Yes, concentrate on that...and on your writing,' he'd advise. Many a time, my director did not like what the writer had produced and would ask me to rewrite the scene. That was great encouragement for me. It [the ability to write scenes] stayed with me throughout my career. I have written lots of scenes in my own movies too.
>
> *Rajendra Kumar Tuli*

On its release *Patanga* became the seventh-highest grossing film of 1949. A duet sung against the backdrop of World War II and picturized on actor Gope and Nigar Sultana, '*Mere piya gaye Rangoon*', became immensely popular.

Following the success of *Patanga*, Rawail began work on his next film, *Sagai*.

Rajendra, his assistant director, who was keen to send his parents ₹100 every month, fervently prayed that for his work on this new film his salary would be raised to at least ₹250 a month.

And to his delight that is precisely what happened. For his work on the sets of *Sagai*, Rajendra Kumar received the monthly salary he had been hoping for.

By this time, he was a full-time employee and had realized that the only way forward was to keep working and meeting influential people. Intuition told him that Rajinder Krishan was somehow destined to lead him on the road to success. Moreover, he had grown very fond of Krishanji, who treated him like a younger brother. Thus, after work hours, he would spend his leisure time at Ranjit Studios, working with the famous lyricist. Now that he had found his path in the world of films, he reminded himself over and over again that he would have to improve his life.

# 5

# Slog, Sweat and Tears

By early 1950, I was settled in my job as an AD. That was my bread and butter. But I would still go to Ranjit Studios to work with Rajinder Krishanji. Therein lay my destiny.

*Rajendra Kumar Tuli*

Ranjit Studios, later renamed Ranjit Movietone, was founded by Chandulal Shah, along with Gohar Mamajiwala. It was one of the three largest film studios of its time. A director himself, with a keen eye for talent, Seth Chandulal Shah hadn't failed to notice the tall, attractive young man coming to the studio every day to meet Krishanji.

One day, he called out to Rajendra, '*Aye, chhokra!* Hey, young man!'

'Namaste!' Rajendra greeted the stranger in response.

'Can you act?'

'Yes, Sethji, I can. But I am not really an actor. I work as Rawail Sir's AD and hope to direct a film soon.'

'Okay, wait for my call,' Chandulal Shah told him. 'There may be a job for you.'

His words filled Rajendra with hope, but he reined in his feelings. *Let's not read too much into this*, he decided. *Who knows what he really meant?*

The answer to his unspoken question was delivered a few days later when Chandulal Shah beckoned to him once again, this time inviting him up to his office. The studio head then offered him a small but important role in his next production, *Jogan*, a film to be directed by Kidar Nath Sharma.

'Are you offering me an acting job?' Rajendra asked, trying to contain his excitement.

Shah nodded. 'Yes,' he replied, 'to play the leading man's friend.'

'The leading man's friend?'

The leading man was none other than Rajendra Kumar's screen idol – the great Dilip Kumar!

*What an auspicious start,* he thought, his heart pounding at the unexpectedness of the development. Yet, his inner voice told him to be cautious. *Stop right there*, it said. *Let it happen first.*

That, however, was near impossible as the jubilant Rajendra's mind raced in excitement and his happiness knew no bounds. *Dilip Kumar!* This veteran actor was the 'tragedy king', a title

*With Dilip Kumar, Raaj Kumar and director C.V. Sridhar*

that, some said, lay heavy on the superstar's brooding persona. But the audience was able to identify with his intensity and relate to the pathos he evoked in his roles. Appropriately, *Jogan*, the film in which Rajendra Kumar had been given a role, was a complex love story in which a city-bred atheist played by Dilip Kumar falls in love with a married woman (enacted by Nargis) who has renounced the material world.

Of the twenty-nine days during which the film was shot, Rajendra's scenes required him to be on set for a mere four days. But nothing could dampen his euphoria. What a learning it was! The expressions of the leading pair, eloquent with unarticulated feelings as they gazed at each other; the pregnant silences that spoke volumes, their understated passion that seemed to set the screen on fire, the soulful dialogues of love and devotion they exchanged and Dilip Kumar's magnetism, along with the gestures that were so characteristic of the great star, became integral to Rajendra Kumar's education as an actor.

For the four days of filming, Rajendra received ₹50 per day – *the mystical number yet again*, he thought – leaving him ₹200 richer. He felt he could now indulge himself a bit and splurged on two pairs of silk trousers and some silk shirts. He also moved from Mumbra to Marina Guest House in Bandra.

> *Jogan* released on 24 February 1950. It featured the song '*Ghungat ke pat khol*' sung by Geeta Dutt. A box-office success, the film became the fourth-highest earning film of 1950 and made Dilip Kumar the highest paid actor of the time, with an asking fee of ₹1 lakh per film. After the release of *Jogan*, people started recognizing me, even though I'd played a very small role in it. I started giving autographs too. It was a nice feeling.
>
> *Rajendra Kumar Tuli*

But even as Rajendra revelled in the love and newfound attention of cinemagoers, his director H.S. Rawail soon brought him back to earth.

'You did get a break, but acting is not for you,' he told him. 'Concentrate on the job at hand.'

*Rawail Sir is right,* Rajendra Kumar humbly acknowledged to himself. *But if I get acting parts, I will go ahead and do them. People do like my work, as did Chandulal Shah.*

A week after *Jogan*'s release, Shah summoned him once again and offered him another role in his next film, *Humlog*, to be written and directed by Zia Sarhadi. Rajendra couldn't believe his luck; this time, he had been signed on to play the lead opposite actor Nutan and alongside other stars like Shyama and Balraj Sahni. It was his big break.

Soon, shooting commenced and *Humlog*'s director, Zia, introduced Rajendra to everyone.

'Meet Rajendra Kumar,' he announced. 'It makes me proud that I am going to create a star.'

But after only a few days of filming, Rajendra received a message that *Humlog* had been stalled for some time. He urged himself to be patient and went about his daily chores on Rawail's sets, trying to keep at bay the depressing thoughts that kept surfacing in his mind. But when a week went by with no further updates on the film, Rajendra was overcome by a feeling of dread. He sensed that something was seriously amiss and decided to talk to the film's assistant director. Straight up, he asked the assistant what the problem was, even as his subconscious told him: *You already know the answer.*

'Sorry, Rajendra,' the assistant director told him. 'You are no longer a part of *Humlog*. The actor Sajjan has been signed in your place.'

A cold sweat broke out on Rajendra's skin. How could they do this to him? His career had not even begun and… Turning away to hide his crestfallen expression, the young man walked away in a daze. *Where do I go from here*, he wondered. His eyes welled up with tears and almost simultaneously, as though reflecting his pain, the skies suddenly opened up, drenching the city in rain. But, unmindful of the downpour, Rajendra walked aimlessly all day, until late evening found him at the Santacruz railway station. Here, he finally came to his senses. Pausing for a few seconds, he asked himself: *What am I doing? I should find a solution or try to reason with Zia Saab.*

Having come to a decision, Rajendra turned around and, with fresh determination, strode out of the station and headed for Juhu. It was 18 July 1950, and so firm was the young man in his resolve, so intent on his purpose to seek redressal for the wrong done to him, that even the storm that had been unleashed on Bombay, practically shutting it down, did not deter him from wading through the flooded streets to his destination. *I will meet the director*, he told himself.

The rain fell in furious sheets, swiftly flooding the island city. Lightning zigzagged to the ground, thick clouds rolled by and thunder rumbled menacingly. Still, Rajendra continued to plough his way through the flooded streets, until, exhausted and soaked to the skin, he finally arrived at Zia's doorstep.

Dripping water, he repeatedly struck the metal clanger of the narrow exterior gate that led up a flagstone path to the porch of the house, until he saw a figure with an umbrella emerge from the main house. It was the director himself, peering through the dense sheets of rain and wondering who could be visiting on such a stormy night.

'What do you want?' he grumbled, distaste evident in his expression as he eyed the bedraggled man shivering with cold outside his gate.

'Zia Saab,' Rajendra began imploringly, 'if I have displeased you in any way, please forgive me. Let me make amends for that, but do not oust me from the film. I will work very hard. Please, sir.'

'I'm sorry,' the director replied, obviously furious at being disturbed. 'There's nothing I can do. Go away!'

Rajendra Kumar's lips quivered with emotion. He was close to tears. Despite his distress, he put his palms together in a gesture of entreaty and pleaded, 'Zia Saab, I…' he began.

But even as he stared in dismay at the other man's retreating back, the door swung shut in his face with a loud bang. Rajendra almost wailed in desperation and tried calling out to the director, but no words emerged from his lips.

Burning with humiliation at the rebuff, he turned away, his bowed head filled with thoughts of anger and disillusionment, his mood alternating between that of failure, revenge and hope. *I am finished. No, I'm not! I will show this man, one day, what I am capable of. There's nothing I can do. Rawail Sir had warned me I could never become an actor.* A wave of hysteria swept over him and he laughed aloud. *I'll be the best and most successful star one day!* Then he mocked his own dreams and ambitions. *Rubbish!*

It was in this mental condition that he suddenly realized that he was back at the Santacruz railway station, which now stood deserted. Due to the torrential rains and the flooding of the railway tracks, all trains had been cancelled.

A sense of doom hung over the young man's head. *My life is over*, Rajendra sighed, shuffling to one of the benches at the station. Now exhausted and utterly defeated, he lay down on it, shivering with fear and an overwhelming feeling of failure.

*But justice will be meted out,* he thought to himself, sending up a prayer to God. Then his eyelids drooped over his deep brown eyes and he fell into an uneasy sleep.

Rajendra Kumar sat up with a start. Had someone shaken him awake? He had felt a hand on him, he thought. He held up his wrist to check the time by his watch.

'Oh no!' he cried out. 'My watch… Oh my God! I've been robbed!'

Frantically, he felt for his wallet, fearing the worst. Gone! His eyes scoured the station, but he was alone, save for a few pigeons fluttering overhead. Bombay, the city of dreams, had broken his spirit. *I hate this city,* he told himself. *Full of cruel people. Only the rich are happy here. I am in the wrong place, the wrong profession…*

A train whistled in the distance and at last, he looked up, his eyes red and swollen from weeping. He noticed that a few passengers had walked into the station. Rajendra Kumar rose wearily from the bench and, dragging his feet, boarded the near empty train. Time seemed to stand still for him as he stared blindly at the maze of metal railway tracks weaving in and out of his range of vision.

Thirty minutes later, he arrived at Marina Guest House, where he collapsed onto his bed. He lay there all through that day and night, his mind seething with feelings of rejection and humiliation while his body burned with fever. On the following day, he was diagnosed with jaundice.

Bedridden for a while, he now indulged in introspection. The treachery and egos of the people in Bombay city! The lure of money and fame! How would he fight against these monsters and overcome them? Could a principled and sincere man combat the unscrupulous? He was willing to take up the challenge, but first he had to master his fears and desires. With his family oblivious to the trauma he was going through, he lay there all alone, determined not to burden them with his problems or cause them anxiety. *They have enough on their plate as it is*, he told himself.

In the days that followed, a much-needed healing of mind, body and spirit took place while he recuperated from his bout of jaundice. It reinvigorated the broken Rajendra and restored in him his powers of resilience.

In no time, with all pretences and dreams cast off, he returned to assist Rawail on his next film, *Saqi*, a Madhubala starrer that would be released in 1952. His acting stint was soon a thing of the past. The fleeting fame that *Jogan* had brought him faded, plunging him back into the anonymity he had become accustomed to in Bombay. Rajendra had all but forgotten about the acting phase of his life when providence smiled on him.

One day, when he had arrived at Famous Studios in Mahalaxmi where H.S. Rawail's office was located, Rajendra became aware of a gentleman staring at him.

*Looks familiar*, Rajendra thought, rubbing his jaw as he bought his cigarette pack from the little kiosk at the gates of the building and headed for the elevator.

Just as he was about to enter the elevator, Julie, the receptionist, called out to him.

'Rajendra, there is a message for you,' she said.

He accepted the handwritten note and turned back towards the elevator. The well-dressed gentleman who'd been looking at him earlier was there too.

'You acted in *Jogan*, right?' he asked as the elevator carried them up.

'Yes, that's right,' Rajendra replied with a smile.

'What other films are you working in currently?'

'I am not really an actor,' Rajendra told him frankly. 'I work as an assistant director with Rawail Sir.'

'Ah! But I see you as an actor. Come, let's have a cup of tea together. My office is on the second floor.'

'Thank you… uhh…'

'My name is Devendra Goel and I am a director.'

'Goel Sir!' Rajendra exclaimed, unable to believe that he had actually met such a famous director, that too by chance. 'I have seen your film *Aankhen*.'

'My gut instinct says that with your looks, style and talent you should act in films,' Goel went on. 'You should become a hero.'

'That's what everyone advises me to do so, sir, but no one signs me on.'

'Hmm...'

'If you feel I am hero material,' Rajendra ventured, 'do give me a chance in your film, won't you?'

'I will,' Goel promptly replied.

But months went by, with no word from the director. Rajendra was back to square one.

Thereafter, with no acting job coming his way, Rajendra Kumar continued working on *Saqi*, and later, through 1952, he went on to assist Rawail with *Shagufta* and *Lehren*.

# 6

# The Turning Point

According to Khalil Gibran, life is just a tear and a smile. I assisted Mr H.S. Rawail in about seven films – *Patanga, Sagai, Saqi, Shagufta, Lehren, Pocket Maar* and *Mastana* – over a period of four years, as I had decided that I would become a good director.

*Rajendra Kumar Tuli*

In 1954, with Rawail's *Mastana*, starring Motilal and Nigar Sultana, under way, followed by the filming of *Pocket Maar*, with Dev Anand and Geeta Bali in the lead, Rajendra Kumar was completely focussed on honing his directorial skills. Little did the twenty-seven-year-old know that a new chapter was about to open in his life.

Earlier the same year, Rajendra's college friend Sansar Behl had come to Bombay on a month's holiday. Every evening after work, the two men would get together and often visit relatives and friends. On one such occasion, Behl invited Rajendra to his aunt's home in Mahim, where she lived with her family – a son, two daughters and a son-in-law.

'What do you do for a living, *beta*?' Sansar's aunt Kartar Devi Behl asked the handsome young visitor.

'I am an assistant director,' Rajendra replied.

'Ah! You work in the film industry!' Kartar Devi smiled, having taken a liking to the young man. 'Son, do feel free to visit us whenever you want to,' she told him. 'I'm sure it isn't easy living a bachelor's life in the big city.'

'I certainly will,' Rajendra responded. 'Thank you!'

But in the days that followed, a busy schedule barely left him any time to spend with Sansar himself, let alone visit his relatives. Too soon, his friend's stay in Bombay came to an end. On their last day together, Rajendra accompanied Sansar again to the Behls's home. His friend wished to bid his relatives goodbye before leaving town.

'The house seems to be livelier today,' Rajendra remarked, as they settled down in the living room.

'You're right. Our cousins from Punjab are here on holiday,' Kartar Devi explained, offering the guests almonds and hot samosas.

'Just my luck!' Sansar laughed. 'I leave tomorrow and all the fun begins now. I'm sure you all have planned lots of sightseeing and movies, right?'

'We did,' Kartar Devi replied, 'but I must share this with you – since your cousins arrived, they've been asking for only one thing: they want to watch a film shoot!' Turning to Rajendra, she asked, '*Beta*, can you arrange it?'

'Of course,' he assured her. 'We are currently shooting for *Mastana*. They can come and watch it tomorrow.'

The next morning, a group of giggly youngsters landed up on the film's sets.

Shukla, Kartar Devi's youngest daughter, was also with them. She loved films and was thrilled at the opportunity to watch *Mastana*'s leading stars, Premnath and Nigar Sultana, in action, that too live. But the man who had invited them for the shoot had not escaped her notice either.

'A hero,' her cousin commented, eyeing Rajendra, who looked dapper in a silk shirt and brown pants.

'So handsome and so elegant! He has such large brown eyes too,' another commented.

Meanwhile, director Rawail called out to his assistant director and asked, 'Who are these girls? Your friends?'

'No, no! They are my cousins,' Rajendra clarified.

'And that girl in the black salwar kameez?'

'Oh, she too is a relative.'

'Pretty girl! Marry her. One look, and I can tell she will be a fantastic wife and mother.'

Rajendra looked across at Shukla. *She is so beautiful*, he mused, *but...*

'*Ullu ke patthe!* You fool! Instead of having affairs with so many, you'd do well to settle down with her,' Rawail said with a laugh.

Rajendra didn't take the conversation too seriously and brushed off the suggestion. But a few days later, when he visited the Behl home again, Sansar's aunt too broached the subject of marriage.

'You live alone?' Kartar Devi asked the young man, then probed deeper. 'No life partner yet?'

'No, Auntyji,' Rajendra replied. 'I am still single. All I can afford on my monthly salary of three hundred and fifty rupees is paying-guest accommodation. Where would my wife stay, if I had one? I have to earn more money and buy my own home, before thinking of getting married.'

'Hmm...that's true,' Kartar Devi agreed. 'But do let me know as soon as you decide to marry.'

'My mother too keeps pestering me to get married,' Rajendra admitted. 'She worries that living alone in Bombay I don't take care of myself and need a companion to do so.'

'She is right, you know,' Kartar Devi murmured. 'Does she have someone in mind?'

'I really don't know,' Rajendra replied. 'But I am leaving for Delhi tomorrow to attend my sister's wedding and I have a feeling my parents will have lined up a few prospective brides for me.' He smiled. 'So let's see!'

'Well, do think over what I said, before you decide. I would like my youngest daughter, Shukla, to marry you.'

'Your daughter!' Rajendra Kumar's head shot up in surprise.

*What a coincidence*, he thought, and looked across with fresh interest at the seventeen-year-old who stood out of earshot and seemed oblivious to the conversation taking place in the drawing room.

*She really is pretty*, Rajendra reflected. *Even Rawail Sir had picked her out of the group for me. Maybe, she's the one*?

'I feel I should talk to my parents and seek their permission first,' he told Kartar Devi.

'Yes, of course,' she agreed.

After Rajendra had left, Kartar Devi summoned Shukla and asked, 'What do you think of that young man?'

'Who, Sansar's friend?' Shukla enquired. 'Why do you ask?'

'I'm considering him as a prospective groom – for you. Sansar has already told me about his background. He comes from a very affluent and educated family. Of course, they lost it all when they migrated to India, but still…'

'He seems nice… Anyway, mothers know best,' Shukla replied, busy clearing the table.

The proposal of marriage had come as a bolt from the blue for Rajendra Kumar. But that same evening, something else was to take him by surprise. As he walked into work, writer-director Mahesh Kaul beckoned him over.

'Come here, Rajinder,' he said. 'Show me your palm.'

'Kaul Saab,' Rajendra said to him. 'Tell me, what does my kismet say? How long must I wait to enjoy success?'

'Hmm…' said the other man, examining the lines on his palm. 'Get married and your kismet will change. You will become rich and famous.'

Meanwhile, back in Delhi, Rajendra's parents had zeroed in on a girl from an affluent family who, aware of the immense wealth and formidable reputation the Tulis had enjoyed back in Sialkot, readily agreed to the betrothal.

Rajendra, however, was reluctant to give his consent. 'I do not want to marry a girl from a rich family,' he told his parents. 'The standard of living to which she is accustomed, her desires… How will I ever fulfil her needs? And who knows about tomorrow? Whether success comes or not is a matter of destiny.'

Although Lakshmichand Tuli appreciated his son's honesty, he felt it was time for the boy to settle down. It was at this moment that Rajendra told his parents about Kartar Devi's proposal.

'I like their youngest daughter, Shukla,' he confided. 'I feel she is the one for me.'

'You have her photo?' Lakshmichand asked.

'No, I don't, but as soon as I reach Bombay, I will send it to you.'

And so he did. His parents liked the girl instantly – so much so that Laksmichand framed her picture and put it up on a wall of their house. Then with great pride, he began introducing his friends to his 'future daughter-in-law'.

Things moved fast thereafter and a week after returning to Bombay, Rajendra Kumar was officially engaged to Shukla.

By this time, Rajendra's income had increased considerably. However, he could not help brooding over the fact that although the years were passing by and he was now twenty-seven years old, he was still nowhere close to directing his own film. *I have to break out of this 'assistant director' mould*, he told himself. But how? He could not risk jeopardizing the steady income his salary brought him by branching off in another direction to fulfil his dream; after all, his family depended on him financially. And now with his engagement to Shukla, he had to find a way. *I must do something*, he told himself.

It was at this point that the name of the filmmaker who had approached him long back came to mind. Devendra Goel had promised him a break in films. He'd said he would sign Rajendra as the hero of his film. But two years had gone by since… So Rawail Sir had been proved right, yet again. *Acting is not for me*, Rajendra told himself in despair. *I must approach producers to direct films. But will they trust me to carry an entire film on my shoulders?*

Insecurities and fears weighed him down as he went about his daily tasks, unaware that the universe was conspiring to bestow upon him what was meant to be his.

It happened a week later. One evening, as he sat smoking in his room at Marina Guest House, a peon came up with a note sent by none other than Devendra Goel.

'Meet me in my office tomorrow morning,' was the message written in the note.

Although Rajendra had to report for Rawail's *Mastana* early the next day, he followed his instinct and landed up at Famous Studios. Rajendra was sure that Goel would offer him a film. But there could be many a slip between the cup and the lip, he reminded himself, as he sat across the producer in his office.

Thankfully, Goel came straight to the point.

'We'd met in 1952 and I'd said that I'd give you a chance,' the producer began. 'The time has come to fulfil my promise.' With that, he placed an agreement on the table in front of Rajendra. 'You are working in my next film, along with Balraj Sahni and Geeta Bali,' he elaborated.

Rajendra looked from Goel to the agreement and back in wonder.

'Go ahead. Read it!' the producer prompted.

Rajendra read through the contract, but among the lines of typed words that his eyes went over, what stood out starkly against the white paper was a number: 1,500.

One thousand five hundred rupees! A fortune! Rajendra couldn't believe his luck. He did tell himself, though, that however lucrative the payment he had been promised might seem, what was invaluable was the full-fledged role he had been offered in a film.

Without further ado, he signed on the dotted line.

'Congratulations, my boy! You are on your way to stardom,' Goel said with a smile, handing Rajendra ₹101 as the signing amount.

A jubilant Rajendra Kumar almost floated out of Famous Studios, reaching the sets of *Mastana* far later than when he had been expected to report for duty.

A furious Rawail confronted him. 'You, a mere assistant director, have the audacity to keep the great Motilal waiting?' he yelled.

'I am sorry, Rawail Sir. But please hear me out first,' Rajendra said, unable to contain his joy. 'Today, I have become an actor in the true sense of the term.'

'What are you talking about? What actor?'

'I have signed a film with the famous Devendra Goel.'

'Who is he, anyway? And you can't call every second film "a film"!' Rawail said disparagingly.

'Rawail Saab,' Rajendra told him firmly, 'film or no film, Goelji has offered me a chance of a lifetime today and that too with a signing amount. Today, I gave nothing and lost nothing, but my gain is immeasurable. Today is special for me.'

With a look of disdain, Rawail turned away from his assistant director. 'Silence on set!' he shouted, calling his crew to attention.

Goel's *Vachan*, starring Geeta Bali and Rajendra Kumar in the roles of siblings, released in early 1955 and was a huge box-office success. In the film, Rajendra Kumar sailed through his first major role, a lock of hair falling on his brow, his fingers splayed across his face in a gesture adopted from 'tragedy king' Dilip Kumar's characteristic technique, or his arms crossed behind his back. But he did seem cockier and more confident in the romantic scenes.

*The visiting card Rajendra's father got printed for himself after his son rose to stardom*

When we started shooting the film, Devendra Goel was going through a financial crisis. I was a newcomer in the cast; it was Mr Goel's assistant Rajrishi's directorial debut and also music director Ravi's first film. The distributors were wary of signing so many first-timers, but finally agreed because the story had been written by the famous Mukhram Sharma and Geeta Bali was playing the lead. When Mr Goel made the film's trailer, he put my name down as 'Rajendra Kumar', along with the words 'the star is born'. I was shocked! 'What is a star? I am not a star,' I told him. But he said, 'Be quiet. I know what I am doing.' And so his prophecy was fulfilled. *Vachan* was completed with a lot of difficulty, but once it released it proved to be one of the biggest hits of 1955. A silver jubilee film, *Vachan* brought me everything in my life. Thereafter, I never looked back.

*Rajendra Kumar Tuli*

# 7

# Marriage, Love and a Taste of Fame

On 5 December 1954, three months before *Vachan* released, I got married to the beautiful Shukla Behl.

*Rajendra Kumar Tuli*

Neither Shukla Behl nor her family had ever imagined that she would become the wife of a superstar one day. Born on 27 April 1937 in Amritsar's Namak Mandi, she was the youngest offspring and a much-pampered child. Following the partition, Shukla, then ten years old, had to relocate with her family to Bombay, where she would initially put up with relatives in Girgaum, before moving to Mahim's Sindhi Niwas. She completed her graduation at Dadar's Ahuja College.

Shukla's brother-in-law was a photographer and had set up shop with her brother as partner. But her father, a conservative and old-fashioned man who had an aversion to city life, had preferred to stay back in Punjab to look after their vast ancestral property. When he learnt of his daughter's engagement to Rajendra Kumar, he was filled with trepidation. Never having

*At his wedding with parents, sister and others*

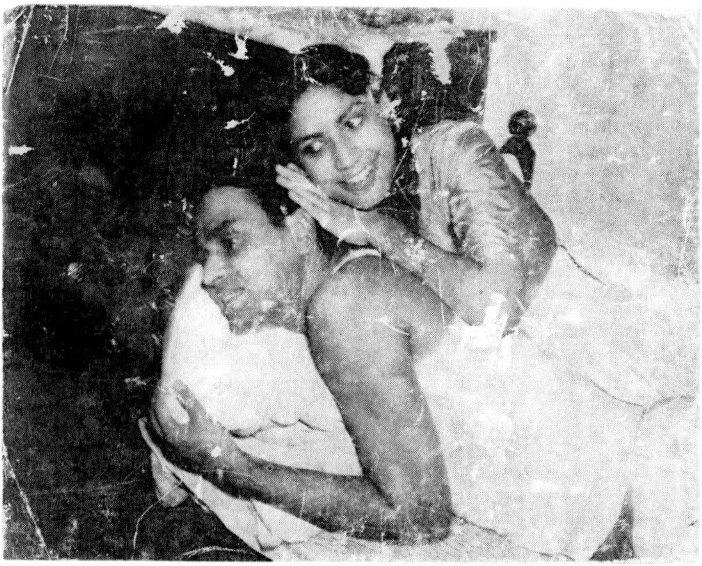

*The newly-weds, Rajendra and Shukla, 1959*

watched a movie in his life, he expressed his reservations about his future son-in-law.

'The boy works in films,' he observed. 'What if he forces my daughter to act too?'

Despite such misgivings, on 5 December 1954, a few months before the release of his first big film, *Vachan*, Rajendra Kumar Tuli wed Shukla Behl in a simple ceremony conducted on her building's terrace in Mahim. Only close friends and family were part of the celebrations.

The newly-weds then moved into a room in a small bungalow in Mahim. It belonged to a friend of the family, a woman who lived alone. Initially, all went well, but as the days passed the landlady began nagging and complaining about every little thing. Soon, fed up with her daily bickering, Rajendra and Shukla made up their minds to move elsewhere. Fortunately for them, film comedian Randhir, who was working with Rajendra in a film, offered them half of his four-bedroom apartment to set up their home.

> When I first met Rajinderji [Rajendraji], I was a second-year student at Dadar's Ahuja College. He and my cousin Sansar had been friends since their college days in Lahore and Sansar had brought him along on one of his visits to our home in Bombay. Before I knew it, Rajinderji had consented to marry me and we were engaged. He had lots of girlfriends before he knew me. I knew about them... All my college friends too were crazy about him and were shocked that the simplest of us had got him. He was also popular as an assistant [director]. Our romance began only after our engagement. In those days, letters were the mode of communication. We started writing to each other and through our 'love notes' romance blossomed – not a physical romance, but full of feeling, pure and platonic. We were never allowed to go out unaccompanied. My cousins always chaperoned us. One day, we were

watching a movie and he placed his hand on mine. That feeling I can never forget. I felt as if a current had run through my arm. I pulled away. After that, it became impossible for us to spend time away from each other. But the waiting period gave us time to nurture a friendship. I was ten years younger than Rajinderji, but mentally very mature. We were engaged for a year and a half and were married before *Vachan*'s release. Our families insisted that I was his lucky mascot. *Vachan* became Miyan's [the Urdu word for spouse] first silver-jubilee hit.

*Shukla Tuli*

Just days before *Vachan*'s release, an excited Rajendra Kumar had turned into a nervous wreck from obsessing about the film's fate. As the date of the premiere closed in, the fear of impending failure seized him and nibbled at his confidence. Numerous what-ifs beset him: What if the film failed? What if people didn't like him in his role? What if… Endless questions emanating from self-doubt ran through his mind.

On the eve of the film's premiere, he couldn't help sharing his apprehensions with his wife.

'Just in case my future as an actor fizzles out, there's no need for you to worry,' he reassured her. 'I still have my job as an assistant director, so…'

'Don't stress yourself out. Everything will be fine,' Shukla said, trying in vain to calm down her overwrought husband.

'At such times in my life, I feel that maybe Rawailji was right,' Rajendra muttered, continuing to brood. 'I wasn't meant to be an actor.'

'*Arre*, Miyan!' his wife protested. Then she had an idea. 'Why not invite Rawailji for the premiere tomorrow? That will put your doubts to rest.'

So the next day Rajendra and Shukla invited H.S. Rawail and his wife to accompany them to the premiere of *Vachan*.

*A young Shukla reading* Filmfare *magazine, 1959*

*With Shukla, at their first apartment, 1959*

For the premiere of *Vachan*, I took along Rawail Saab and his wife Mrs Ranjana Rawail, who loved me the way a mother would her son. After the film was over, Rawail Saab drove us home. Throughout the drive, I didn't bring up the topic of the film in conversation, because I was nervous, still apprehensive that the director might not have cared for my performance. But when we reached home and I stepped out of the car, he too did so. Then he just stood there, gazing at me… I had no idea what he could possibly want to say, but suddenly he hugged me and kissed me on the forehead. 'Son,' he said, 'I am proud of you!' Tears rolled down my eyes. I was overcome with emotion at the thought that this man, who'd never believed I could act in a film, was now acknowledging that he was proud of me!

*Rajendra Kumar Tuli*

*With H.S. Rawail and Raaj Kumar*

Following *Vachan*'s success, word spread in the industry that Rajendra Kumar, the new actor on the block, was lucky. *Lucky I may be*, Rajendra said to himself, *but my hard work and talent cannot be ignored.*

The next film he signed was *Toofan aur Deeya* with V. Shantaram, better known as Anna Saab, India's greatest filmmaker. Following the success of *Dr Kotnis ki Amar Kahani*, it was Shantaram's Raj Kamal Studios that would produce *Toofan aur Deeya*, a 1956 film directed by Prabhat Kumar. The film would also mark the debut in an adult role of Shantaram's seventeen-year-old niece, Nanda, who was already familiar to cinema audiences from the time of her debut in 1948 as child star Baby Nanda.

*Toofan aur Deeya*, a touching story about those who had toiled ceaselessly to rebuild their lives after the partition, underscored the importance of grit and determination in achieving success. This struck a chord in Rajendra Kumar, who had been through the same ordeal in his own life. As a result, he was able to relate closely to the small but important character he was playing in the film.

After almost three-fourths of the film had been shot, however, Shantaram watched the rushes and was clearly unhappy with the way the film was turning out. He then decided to direct the remaining portions himself. His obvious dissatisfaction with the film brought Rajendra's insecurities to the fore, yet again. But before he could start brooding over them, as was his inclination, the actor received a call from none other than the great Mehboob Khan.

It so happened that one day, writer S. Ali Raza, who was also actor Nimmi's husband, dropped in to see Rajendra Kumar on the sets of *Toofan aur Deeya*.

'Mehboob Saab would like to meet you,' he told the young actor, offering him a paan from a small silver box.

'*The* Mehboob Khan!' Rajendra exclaimed, declining the betel-leaf triangles.

*With fellow stalwarts of the Hindi film industry, Mehboob Khan and Dilip Kumar*

He could hardly believe his ears, but was compelled to do so when he found himself actually sitting across from the great man in his office at the iconic Mehboob Studio in Bandra, named after its owner, the famous Mehboob Khan. But Mehboob Saab's humility, as he rose from behind his desk to embrace the newcomer, was a lesson in itself.

'Let's sit out in the garden,' Khan suggested, leading the way.

Once they had settled themselves comfortably on cane chairs, he asked, 'Would you like to work with me?'

'Mehboob Saab,' Rajendra began, 'for a newcomer like me, there can be no greater honour than to work with you. I am grateful for this opportunity.'

'Done, then!' the director responded. 'What are your charges?'

'That I will be working in your film is payment enough. Please don't place the "money" burden on my shoulders; they aren't as strong as yours,' Rajendra said humbly.

A smile broke out on Mehboob Khan's face. 'Dialogue *achha bolta hai!* A whiz at mouthing dialogues!' he remarked, and the deal was duly consolidated.

As if this were not enough, the next day, Rajendra received another call, this time from Wadia Movietone. *Things seem to be on the up and up,* he thought, smiling to himself as he sat looking out of the train window en route to the Wadia office.

No sooner had he been ushered into the office and he'd taken a seat than they made an offer.

'We would like to offer you a three-film contract.'

Although thrilled beyond words, Rajendra played it cool. 'What will the payment be?' he enquired.

'The signing amount is a new car,' they told him. 'So you can imagine how generously we will be paying you. Tomorrow, you will have a Fiat at your doorstep. But there's one condition: no other movie release till our films are in the theatres.'

'Hmm...' Rajendra leaned back, as if considering the terms. But at the back of his mind was an image of Shukla opening their front door and gasping with shock and delight at the sight of the new car.

'I would love to work with you,' he finally told them. 'But I need a day to finalize things, before we sign the contract.'

'Sure. Tomorrow it is, then.'

Carried on a wave of euphoria, Rajendra made his way straight out of the Wadia office to Mehboob Khan's office.

When he reached there, before he could utter a word, the director announced, 'I have finalized a major role for you in my next project, *Mother India*, with Nargis and Raaj Kumar. You, along with another actor called Sabu, are to play Nargisji's sons – the good son and the bad one! But before that comes along, I want you to act in my current film, *Aawaz*. It's a small part, but I promise you that the *Mother India* role will follow. Also, you will be paid one thousand rupees per month.'

'All right, sir!' Rajendra said with a nod, feeling a little bemused as he left the studio for the sets of Rawail's film, where he was still holding on to his job as an assistant director.

By this time, Shukla was expecting her first child and they'd shifted into a one-bedroom-and-hall apartment in Santacruz. On reaching home that evening, Rajendra lifted the petite Shukla and twirled her around, before announcing, 'My dear, pretty wife, when you wake up tomorrow morning, there will be a surprise for you at our doorstep.'

'Really? How will that happen?' Shukla asked, cool as a cucumber, as she led her husband to the dining table where the evening meal was waiting.

As she started serving him, Rajendra began relating the day's events.

'I've received two offers today – one from the Wadias and the other from Mehboob Khan,' he told her.

'Hmm! Great news!' she said, sitting down opposite him and sipping water from her glass as she considered the development.

'Now our life is about to take off,' Rajendra said happily, between bites.

'Miyan,' Shukla said with a smile, 'I may be quite a bit younger than you, but I am mature beyond my years. Do you know that the one passion in my mother's life was movies? I have been watching films from the time I was a toddler and would sit on her lap in theatres. I know films.'

'So what's the connection?' her husband enquired, puzzled. 'What are you trying to say?'

'The owners of the Studio have recently sold Movietone... and they're reworking their film-making economics.'

'I see...'

'On the other hand, there is Mehboob Saab!' she went on. 'Incomparable!'

'I agree, but...'

'If you keep the company of big people,' Shukla persisted, 'you will become a big man some day. But if you associate yourself with the more commercialized...'

'I understand what you're trying to say,' her husband told her, 'but it is for you that I want a new car, especially now that we are expecting a new member in the family.'

'Greed isn't one of my shortcomings and I certainly didn't marry you for money, Miyan,' Shukla told him firmly. 'Fiat-*shiaat ko maro goli!* To hell with the promised Fiat! We'll not be wanting for homes and cars when the time is right. Think long-term.'

The next day, Rajendra signed a contract with Mehboob Khan.

He returned home that evening, not with the Fiat that had been dangled before him by Wadia Movietone as the signing amount, but with the princely sum of one thousand rupees. Husband and wife spread the notes out on their bed, gazing at the money in awe.

*With his wife, Shukla Kumar – love shining through*

'So much!' Rajendra beamed with happiness. 'How shall we spend it?'

'First, we must send money to Papa,' his wife reminded him, her thoughts going to her father-in-law. 'He struggles with that little cloth store in Delhi. Then we will decide what to do with the rest.'

'Your wish is my command,' Rajendra said, taking her in his arms again.

My mother-in-law would often tease my mother by asking her, 'How did you even consider getting your daughter married to my son? He had nothing!' But the thrill of that first thousand rupees was something else! Six months after my husband received that signing amount, we had everything and more. But even with lakhs of rupees coming in, we would never experience that first thrill ever again.

*Shukla Tuli*

# 8

# The Rising Star

Despite the period of struggle I went through in Bombay, in the coming years, I could look back and say, 'To go and start afresh in a strange city can be a very beautiful experience, if you find space in it.'

*Rajendra Kumar Tuli*

The year 1956 began with the promise of a bright future for the young Tulis.

In his Santacruz home, Rajendra stood at the window with a cup of tea in one hand and a 555 cigarette in the other, watching the sun rise over the horizon. Today was his first day of shoot for the Mehboob Khan production *Aawaz.* He was excited, but apprehensive too. In a strange twist of fate, the director of the film had turned out to be none other than Zia Sarhadi, the man who had not only replaced Rajendra with another actor in his film, but shooed him away from his doorstep on that stormy night in July when the desperate young man had called on him.

By 9 a.m. sharp, Rajendra reported on the film's set, ready with his make-up and well-rehearsed dialogues. But as soon as he set eyes on the director, he found himself breaking out in a cold sweat. A sense of déjà vu seized him momentarily, filling him with panic. At the same time, he couldn't help appreciating the irony of the games karma played in the lives of humans. *Today, the man who had once rejected me has no choice but to direct me in this film*, he observed silently.

'Action!' the director called out, and both director and actor played along as if nothing had ever happened between them to sour their relations.

However, two days into the shoot, an intuitive Rajendra began to sense Sarhadi's latent antagonism directed towards him. *Why? What have I done that Zia Saab dislikes me*, he wondered. But he resolved to stay focussed on his work.

A few days later, Mehboob Khan watched the little footage that had been shot and was taken aback by Rajendra's unbecoming appearance in the film.

'Zia Saab, why is this handsome lad looking so shabby?' he asked the director. 'Even his clothes seem too big for him.'

'Well, he was your choice, not mine,' came the cocky reply, bringing a frown to the showman's brow.

'Hmm…' Mehboob Khan remained silent for a few seconds, then observed, 'When Rajendra's first film released, everybody was praising him. And today you doubt my casting choice.'

'I cannot make him what he isn't,' Sarhadi said defiantly, his arrogance coming to the fore.

'No problem,' said the producer. 'If you cannot, then leave the film. I will take over from this point.'

Mr Zia Sarhadi was removed from the film exactly the way I had been thrown out of an earlier film at his behest. We have an apt saying to describe such a situation: '*Khuda ki lathi mein awaaz nahin hoti, magar takat bahut hoti hai.* A knock on the head from God makes no noise, but packs a punch.' *Aawaz* was subsequently completed by Mr Mehboob Khan. Not only was he a superb director, he

> was a great actor himself. Even truly gifted actors could not match the quality of Mehboob Saab's performances. He was like a father figure to actors like us, full of empathy. He was also such a down-to-earth man. Without any expectations from his artistes, he would encourage and guide newcomers by acting out the scenes himself. But yes, he sat with a cane in hand on the sets of the film [to maintain discipline and his high standards]. I don't believe I have met anyone quite like him in my entire life.
>
> *Rajendra Kumar Tuli*

Even as work on *Aawaz* continued, Mehboob Khan began shooting for *Mother India* with actor Nargis, whose career had taken off with the film *Tamanna* in 1942. Her leading man was Raaj Kumar, who had begun his acting career with the 1952 Hindi film *Rangeeli*. Hollywood actor Sabu was to play their rebellious son in the film. Sabu Dastagir was the son of an Indian mahout, who'd got his lucky break when he was chosen to act in the 1937 British film *Elephant Boy*. He'd then been given roles in similar kinds of films, like *The Thief of Bagdad*, *Jungle Book*, *Arabian Nights* and *Song of India*. *Mother India* was to mark Sabu's debut in Hindi cinema, and he duly travelled from Los Angeles (LA) to Bombay and was put up at a multi-star hotel in the city.

Thereafter began the battle to get him a work permit. As time went by and there was no permit in sight, Mehboob Khan suffered financial losses and had to forgo dates for shooting committed to him by the other actors. Finally, he decided to replace Sabu with his muse, the legendary Dilip Kumar, who had earlier expressed an interest in playing the defiant Birju. However, Nargis rightfully pointed out that the audience was unlikely to be receptive to the idea of her playing mother to her romantic lead of several films. The role finally went to the dashing, one-film-old actor Sunil Dutt, who had been introduced to Mehboob Saab by Mukri, the film's comedian.

Meanwhile, Mehboob Productions' *Aawaz*, based on the poignant theme of respectable folk struggling to overcome the hardships brought about by enforced poverty, premiered on Friday, 16 March 1956, at Bombay's classic Liberty theatre. Among the illustrious members of the audience were glamorous film stars, filmmakers and film fans. The film proved to be a success and Rajendra Kumar's quiet and dignified portrayal of a young man in love was much appreciated.

The actor was overjoyed. As if to add to his happiness, his first child, Bunty, was born the same year on 11 July in Kashibai Hospital, Santacruz West.

Cradling the baby tenderly in his arms, an ecstatic Rajendra Kumar ordered sweets to be distributed to celebrate the occasion. At that very moment, the beautiful Nargis walked in and became the first woman visitor to hold the newborn in her arms. Settling the infant on her lap, she said, 'Today, my son Ramu has made me a grandmother,' making a tongue-in-cheek allusion to the roles she and Rajendra were playing in *Mother India*. Her laughter, emanating from her feelings of happiness and pride, lit up the hospital room. She had no way of knowing, of course, that one day, her own daughter Namrata would be married to Bunty, the infant in her arms.

Once *Aawaz* had been released, work on *Mother India* picked up speed. The film was a remake of Mehboob Khan's earlier black-and-white superhit *Aurat*, where Khan's second wife, Sardar Akhtar, had played mother to Surendra, in the role of the good, obedient son, and Yakub, in the role of the deviant one. Interestingly, the role of their father had been enacted by Arun Kumar Ahuja, who was none other than popular film actor Govinda's father.

Although Mehboob Khan had been ready with the title and concept of *Mother India* since early 1952, it was only

*With his first-born, Bunty aka Kumar Gaurav*

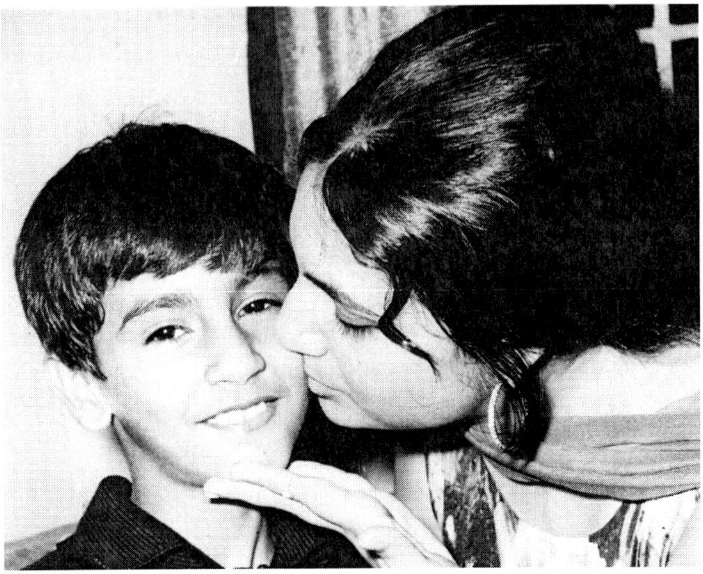

*Shukla with the young Bunty*

two years later that he would be granted permission to begin shooting.

While the crew waited for the necessary permission and the script and cast were yet to be finalized, the film's cinematographer, Faredoon Irani, was travelling to Uttar Pradesh to shoot some scenes of monsoon floods in the countryside. Meanwhile, Nargis and Raaj Kumar, who would be playing the roles of the couple Radha and Shamu, were busy familiarizing themselves with the agricultural work their rural characters were meant to carry out as a part of their daily routine – ploughing, reaping, sowing and picking. It is clear that Mehboob Khan was aiming for realism. With that objective in mind, the film was mostly shot on location in various villages of Maharashtra and Gujarat, with the exception of a few scenes that would be shot in Bombay's Mehboob Studio.

In the role of Radha and Shamu's dutiful son, Ramu, Rajendra Kumar, romanced Kumkum who played a village girl on the song '*Ghoonghat nahi kholoongi saiyaan tore aage* (I will not lift my veil for your eyes to savour my beauty)' Ramu, with his boyish good looks, a lock of hair stylishly brushing his forehead, his distinctive style of acting, presented a stark contrast to Sunil Dutt playing his brother, Birju. With artificially tanned skin, a country-bumpkin-style haircut and a perpetual sulk, Birju the defiant younger sibling rages throughout the film, teasing and taunting the village belles, playing to perfection the quintessential rebel and bad boy with his own peculiar charisma. But *Mother India* belonged, in the true sense, to Nargis. All of twenty-six, she owned the role of Radha, covering the different stages of her life as a newly-wed, a young single mother struggling against all odds to raise her sons after her husband abandons her and, finally, an ageing mother who must make tough, heartbreaking choices. *Mother India* embodied the spirit of Indian motherhood, showcasing

Radha's strength of character and determination to choose the difficult path, rather than give in to the lust of Sukhilala, the local moneylender. 'Radha Rani,' he says as he drools over Radha in the film, infuriating her son Birju enough to take up arms, whereas his brother, Ramu, represents the voice of reason and maintains his composure.

One of the many scenes in the film that encapsulates the sentiment at its core shows Ramu berating Birju for stealing back the gold bangles their mother had pawned to Sukhilala. He insists that Radha return them to the moneylender and promises to earn enough to redeem them in the future.

'*Ma, dede kangan.* Ma, return the bangles,' Ramu urges her in a low, authoritative voice.

'*Yeh kangan nahin utarenge.* They'll never come off!' Birju growls, holding his mother's wrists in a tight grip to prevent her from obeying Ramu.

'*Mujhe chori ke kangan pehnayega? Tu chor hai?* Are you a thief, wanting me to wear stolen bangles?' Radha sobs, as her two sons grapple with each other and cling to her at the same time.

This poignant scene set the stage for the unfolding of subsequent events. The bond shared between the mother and her sons, the banter exchanged between them, the tussle between the siblings, the emotional outbursts that result from their conflicts and the coming to blows were so movingly depicted by the three principal characters that *Mother India* touched a chord with its audience and became a stupendous success. The songs '*Holi aayi re, Kanhai, rang chhalke bajaa de zara bansuri* (Oh, Kanhai, play your flute for me and spray the colours, for Holi is here!)', '*Na main bhagwan hoon/ Na main shaitaan hoon* (I am neither god nor the devil)', and '*Duniya mein hum aayein hain toh jeena hi padega* (Since we are born into this world, we have to live life undeterred)', among others, helped carry the story forward.

*In* Mother India, *with Sunil Dutt and Nargis*

*Mother India*'s tragic climax is embedded in the memory of cinemagoers of that era, but what would become a part of the film's lore was a crucial scene involving Sunil Dutt and Nargis that marked the beginning of their real-life love story. In the scene, shot in March 1957 in the Umra area of Surat in Gujarat, Radha is supposed to run between burning haystacks, looking frantically for Birju. But while the shooting was in progress, the wind changed direction without warning, fanning the flames and causing the fire to rage uncontrolled, trapping the film's leading lady within a circle. It was at this moment that actor Sunil Dutt grabbed a blanket and jumped into the ring of fire to rescue Nargis. While both were hospitalized with burns and minor injuries, the unfortunate incident marked the beginning of one of filmdom's most unforgettable love stories. Rumours had it that Sunil Dutt and Nargis were married soon after, and it was only due to Mehboob Khan's earnest plea that they waited for the film's release before making their relation public. Sunil Dutt and Nargis were married on 11 March 1958.

It would turn out to be one of the industry's most enduring partnerships.

Although Mehboob Khan had planned to release *Mother India* on the tenth anniversary of India's independence, it took another two months for the film to premiere at Bombay's Liberty Cinema on 25 October 1957 and was a resounding success. The most expensive Indian film ever made till that time, *Mother India* earned a higher box-office revenue than any of its competitors. A special screening of the film was also held at the New Delhi residence of the then Indian President Rajendra Prasad and attended by Jawaharlal Nehru, the country's prime minister at the time.

While the leading lady Nargis was lauded for what would come to be considered her career's best performance, *Mother India* became the first successful film for both Rajendra Kumar and Sunil Dutt and proved to be a turning point in their careers.

In fact, even before the film had released, people who'd seen the rushes lauded Rajendra Kumar's magnetism and acting skills, and he was soon receiving offers from other directors and producers. With money coming in and his popularity on the rise, Rajendra first fulfilled his dream of purchasing an imported car for his wife.

Sitting beside her star husband in their brand new Impala, Shukla recalled how she had persuaded Rajendra to turn down the earlier offer from Wadia Movietone that had come with the promise of a Fiat as the signing amount. *Thank God,* she sighed, as their car turned into the theatre driveway. Flashbulbs exploded, crowds screamed and cheers rent the air. Stepping out of the car, Shukla walked proudly beside her debonair husband. *Stardom is upon us,* she thought, smiling to herself.

*Mother India* was nominated for the Academy Awards, but lost by just one vote. The film won the All India Certificate of Merit for Best Feature Film and also the Filmfare Best Film

Award 1958. It was dubbed in several European languages, including Spanish, French and Russian.

Naturally, parties and celebrations followed.

When Mr Mehboob Khan introduced us to Nargisji, he said, 'Boys! Here is your mother.' To Nargisji, he said, 'Baby, meet your sons.' Thereafter on the film set she was, indeed, like a mother to us and we behaved like her sons. She was such a good person, such a noble lady. Nargisji came to see my first child, my son, Bunty – his real name is Manoj Kumar – when I became a father in July 1956. She then went off to Europe and brought back imported clothes for Bunty. By the time *Mother India* released, Sunil Dutt and Nargis were married. I remember there was such a hue and cry outside Mehboob Studio, with many saying, 'How could he marry his mother?' It was just a role they played. Consequently, they [Sunil Dutt and Nargis] did not attend the premiere of *Mother India*. Mehboob Saab was very upset about it, but with time everything was fine. With the grace of God, they are living a very happy life. The film's success proved that people [eventually] accepted it. They were not bothered about [the] personal relationships [between the stars].

*Rajendra Kumar Tuli*

# 9

# Two Lucky Dimples

I began getting good film offers. I'd also bought a new Impala car. It was a big honour for me that despite being a newcomer, I was being compared to the great Dilip Kumar from the time I had acted in my very first film. But when it happened repeatedly, it became annoying. Any serious actor would definitely be inspired by Dilip Kumar's style of acting. This underplayed, natural acting style had been introduced by [the actor] Motilal. Dilip Kumar took it forward. And then we came and decided to follow through.

*Rajendra Kumar Tuli*

The period covering the late 1940s right up to the 1960s witnessed the release of Hindi films in a variety of genres. The mood in India following the country's independence was decidedly upbeat and there was a tangible feeling in the air that filmmakers were ready to question the status quo by breaking away from tradition and stepping into new territory. It was, in fact, in the 1950s that Indian cinema would attain its peak of glory.

*With Raj Kapoor, Dilip Kumar and Shammi Kapoor*

Socially conscious directors like Mehboob Khan, Bimal Roy, Guru Dutt and Raj Kapoor, who had entered the film industry in the 1930s and 1940s, would be instrumental in changing the face and character of Hindi films. Their works, like Kapoor's *Awaara* (1951), set in the city of dreams and nightmares, and *Shree 420* (1955) dealt with social themes, primarily working-class urban life and the country's progressive materialism. In the same league were Guru Dutt's films *Pyaasa* (1957) and *Kaagaz ke Phool* (1959).

Marking a complete departure from this trend was the farmer- and landlord-based film, Mehboob Khan's iconic *Mother India*, followed by V. Shantaram's 1957 release *Do Aankhen Barah Haath*. Romance too was integral to films like Bimal Roy's 1958 reincarnation drama *Madhumati* and K. Asif's epic love story *Mughal-e-Azam* (1960). Other Hindi films of the time include those made by Kamal Amrohi and Vijay Bhatt. Musical comedies like *Albela*, released in 1951, and Kishore Kumar's 1958 film *Chalti ka Naam Gaadi* also made it big. The common thread running through all these films remained their rich and meaningful music, their songs and lyrics.

Along with the other genres, drama too reigned supreme, as did the tragic-martyr space that only one person could fill and do justice to: Dilip Kumar. It was believed, however, that the 'tragedy king' image and the roles it brought him weighed heavily on the superstar, prompting him to consciously seek light-hearted roles. There was also the matter of his stature in the industry and the fees he could command for his films, which made the star unaffordable for many producers. The next course of action for the latter was to zero in on the newcomer Rajendra Kumar, who – reviewers had been claiming from the time they watched him in his first major role in *Vachan* – had styled his performances on Dilip Kumar's. No wonder then that he seemed perfect for roles once tailor-made for the tragedy king. The first of these was in Kedar Kapoor's *Devar Bhaabi*, a 'social film' starring Balraj Sahni, Rajendra Kumar and Mala Sinha that released on 1 January 1958. Rajendra Kumar attended the film's premiere with his friend Manoj Kumar, an aspiring actor at the time.

> Rajinder [Rajendra] was shooting at Ranjit Studios. During my days of struggle in the film industry, when I was doing the rounds of the studios, I would go there quite often and see him sitting outside, between shots, reading. He was very fond of reading. One day, he said to a crew member, 'Call that boy.' I was summoned and went and sat across from him. He asked me, 'What do you do?' to which I replied, '*Jo aap kar rahe ho, wahi*... The same thing as you.' From then on, we started meeting frequently. He was from Sialkot and I from Lahore. We had so many stories to share. Gradually, a rapport developed between us. He started giving me the encouragement I needed.

After that first meeting at Ranjit Studios, he took me to watch an English film at New Excelsior – *The Bravados*. Later, he asked me to accompany him to *Devar Bhabhi*'s premiere, where I met Rawail Saab, who liked me and offered me a role in *Kanch ki Gudiya*. And one beautiful evening, I remember Rajinder taking me along to Mr Mehboob Khan's home on Marine Drive for Eid. He also took me to Mehboob Studio for *Son of India*. He had a terrific knack for languages and spoke to Mehboob Saab in Gujarati. 'Take him in your film,' he suggested, pointing to me. The legendary Mehboob Saab then held my head between his hands and checked my profile. It made Rajinder laugh. 'Khan Saab,' he said, 'you don't need to check. Trust me, he is very good.' He took me along to meet many directors and left no stone unturned to help me in my career. He was a symbol of support for us newcomers, like Dharmendra, Feroz Khan and many others. I remember him calling up actor Ajit in my presence for a role in *Suraj*. Ajit was not doing well at that time and by offering him this role Rajinder resurrected his career, as he did for many others. He was a generous man.

*Manoj Kumar*

Despite his rising stature and the number of films promised to him in 1958, Rajendra Kumar had continued to live in his one-bedroom apartment in Santacruz. But in August that year, a heavily pregnant Shukla sat her husband down and said, 'Miyan, we have such a big car, but what about our home? I am due soon and with Bunty growing up, we need a bigger home.'

'I have been thinking about it too,' Rajendra told her absent-mindedly.

'We wear the latest styles, drive to the most exclusive parties in our Impala, but our home really is too small.'

'Hmm... I've been looking for a bigger place since last week,' Rajendra informed his wife. 'It was to be a surprise for you. But I haven't yet found anything suitable. Tomorrow, I will consult Punditji and see what he has to say.'

Pandit Shambhu Lingam, who had, since their wedding, been visiting the young Tulis every Sunday, arrived the following day, right on schedule, at 10 a.m. Punditji was the man who had been instrumental in guiding Rajendra Kumar on the path to success, every step of the way.

'Punditji, I plan to move to a new home,' Rajendra announced, seated beside the holy man on a cushion arranged on the floor. 'I wonder if the time is right.'

'Hmm... Let's see,' Punditji mumbled, scanning Rajendra's horoscope. 'This is the month of August. I do see you in a larger home...but not before February 1959. I see a bungalow by the sea.'

'You can't be serious, Punditji!' Rajendra exclaimed. 'Six months? To find an apartment in Bombay? I'll find not one, but ten in that much time!'

'Son, you can keep trying,' Punditji countered, 'but if you succeed in finding a larger home before February and prove my prediction wrong, I am prepared to give up my practice.'

'I am sure you are right, Punditji,' the ever-polite and respectful Rajendra hastened to say, concerned that he might have offended the family priest. But in his heart he was convinced that he would find a suitable home in the next few weeks.

The weeks passed swiftly, with no tangible results. While Rajendra continued looking for a new home, the upcoming star and his wife lived life to the fullest. Being a popular young couple, they were invited to several gatherings and film parties.

On Friday, 31 October 1958, a *karva chauth* party was organized by the Rawails in their Bandra home. Dressed in their wedding finery to observe the rituals dedicated to the well-being of their respective spouses, Shukla and her friends sat together, waiting for the moon to appear so that they could break the fast they had been observing through the day.

Despite being in the last trimester of her pregnancy, Shukla had been adamant about observing the fast and hadn't had a morsel of food or even a drop of water since dawn. Now as a cold sweat broke out on her body, followed by the first spasm of pain, she felt slightly dizzy.

'I think it's time,' she said to one of the women sitting close to her.

'Are you certain?' the woman asked. 'It must be just the fatigue and dehydration brought on by the fast. You'll be fine, don't worry. Just enjoy the party.'

*Maybe, she is right*, Shukla thought, watching her husband and the other men downing amber-filled glasses as they sang along with the famed vocalist Saeeda Khan and showered her with praise, garlands and rupee notes in appreciation. But a few moments later, a second wave of pain shot through her lower back. Shukla looked around for Mrs Rawail, who was busy overseeing the serving of snacks and dinner.

Clumsy in her advanced stage of pregnancy, she waddled over to her hostess with difficulty and said in an urgent whisper, '*Bhabhi*, I have to go to the hospital.'

Within moments, Mrs Rawail had summoned the driver and was leading Shukla to the car waiting outside.

At that very moment, a very drunk H.S. Rawail called for a halt to the party and announced, 'Shukla is [as dear to me as] my daughter. I will take her to the hospital myself.'

Along with an almost equally inebriated Rajendra, they piled into the car and tumbled out of it on reaching the nursing home.

'The nurses tittered at the sight of the drunken actor and the overdressed mother-to-be. "The men are not in their senses," they remarked, "and look at you, all dressed in your finery. You have come to the hospital to deliver a baby or for a party?" the head nurse teased.'

But before Shukla could launch into an explanation, her mother arrived and took charge, shooing the men away.

'Go back and enjoy your party,' she told them. 'It will be some time before the baby comes.'

The next morning, when a sober Rajendra returned to the hospital, he couldn't take his eyes off the wailing baby girl in his arms.

'So beautiful, but how much she cries!' he whispered.

'The baby was dehydrated because of her mother's fast,' his mother-in-law explained. 'She is crying because she's hungry.'

'Hmm!' Rajendra Kumar smiled and as he gazed down at his little girl a dimple appeared on her plump cheek.

'Dimple! It's an apt name for my baby girl! Dimple – that's what we will call her.'

Back from the hospital, the family continued to live in their Santacruz home, as Rajendra hadn't yet found the ideal apartment.

Then, on 3 February 1959, his real-estate broker called about a flat that seemed to meet the actor's requirements.

'It's on Carter Road,' the man told him. 'Can you come and see it now?'

'Of course!' Rajendra said eagerly. 'I'll meet you there.'

A cool February breeze was blowing in from the Arabian Sea as Rajendra Kumar stood with the broker, waiting for the key of the apartment to be brought to them. *I'd love to stay by the sea*, he thought, looking around him. His eyes came to a rest on a bungalow nestled amid lush branches and tall badam trees. He approached it to get a better view. It had a sloping roof and wide verandas facing the sea.

For Rajendra, it was love at first sight. *Idyllic and so beautiful,* he thought. Then his astrologer's predictions sprang to mind.

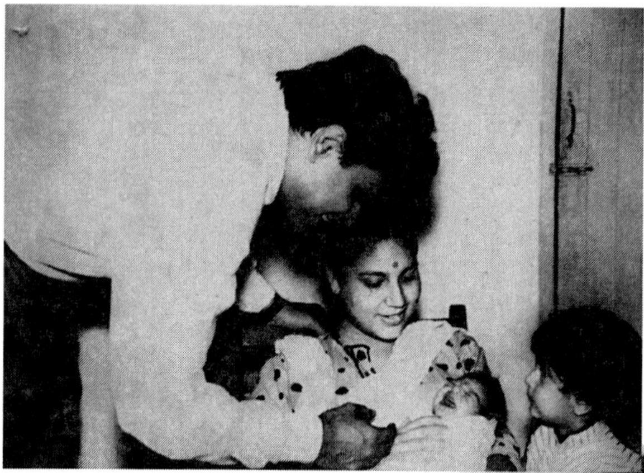

*The doting parents and older brother Kumar Gaurav with Dimple Kumar, born on 31 October 1958*

*With his beloved daughter Dimple*

*At a film location with Bunty and Dimple*

Punditji had been right. His new home stood by the sea. But a bungalow… It looked expensive. Would he be able to afford the rent?

'Who does the house belong to?' he asked the broker, taking a deep drag of his 555 cigarette.

'It belongs to a Muslim…or Parsi family. Look at the name,' said the broker, pointing to the words 'Bano Villa' engraved on the outer wall.

'Would they agree to let it out on rent? How much are they asking for?' Rajendra Kumar enquired, stubbing out his cigarette with his foot.

'I don't think so,' the broker replied. 'At the moment, a writer is living there on rent. I spoke to him some time back and he said the house was haunted.'

'Really!'

'Yes!' the broker laughed. 'Apparently, this gentleman hasn't paid the rent for months, and now that the landlord has given him an ultimatum he's probably spreading rumours to drive off prospective buyers and tenants. Otherwise, why would he continue to live in a haunted house?'

'Hmm. Are you sure the landlord will not rent it out to me?'

'I doubt it, sir. The owner is quite fed up and has decided to sell it. No rentals.'

'Any idea how much he wants for it?'

'Around seventy-five thousand rupees, I think – furniture included.'

'Okay! I like the house,' Rajendra acknowledged, lighting another cigarette. 'See, I am not interested in the furniture. If he is willing to reduce the price a bit and is open to negotiation, then it's a go-ahead.'

'All right!' the broker said. 'I will talk to him about it.'

On his way back home, Rajendra began working out the economics of purchasing the bungalow and as soon as he reached home, he asked his wife, 'How much money do we have saved?'

Taken aback, Shukla replied, 'Ten thousand. Why?'

Rajendra told her about the bungalow he'd seen.

'I think we can make this work,' he said. 'Tomorrow, the broker will let us know if the landlord is ready to negotiate.'

'But…but,' Shukla stammered in protest, 'the broker said the bungalow was haunted, didn't he?'

But her mother, who had joined them in the living room, scoffed, 'In a city like Bombay, even humans don't have a place to stay. And here we are, talking about ghosts!'

Manoj Kumar, who had, at the time, been accommodated in the Tuli home, suggested, 'Just perform a havan and if there are any ghosts around, they will vanish.'

The next morning, the broker called again. 'I've managed to convince Bano to bring the price down to sixty-five thousand,' he said.

'Great! Done,' Rajendra replied, his blood racing with excitement.

'But, Rajendraji,' said the broker, 'if you wait for a couple of days, there's a chance that he might reduce the asking price to fifty-five thousand. The family seems to be in a hurry to sell.'

'No!' Rajendra was adamant. 'I do not want to risk losing it to another buyer. In fact, I am sending over the advance right now.'

'Fine, sir. That will be a cheque for ten thousand rupees.'

As Rajendra Kumar put the phone receiver back in its cradle, he smiled at his own audacity. *I have only ten thousand in my account and, here I am, purchasing a bungalow that costs sixty-five thousand! It was fated to happen.*

I immediately signed a cheque for ten thousand [rupees] and sent it to the broker. Now I had to pay fifty-five thousand more, which I didn't have in my account. So I went to Mr B.R. Chopra, who, a few days earlier, had offered me two films – *Dhool ka Phool* and *Kanoon*. While I had accepted both, we had yet to come to an agreement over the payment for each film. The consolidated fee they were offering for both films was not acceptable to me. So C.V.K. Shastri, the Chopras's production controller, and I were still wrangling over it when this beautiful bungalow came into the picture. I told Chopra Saab, 'Shastriji and I have reached an impasse regarding my fee. So could we please finalize the amount?' Chopra Saab asked, 'How much has Shastri offered you?' 'One lakh fifty thousand for both films,' I told him. 'And I have asked for two lakhs, as I am charging other producers more than a lakh per movie.' He said, 'All right, I will pay you one lakh seventy-five thousand for both.' I agreed immediately, but laid down the condition that he should pay me fifty thousand then and there. And the magnanimous B.R. Chopra immediately handed me fifty thousand rupees. I paid fifty-five thousand to the owner of the bungalow on Carter Road that I had set my heart on and now it was mine. I named the house after my newborn daughter, Dimple. I spent my most successful years as a star in that house. Then my mother, my sister Manorama and my youngest brother, Ranjit, moved to Bombay, with my father preferring to stay back in Delhi, content to run his little cloth store. In 1959, my sister would get married to [producer, director and actor] O.P. Ralhan in that very house.

*Rajendra Kumar Tuli*

# 10

# Going Solo

I never ran after producers and directors in the hope of being offered roles in their films. I never sent my photographs anywhere for work. Having started my career as an assistant director, I had a secure job. So that helped. And soon, by the grace of God, my life became even more secure. After the release of *Mother India*, I never had to look back. I had found the confidence within me to make it big. I signed *Talaq*. It was written by Mr Mukhram Sharma, the top writer of that time, and would be directed by the great Mahesh Kaul. The film's title meant 'divorce', but there was no divorce in the film... It was a comedy drama.

*Rajendra Kumar Tuli*

*Talaq* released in 1959 and was nominated for a couple of Filmfare awards. While writing the screenplay, Pandit Mukhram Sharma, who was known for his progressive film scripts like *Aulad* and *Dhool ka Phool*, could not find an appropriate Hindi word for 'divorce' and, therefore, settled on *Talaq*. As its Urdu title suggests, the film, a social comedy of sorts, dealt with a couple's marital problems, with the impending threat of divorce hanging over their lives all through its runtime. In the role in which he was cast, Rajendra Kumar, who had yet to fall into the image trap, looked suave, confident and dashing in waistcoats and achkans, his chosen wardrobe lending credence to the character he was playing. However, it was in this very film that the mannerisms – quivering lips, cocked eyebrow and dramatic facial expressions – identified with his particular style of acting would first manifest themselves. Interestingly, one of his co-stars in the film was an exceptionally talented child actor – Honey Irani – who played the three-year-old son of the characters enacted by the main leads.

In the midst of shooting for *Talaq*, Rajendra received a message from Vijay Bhatt and rushed over to Prakash Studios in Andheri East to meet the producer-director and his older brother and partner Shankar.

'Rajendraji,' Vijay said, 'we our planning our next film, *Goonj Uthi Shehnai*, and would like you to play the title role of a *shehnai* player.'

'I am honoured,' the actor murmured, his heart skipping a beat.

*The lead, and a* shehnai *player! Wah!* He smiled to himself, but the insecurities that had crept in from the setbacks he had suffered in the past impelled him to seek further reassurance.

'Bhatt Saab,' he began, 'you've offered me the chance to act in *Goonj Uthi Shehnai* and I accept your offer wholeheartedly. But please promise me that when this movie is made I will be the one playing the role.'

In response, both the Bhatt brothers burst into laughter.

'Of course we will!' they assured him. 'That is why we've called you over – to sign you for the film. How much will you charge?'

'Whatever you wish to give me,' Rajendra said humbly.

'No, please tell us what your fees will be.'

'Well, I have just signed another film for sixty thousand, so...'

'Sir, that is far too much,' Shankar Bhatt promptly cut in. 'We can't afford it.'

'Okay, then,' Rajendra conceded, 'I suggest you pay me whatever you have decided upon.'

'We had planned on thirty thousand for the central role.'

'That's fine, then,' Rajendra said with a smile. 'I am your *shehnai* player.'

Without much ado, Bhatt placed the contract in front of the actor for him to sign.

Rajendra Kumar put his signature to the document, accepted the thousand and one rupees he was given as the signing amount and left the office. Once outside, he patted himself on the back. He was sure that this was his great chance. This film would change the course of his life.

> We made *Goonj Uthi Shehnai* in four to five months. Following its completion, I signed my next film for a fee of one lakh rupees. The amount justified an earlier conversation that I'd had with Bhatt Saab. Shankar Bhatt had asked me, 'Tell me, son, why did you accept *Goonj Uthi...* for a sum that was lower than your asking price?' I had replied, 'I am the son of a businessman and a good business grows with investment. I charged thirty thousand less than my asking price of sixty thousand for your film, but now I am charging forty thousand more.'
>
> *Rajendra Kumar Tuli*

*Goonj Uthi Shehnai* released on 29 May 1959. The film opened with a scene where all that was visible was the silhouette of a *shehnai* player. He could easily have been mistaken for the legendary Dilip Kumar, but when the actor playing the role turned to face the audience and his features caught the light, the viewers sighed with pleasure – it was Rajendra Kumar!

The handsome actor in the role of the talented Kishan, the quintessential lover, lit up the screen, breathing life into melody through his musical instrument. A romantic tragedy, riding on the crest of the emotions it evoked and its hauntingly beautiful music, *Goonj Uthi Shehnai* turned out to be a treat for the senses, elevated to the level of the sublime by Ustad Bismillah Khan's *shehnai*. So much so, that by the time the end credits rolled the music flowing from the double-reed instrument had touched every heart and stirred every soul in the audience, validating a few lines from the film that went: '*Sangeet cheez hi aisi hai... joh uss mein kho nahin jaata, woh usse paa bhi nahin sakta* (Music is such a creation that those who aren't carried away by it won't be able to capture its essence either)'.

In the film, Rajendra Kumar, with eyebrow cocked and head swaying to the notes of the *shehnai*, exuded an innocent charm as he wooed the audience, along with his leading lady, played by the pretty Ameeta, who cavorted around her beloved, singing, '*Jeevan mein piya tera saath rahe/ Haule haule ghunghat pat khole/ Tere sur aur mere geet* (We remain together all our lives/ Slowly, my veil lifts/ On your melody and my songs)'. The audience responded with equal fervour to the pathos of '*Dil ka khilona hai toot gaya* (My heart, a toy now shattered)' and '*Keh do koi na kare yahaan pyaar* (Let it be known that none should fall in love here)'.

In addition to Vasant Desai's memorable compositions, with lyrics by Bharat Vyas, the mesmerizing *jugalbandi* between Ustad Bismillah Khan and sitar player Abdul Halim Jaffar Khan helped the film break all records. *Goonj Uthi Shehnai* was not only the fifth-highest grosser of the year, but was also declared a hit at Box Office India. It became Rajendra Kumar's first big commercial success, following his previous releases *Khazanchi*, *Devar Bhabhi*, *Ghar Sansar* and *Santan*.

For the rising star, the *shehnai* that was said to bestow sanctity on those within its environs had stayed true to its notes. It had brought the actor considerable luck, as had his newborn daughter, Dimple, and, of course, 'Dimple', the Tulis' new home by the sea. It was from here that Rajendra Kumar was soon allotting dates for new films that would be made four years from the day he had signed contracts confirming his commitment to these productions. In fact, all his films that year – *Do Behnen*, *Chirag Kahan Roshni Kahan* and *Dhool ka Phool* – would have a successful run at the box office.

*Chirag Kahan Roshni Kahan* released in August 1959. In this film, the benevolent hero Rajendra played the benevolent Doctor Anand, who, in a bid to save the life of a recently widowed patient, Ratna (played by Meena Kumari), decides to give his own son up to her when the baby she delivers dies at birth. Heartbroken and dejected at being separated from his son Raju, Dr Anand finds solace in his periodical visits to

*With Meena Kumari in a scene from* Chirag Kahan Roshni Kahan

the child. While the film's evergreen songs '*Chal mere ghode, tik tik tik* (Trot on, my horse, tik tik tik)' and '*Tim tim karte tare* (The stars twinkling in the night sky)', expressing the love between Raju and his adoptive mother, won hearts, Rajendra Kumar, playing the lonely and despondent Dr Anand, was lauded for his ability to hold his own against the formidable talent of 'tragedy queen' Meena Kumari, as he portrayed the latent tenderness of a father denied the right to acknowledge his son as his own and the pathos inherent in his predicament.

Recalling his own association with the film many years later, actor Manoj Kumar would say, 'I used to write. At the time Rajinder was shooting for *Chirag Kahan Roshni Kahan* with Meena Kumari, I reworked some scenes [from the film]. Although nervous about his reaction, I read out my versions to him. He loved them and said, "Yaar, you look so simple [unassuming]. From where did you get such depth in your writing?"'

Earlier that year, Rajendra had begun shooting for B.R. Chopra's films. The first was *Dhool ka Phool*, marking the directorial debut of Yash Chopra, an English literature student from Lahore University who had subsequently worked as a journalist with *Cine Herald* in Lahore. Known for his progressive ideas and intrepid writing, he'd begun by assisting his older brother B.R. Chopra. Deeply influenced by his sibling's social activism, his film *Dhool ka Phool*, an epic melodrama, dealt with pre-marital sex and its consequences – the stigma of motherhood without the endorsement of marriage and the social ostracism of children branded as illegitimate.

*Dhool ka Phool* released on 4 December 1959. The film opens with a scene where two bicycle-riding college students, played by Rajendra Kumar and Mala Sinha, collide head-on with each other. Inevitably, the encounter ignites a spark of attraction as the duo sing, '*Tere pyaar ka aasra chahta hoon* (I need the assurance of your love)', and blooms into full-fledged love during a duet in the garden that ends with the two young lovers taking shelter from a thunderstorm. A night of passion follows. Predictably, the young woman becomes pregnant and bears an illegitimate child, while the man she loves goes on to marry another woman (played by actress Nanda) and have a family of his own. The former girlfriend is literally left holding the baby and singing, '*Tu mere pyaar ka phool hai* (You are the fruit of my love)'. The child born out of wedlock is brought up by the character played by Manmohan Krishnan, who defies prevalent religious dogma with the song: '*Tu* Hindu *banega na* Mussalman *banega* (You will be raised neither as a Hindu nor as a Muslim)'.

In what was a departure from the norm in those days, Yash Chopra dared to make this woman-centric film and question the social taboos of the time. As if that were not enough, the story of *Dhool ka Phool* was bold enough to allow both the hero and the heroine a chance to find love again.

Although the film turned out to be a silver jubilee hit, Rajendra Kumar's many fans, who had become accustomed to his earlier image of the earnest lover of *Goonj Uthi Shehnai* and the disconsolate, self-sacrificing doctor of *Chirag Kahan Roshni Kahan* were shocked by his role reversal in *Dhool ka Phool.* Interestingly, this reinvention of the actor's conventional image hardly made a dent in his growing popularity. Women of all ages were infatuated with the good-looking star. Having played dutiful son, loyal brother, caring boyfriend, faithful husband and loving father with equal élan, Rajendra Kumar had created a particular image of himself that in the eyes of the film-going public stood for integrity and dependability.

While the star's female fans, whose number seemed to be increasing by leaps and bounds, were aware of his pretty wife, Shukla, for her part, understood the kind of temptations that lay in the path of her husband's growing fame and success. In this regard, she was very clear in her mind about the dynamics of their relationship and outlined its boundaries for her husband.

'Rajinderji, I understand the film line well enough,' she told him, before going on to explain her expectations of him and the kind of support she would extend to him. 'I will never question or nag you about what goes on at your workplace. Nor will I visit you at the studio where you are shooting. You have complete freedom there. But there's just one thing I expect from you: when you return home from work every evening, please don't carry the film world back with you. Do not bring that atmosphere into our home. Our home is our temple. Here [your priority] will be our time and our children's time.'

> Agreeing to do the role in *Dhool ka Phool* was a bold step, but I felt I had to take it. The thought of losing female fans for whatever reason, including the fact that I was a married man, never occurred to me. Nor, thankfully, did it ever happen. In fact, I was the most popular actor where women fans were concerned. They would say, 'Look at the man. He is married and still playing romantic roles so convincingly.' My wife never felt insecure about my ladies' fan club, because I kept my two identities [as an actor and a family man] separate. I never carried my home [or any issues connected to my personal life] to the studio. Nor did I ever carry my studio [and any work-related problems] back to my home. So Shukla and I were a very happy couple. I would go to the studio like any other working man goes to the office. So my wife was reassured that I was simply going for my job and coming back in the evening. I used to be very regular and maintained a professional routine, doing 9.30 a.m. to 6.30 p.m. shifts. Once that

was over, we would go for parties, functions and so on. So Shukla had no reason to be troubled by a sense of insecurity. She was very happy and proud of me. And it wasn't just her; the entire atmosphere at home was one of contentment, because we are an ideal couple from the film industry. The way I led my life was not simply related to the promise I had made my father [that I would always abide by a certain set of principles], but also guided by my own instincts. I am not sure whether I have managed to live up to the promise I made my father and lived by the principles Prithviraj Kapoor had followed, but I definitely have tried to live like a true gentleman.

*Rajendra Kumar Tuli*

# 11

# The Making of Jubilee Kumar

I was very choosy about selecting my films and never worked in more than three at a time. In a career spanning twenty years, from 1955 to 1975, I acted in about sixty-five to seventy films in all. This happened because I was only interested in working with the industry's top filmmakers. The strategy of working with renowned filmmakers worked well for me, especially in the 1960s. Since the very beginning of films, there have been stars. Then came an era when people started calling themselves superstars. But after every few films, these 'superstars' would be toppled from their position by yet another hero who had become a superstar. From 1955 till date, however, there has been only one 'Jubilee Kumar' in the film industry – Rajendra Kumar. It's not a title I chose for myself. It was given to me by my audience, the press and the film industry. I am so happy and so proud of it, and of the fact that this title has never been given to anyone else and, perhaps, never will be.

*Rajendra Kumar Tuli*

The swinging sixties were the harbingers of breezy, light-hearted films. Based on upper-middle class preoccupations, they marked a departure from the earlier ones whose primary focus had been urban deprivation and immorality. Among them, the trendsetters turned out to be the 1960 release *Love in Simla*, starring Joy Mukherjee and a new entrant to the industry, Sadhana; *Jab Pyar Kisi Se Hota Hai* (1961), with Dev Anand and Asha Parekh in the lead; and the Shammi Kapoor starrer *Junglee*, another 1961 release, which marked actor Saira Banu's debut. Indian film sets were now travelling to far-flung corners of India with their sunlit mountain ranges and snow-covered slopes and to other exotic and enchanting foreign locales, quite effectively erasing the memory of the ideal-driven revolutionaries of the 1950s from the minds of a younger audience that thirsted for undiluted entertainment and was drawn to the attractions of a progressive, Westernized culture. Thus, on screen, realism gradually gave way to adventure, jollity and romance.

For Rajendra Kumar, the fortuitous 1960s began with him playing a doctor, yet again, in *Patang* (1960), following which released Manhar Raskapur's Gujarati film *Mehndi Rang Lagyo*, a classic drama. Bipin Gajjar, the cinematographer of *Goonj Uthi Shehnai*, had asked Rajendra during the making of the film, 'Sir, when I work on my first Gujarati film, will you star in it?'

The star had laughed and replied, 'Only if it's in Gujarati.'

To his surprise, Gajjar soon approached him with a Gujarati film. A man of his word, Rajendra accepted the offer. The film was declared a hit and was particularly remembered for its soundtrack by the famous Gujarati music composer Avinash Vyas.

*Maa Baap*, a family-oriented drama, followed and became the first movie to run for twenty-five weeks in the same theatre.

It also offered Rajendra Kumar an opportunity to travel abroad for the first time.

It so happened that one evening, a certain Mr Gandhi turned up at Rajendra's home.

As he greeted the man, the actor realized that he had never met him before.

'Good evening, sir,' the stranger said, 'my name is Gandhi and I am the East African distributor of *Maa Baap*. I have come here to invite you over to Kenya for the film's silver jubilee function.'

'Oh! That's good,' Rajendra said.

'Yes, sir. People in Kenya have loved the film and especially your role in it. It would be an honour to have you visit your fans there.'

'I'd be happy to meet them too,' the actor replied.

He was delighted to receive the invitation for several reasons: the film was evidently successful enough for its African distributor to desire his presence in Kenya; the visit to that foreign country would be his first trip abroad; and he was getting a chance to meet up with his younger sister Kamla who had settled in Kampala, Uganda's capital city, after her marriage. For months, he had been longing to see her and here was the opportunity.

A week later, Rajendra and Shukla were on their way to Kenya, where they would spend ten wonderful days, before visiting Kamla's home in Uganda.

*Maa Baap* was followed by Rajendra's second B.R. Chopra film, *Kanoon*, a courtroom drama centred on a murder. Here, the actor played the role of a lawyer, with Nanda, Ashok Kumar, Mehmood, Shashikala, Jeevan and Om Prakash as his co-stars. The film, produced and directed by the radical Chopra himself, was India's second songless talkie film.

Simultaneously, Rajendra Kumar had begun shooting for a cameo in Yash Chopra's second film, *Dharmputra*. While in the poignant *Dhool ka Phool* a Muslim man was seen raising a child born to Hindus, in *Dharmputra* Chopra reversed the roles, with the depiction of a Hindu family bringing up a Muslim child. The film released in 1961, but provoked public outrage, leading to communal riots breaking out at the screenings. The outcome was inevitable: *Dharmputra* died a premature death.

The film did leave an enduring legacy, however: the immortal patriotic song '*Sare jahan se accha*', whose lyrics had been penned by poet Muhammad Iqbal, and '*Yeh kiska lahu hai? Kaun mara?* (Whose blood was shed? Who has died?)', the one song picturized on Rajendra Kumar, where the sincerity of his portrayal, embodying the pain and angst of all humanity, came through vividly.

Yash Chopra, however, never made another political film for obvious reasons.

Despite the trouble stirred up by *Dharmputra*, the same year would see the release of a total of six Rajendra Kumar starrers.

It began with *Aas ka Panchhi*, the debut film of both producer J. Om Prakash and director Mohan Kumar. Rajendra Kumar had signed the film in 1959 to honour a promise made in the early fifties to J. Om Prakash, his neighbour and friend from his early days in Bombay when he was desperately trying to gain a foothold in the industry. In those days, J. Om Prakash had been working as Mohan Segal's manager and would often encourage Rajendra in his efforts to build a career by urging him to 'focus on becoming a good director'. But J. Om Prakash's wife Padma hadn't quite agreed with her husband's point of view.

'No, Bhai Saab!' she'd told the young Rajendra. 'Focus on becoming a good actor. That's where your future lies.'

In fact, to affirm her faith in the good-looking, fledgling assistant director's potential as an actor, she had, on one occasion, placed a couple of copper coins in his palm and

*A scene from* Kanoon *(courtesy B.R. Studios LLP)*

*A still from* Kanoon *(courtesy B.R. Studios LLP)*

announced, 'This is my advance. The day my husband makes a film, you will be the hero. This is your signing amount.'

That day would arrive in 1959. One morning, J. Om Prakash and his wife dropped in for a visit at Rajendra's magnificent bungalow on Carter Road. After exchanging warm greetings, the friends made themselves comfortable in garden chairs to enjoy a cup of tea.

It was at that moment that Padma asked, 'You remember your promise and the coins I gave you?'

'Absolutely! Of course I remember,' Rajendra replied.

'My husband is making a film and he wants you as the hero.'

'Hmm… Who is the director?' Rajendra enquired after a long pause.

'Mohan Kumar.'

'*Woh kaun hai,* bhai? Who is he?'

'He is Mohan Segal's assistant director.'

Rajendra nodded politely in response. But as he leaned back in his chair and lit a cigarette, his mind was whirling with countless questions.

*Om's first production, with Vyjayanthimala in the lead and music by Shankar–Jaikishan… He could easily have signed Mohan Segal himself. Why the new director? There could be only one reason: Mohan Kumar must be very talented. He must be a good director.*

'Oh, he is brilliant!' J. Om Prakash declared in the ensuing silence, smiling with satisfaction at his choice of director.

'Fine,' Rajendra said, after a pause, 'let's give your new director a chance to prove himself.'

With that decision, the far-sighted jubilee star struck gold.

Shooting for the film commenced. From his very first meeting with Mohan, Rajendra took to the young director. Impressed by his expertise, he asked him, 'Mohan, how old are you?'

'Twenty-seven,' the young man replied.

*With producer J. Om Prakash*

'Mark my words,' the actor told him, 'this debut film of yours will run non-stop for at least twenty-eight weeks, that too in the same theatre.'

And that's what happened. The film [*Aas ka Panchhi*] ran for twenty-eight weeks on its own merit at Novelty Cinema. But at its premiere, I remember how B.R. Chopra Saab had put his arm around my shoulders, taken me aside and murmured, 'Bhai, *maaf karna, magar*... I'm sorry to say this, but it's a bad film.' I had felt slighted, but had managed to say, 'Bhai Saab, don't forget to come for its silver jubilee function.' He was really startled. 'Huh?' he'd said, open-mouthed. 'Yes, do come,' I'd repeated. And when that moment arrived, Chopra Saab was invited for the silver jubilee function at the Taj Mahal Hotel. Of course, he accepted the invite graciously. The chief guest was Raj Kapoor, who subsequently became my lifelong friend. Raj and I would experience a strange series of career crossings, beginning as early as in 1956, during the shooting of *Mother India*.

*Rajendra Kumar Tuli*

One morning in 1956, while the leading stars of the film *Mother India* were waiting for the shot to be set up, Nargis had said to Rajendra, 'Ramu, Mr Raj Kapoor is making a film called *Gharonda*. He had cast himself, Dilip Kumar and me in it. But for some unexplained reason, Dilip Kumar has suddenly opted out and Raj has gone into depression. Yesterday, he asked if you could meet him at R.K. Studios to discuss the same role.'

'That's great, Mummy!' Rajendra had exclaimed, pleasantly surprised that Raj Kapoor himself would consider offering him a role in his new film.

But in the same breath Nargis had continued, 'Yes, it is. But I had to turn down his offer. You are my son in *Mother India*. I can't play your lover in *Gharonda*. So I had no option but to reject it.'

Perhaps, Nargisji was right. Perhaps, that film was not in my destiny – or was it? Because a year later, *Gharonda* became *Sangam* and Nargis walked out of the film, as she had married Sunil Dutt by then. My next encounter with Rajji occured in 1959. That's when I first met him in person, while I was shooting for *Aas ka Panchhi* in Mohan Studio. Rajji was shooting there too.

*Rajendra Kumar Tuli*

In those days, absolute silence was mandatory on the set. This required fans and air conditioners to be switched off during shoots, causing actors much discomfort in the summer months.

*In* Aas ka Panchhi

*In a scene from* Aas ka Panchhi *with Vyjayanthimala*

It was in these conditions that Rajendra Kumar was shooting for *Aas ka Panchhi*.

When J. Om Prakash okayed a shot by calling out 'Cut!' spot boys hastened to the stars with napkins and spray bottles to refresh them. In the flurry of activity that ensued to set up the next scene, Rajendra, who was desperate for a smoke, walked off the floor and stepped out. Leaning against his car, he tapped out a 555 from his cigarette case, lit up and blew out a ring of smoke, his upturned face presenting a perfect profile for anyone who might be observing him. It was at this moment that he spotted Raj Kapoor from the corner of his eye. The artiste was emerging from the adjoining sets.

Rajendra greeted him from afar with a pranam. Kapoor responded with a smile and sauntered over to the younger actor. But in the very next instant, Rajendra's heart sank. Raj Kapoor had hoisted himself onto the bonnet of the other actor's shiny new car. As the car heaved under the senior star's weight, Rajendra groaned inwardly. But, oblivious to his misgivings, Raj Kapoor slid over the bonnet, his head reclining against the windshield, and puffed away on his own cigarette. For a few moments, both stars continued to smoke in silence. Then Raj Kapoor turned to face Rajendra Kumar.

'Yaar, *woh* film *banaye*? Buddy, shall we make that film?' he asked, his eyebrow cocked quizzically.

Rajendra knew instinctively what he was talking about and replied, 'I'll be happy to! *Karte hain.* Let's go ahead with it!'

'*Theek hai.* Fine,' the other man said in response. 'So what time do you pack up this evening?'

'Six-thirty.'

'That early! I pack up at ten every night.'

'Oh, but I don't work beyond six-thirty,' Rajendra told him.

'All right, then. I too will pack up early today and we can go to my studio and discuss the film.'

'Done!' Rajendra agreed, stubbing out his cigarette.

At 6.30 that evening, the two actors drove down to Chembur in Raj Kapoor's blue Buick convertible, with Rajendra's chauffeur following them in the other car. This was the jubilee star's first visit to the famous cottage in R.K. Studios.

As Rajendra made himself comfortable on the all-white divan placed on the floor in one corner of the room, Raj went in to freshen up, asking his attendant John to bring in drinks for them. Over the next few hours, the two stalwarts lounged against the white cotton bolsters, discussing films, their likes, dislikes and film philosophies. Then, finally, they came to the crux of the matter that had brought them together: *Sangam*,

*With his lifelong friend, Raj Kapoor*

*Having a jolly good time with Raj Kapoor*

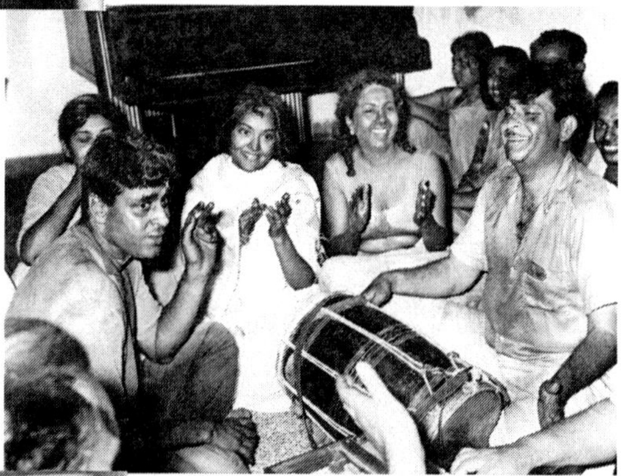

*Holi celebrations with the Kapoors and co-star Vyjayanthimala*

*Holi celebrations with Shammi and Shashi Kapoor and the famous screen villain Pran*

a story that would have the two leading men Raj Kapoor and Rajendra Kumar playing best friends. That day would set the course for their lifelong friendship.

On most evenings thereafter the two friends would get together for a drink. Although Rajendra was not particularly fond of alcohol, he empathized with his friend and gave him company to divert his mind, as Raj Kapoor tended to become sad and nostalgic while talking about friends he'd lost.

But as a man obsessed with cinema, Raj Kapoor also had the ability to snap out of his melancholia just as easily as he'd slipped into it. At the mere mention of films, his blue-green eyes would light up and he would launch into a discussion about whom they should cast in the supporting roles in *Sangam*, where the film should be shot, how they could improve on the script and similar matters.

Then there was the big question that Raj Kapoor kept coming back to: who would play Radha, the girl the two friends in the story were in love with?

'What about Meena [Kumari]? She'd suit the role, wouldn't she?' Rajendra asked.

'She would,' Raj replied, 'but I am not so sure...'

'Maybe Nutanji or Waheedaji?'

'I don't know. Radha's is a pivotal role and the casting has to be perfect. I have an image of her in my mind. Let's mull over it for a few days,' Raj Kapoor replied, lost in thought.

The two friends left it at that. Months went by and even though they met whenever possible, both were too busy with their individual commitments to discuss the subject further.

The next time our career paths crossed was in 1961 when I, like Rajji and Dilip Saab, began working with the south Indian film industry.

*Rajendra Kumar Tuli*

Since the advent of cinema, it was sheer good fortune, among other factors, that lay behind the silver and golden jubilee hits emanating from the Hindi film industry. Luck had simultaneously blessed the regional film industries, including the south Indian film industry with its many grand film studios.

AVM, the oldest surviving studio in India that had churned out several superhit Tamil films, subsequently set off the trend of dubbing their films in Hindi and other languages. With their organized studio culture, they eventually graduated to producing full-fledged Hindi films, completing them quickly and on schedule. AVM's debut Hindi production, *Bahar* (1951), had brought in the beautiful and gifted dancer Vyjayanthimala, the first south Indian actress to pave the way to Hindi films for others like her. These leading ladies from the country's southern states would bring films alive with their natural grace and eloquent eyes, and were much sought after.

As for the leading men from the Hindi film industry, it was after the success of the Dilip Kumar starrer *Azaad* in 1955 that other north Indian actors had begun gravitating southwards. As early as in 1956, Raj Kapoor, one of Bollywood's legendary triumvirates, the other two being Dilip Kumar and Dev Anand, had signed the film *Sharada*, L.V. Prasad's Hindi directorial debut under his newly established Prasad Productions, with Meena Kumari as his leading lady. Prasad then produced *Miss Mary* (1957), also starring the actress, and *Chhoti Bahen* in 1959, with the same actress in the lead, yet again. But for his next film, *Sasural*, he signed on Rajendra Kumar, with south Indian actress B. Saroja Devi as the leading lady. Simultaneously, Raj Kapoor became a part of another southern remake – S. Krishnamurthy's *Nazrana*, a film that had first been offered by its director, C.V. Sridhar, to Rajendra Kumar through the star's mentor in the world of films – Rajinder Krishan. Rajendra

Kumar, however, had turned down the offer, preferring to focus on his very first south Indian film, *Sasural*.

Meanwhile, back in Bombay, *Sangam*'s leading men needed to find their leading lady soon. But with no further developments on that front, the two stars didn't meet for some time.

Then, one day, Raj, who had just returned from a shooting stint in Madras, called Rajendra over.

'I want to show you something,' he said as soon as Rajendra walked into the other actor's cottage.

'No "hi-hello", Rajji? What is so urgent?' Rajendra smiled, joining his friend on the white floor mattress.

'Look at these transparencies,' Raj urged, indicating the glossy pictures spread out in front of him.

They were photos of the beautiful Vyjayanthimala.

'How would she be as Radha?' Raj Kapoor asked his fellow actor, trying to gauge his reaction.

'Hmm… Rajji, she is a big star, a beautiful and talented actor and a fantastic dancer,' Rajendra finally replied, 'but I don't see her as Radha. Anyone playing Radha's role will need to emote well.'

'I think she will be perfect,' Kapoor insisted.

'Perhaps she will. After all, you are the filmmaker,' Rajendra said tactfully. 'What your eyes see, maybe I cannot… Your choice will definitely be the right one.'

'You are working with her in several films, so…' Raj Kapoor trailed off, leaving the words unsaid.

'Yes, I have films with Vyjayanthi,' Rajendra told him, instantly sensing what the other actor wanted of him. 'If you wish, I can speak to her.'

'Done, then!' Raj Kapoor raised his amber liquid-filled glass, merriment gleaming in his light eyes.

'Cheers!' The men clinked their glasses and downed the contents in one go.

*With producer Krishnamurthy, director Sridhar and co-star Vyjayanthimala*

Raj Kapoor then set out to woo the beautiful Vyjayanthimala and even signed *Nazrana* with her in the lead. Meanwhile, Rajendra began work on *Sasural* with Saroja Devi, who had been unceremoniously replaced by Vyjayanthimala in *Nazrana* and, therefore, had dates to allot for *Sasural*.

Both Rajendra Kumar's *Sasural* and Raj Kapoor's *Nazrana* released at around the same time in late 1961. While *Sasural* was a silver jubilee hit, *Nazrana* did average business at the box office.

In *Sasural*, Rajendra Kumar, clad in a checked shirt tucked into smart trousers, his bushy eyebrows raised, his eyes teasing, moved from one tree to the next in the old style of courtship, serenading Saroja Devi with the iconic song '*Teri pyaari pyaari surat ko/ Kisi ki nazar na lage* (Let no envious eyes be cast on your lovely face)'. Later in the film, he sang, '*Ik sawaal main karoon/ Ik sawaal tum karo* (I'll ask you a question; you ask one of me)'.

With his career graph on the rise, *Sasural*'s success not only endorsed Rajendra Kumar's reasoned choice of films all over again, but also mollified Saroja Devi, who had, understandably, been miffed over her ouster from *Nazrana*. In the very same year, Raj Kapoor's *Sangam*, with his co-stars Rajendra Kumar and Vyjayanthimala, finally took off.

> The second time I travelled to a foreign country was for the shoot of *Sangam*. But after the initial shooting schedule the film progressed in fits and starts, during which time both Raj Kapoor and I had several other releases.
>
> *Rajendra Kumar Tuli*

Rajendra's *Zindagi aur Khwab* released in 1961. In the film, he was cast in the role of a police inspector, a position he'd actually been offered when he was looking for work in Delhi and had turned down to pursue a career in films in Bombay. *Zindagi aur Khwab* was based on a story by Kamal Amrohi and also starred his estranged wife, Meena Kumari. What the audience took back home from this film was the song composed by Dattaram: '*Na jaane kahan tum the/ Na jaane kahan hum the/ Jadoo yeh dekho hum tum mile hain* (Who knows where you were/ Who knows where I was/ It's some kind of magic that has brought us together)'. The lead actors merely went through the motions in *Zindagi aur Khwab*, as they would in their subsequent film together – Devendra Goel's *Pyaar ka Saagar*.

*Gharana,* Rajendra Kumar's next 1961 release, was with Asha Parekh, who had started her career as a child artiste under the screen name Baby Asha Parekh. The dashing Raaj Kumar was the third actor playing a leading role in the film. Directed by S.S. Vasan, *Gharana* turned out to be a box-office

*With Meena Kumari*

hit. In the film, Rajendra played a lovelorn college student, yet again wooing his leading lady in his inimitable manner, with the exception that, this time, he held a policeman's baton in his hand as he sang, '*Husnwale, tera jawab nahin* (Pretty lady, you are incomparable)'. The other memorable songs in the film were '*Dadi Amma, Dadi Amma, maan jao* (Grandma, do relent)', and '*Ye duniya usi ki* (This world is his alone)'.

> We shot *Gharana* in Mysore. I clearly recall a particular incident. While [we were] shooting for a song in Brindavan Gardens, one of the bystanders made a crude remark about us. Rajinderji, with stick in hand, ran after that guy to hit him! I realized then how much he respected women and how well he took care of them.
>
> *Asha Parekh*

The very same year, Rajendra Kumar surprised his audience by veering away from his romantic, light-hearted lead roles and appearing in *Amar Rahe Yeh Pyar*, a Hindi/Urdu family drama co-starring Nalini Jaywant and Nanda that was set against the backdrop of the country's partition. Ravi, who had composed the music for *Gharana*, was also the music director of *Amar Rahe Yeh Pyar*. Both films did well at the box office. In fact, through the initial years of the 1960s, and right up to 1966, the Hindi film industry seemed to be at its peak. Simultaneously, Rajendra Kumar's career was reaching its zenith with an incredible number of jubilee hits, along with six consecutive box-office hits, a record unmarred by a single flop in between. It was for this very reason that he would come to be known as the 'jubilee star', an honour that has remained forever associated with his name in the Hindi film industry and has never been conferred on another.

# 12

# Fame and Fortune

I led a life of ease. I had a beautiful home and designer clothes, shoes, jewellery. French chiffon sarees were especially imported for me from Paris. My husband was a star, I would wear gold and diamonds and go for premieres in big cars. However, over time, I began to sense an emptiness within myself. *All this luxury and comfort is fine, but this is not the purpose of my life*, are words I frequently told myself. I was happy, yet unhappy. I was in search of my higher self. I'd been spiritually inclined from the time I was a young girl. Then, one day in 1962, this latent spirituality came to the fore and I found my first guru.

*Shukla Tuli*

The year 1962 was an eventful one in the life of the jubilee star and his wife. It began with a happy occasion: on 18 September, Shukla gave birth to her third child, a daughter. The Tulis named her Kaajal. However, a month after the baby's birth, Shukla slipped while descending the stairs of her home and had a bad fall, seriously injuring her back. The doctors informed her that she'd suffered a slipped disc and prescribed

bed rest for nearly a month. Though she did have help from her mother and her household staff, she had no option but to run her home and take care of her children while being bedridden.

It was in the same year that her husband began shooting for *Ayee Milan ki Bela.* His leading lady in the film was Saira Banu. Rajendra subsequently had to leave for the hills for outdoor shooting. Under normal circumstances, Shukla would have accompanied her husband. But on this occasion she had to lie helplessly in bed, with acute pain shooting through her body if she so much as moved or turned. Painkillers were of some help, but on most nights she slept restlessly, her dreams full of visions and strange images.

A month passed. While Shukla's body healed bit by bit, her restlessness kept growing. By the time her husband returned home, she was well enough to move around again, although she'd had to give up the comfort of her bed after being advised to sleep on a mattress on the floor. Rajendra Kumar too insisted on doing the same.

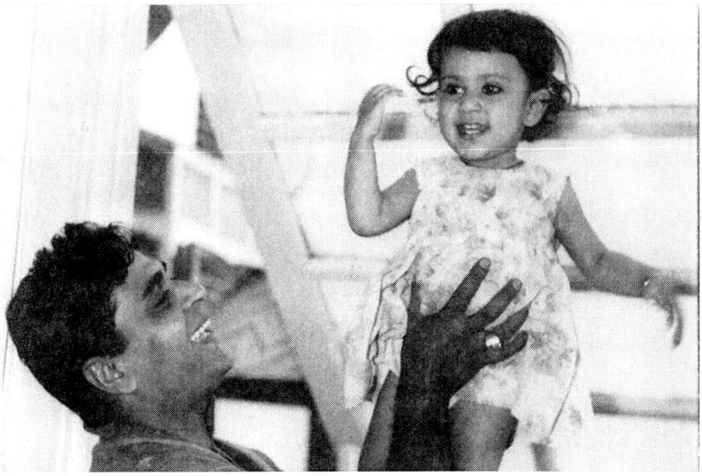

*With his youngest daughter, Kaajal*

'You are being too nice,' Shukla teased him one night, as they lay together.

'I've always been nice to you.'

'True, but this time around, I feel that even those love letters you sent from your last outdoors were a bit much!'

'Nothing is too much. Now rest and get well soon.'

Needing no further prompting, Shukla dozed off, only to awaken with a start an hour later. In a state of great agitation, she shook her husband awake.

'What is it? Are you in pain?' he asked groggily.

'An image of Sai Baba appeared before my eyes,' she told him. 'He was calling out to me. I feel a strong urge to meet him.'

'Are you mad? It's midnight!'

'Sai Baba has called me and I have to go to Shirdi right now.'

'Go to sleep,' Rajendra advised his wife. 'I will arrange for a car first thing in the morning, that is, if your health permits you to travel.'

Shukla left for Shirdi at five the next morning, and six hours later she was standing in front of the saint's idol in a state of complete surrender.

'I have come to the right place,' she murmured to herself, overwhelmed by a feeling of deep devotion.

From that moment onwards, she would never miss out on her monthly visits to Shirdi.

Whenever Baba's loving eyes fell on Shukla's troubled ones, her tears would flow spontaneously. It was only when a sense of tranquillity permeated her entire being that she felt purged and somewhat healed of the turmoil within her.

*What's happening*, she asked herself, beset by uncertainty, yet aware of a growing transformation within herself, a closer connection with her consciousness.

Meanwhile, Rajendra's career was on its meteoric rise. He was the star of all stars for his countless fans, who went into a frenzy over his performances, and for all the women who were infatuated with the idea of the ideal man that he seemed to exemplify.

> I am not a lifeless sculpture, but a human being with feelings, like everyone else. During my days of stardom, I would reach the studios for a shoot and a beautiful girl, probably someone's daughter or sister, would be all dolled up and made to stand before me. I was then directed to romance her, to take her in my arms and express my love for her. These were the kind of scenes we had to enact with these pretty girls. For a man, it was a very vulnerable moment – imagine when two young people sigh and their breaths merge, when they embrace and feel each other's heartbeats... For me too, it was a delicate moment. It made me very weak, actually, and almost broke down my defences. But one thought kept running at the back of my mind – that I was a married man; I had a family. So the very connection I had established with the pretty girl during the romantic scenes had to be severed as soon as the director called 'Cut!', bringing me back to reality. That was one difficult bridge I managed to cross in my life. I had many friends too from among my leading ladies, like Meenaji, Nanda and others. However, it was Sadhana with whom I really bonded. I first worked with her in *Mere Mehboob* and we became lifelong friends thereafter. It was my mentor H.S. Rawail who had offered me a leading role in this musical masterpiece one morning in 1961.
>
> *Rajendra Kumar Tuli*

The star was happy to see Rawail, the man who'd helped kick-start his film career, when he dropped in one morning.

*At a function with Naushad and his wife*

Rajendra touched the filmmaker's feet as a mark of respect and asked, 'Daddy, *kaise hain?* How are you?'

'Times are bad,' Rawail replied, a dazed look on his face.

'Hmm… So now what do we do?'

*We?* Rawail's head shot up and he looked at the younger man with renewed hope.

'There's only one thing to do,' he replied. 'Make a film. I have a brilliant script – a musical – set in Lucknow, but no money to make it. And after the fate of my last film, no one is ready to work with me. But if you star in the film, then…'

'Lucknow, you say, and it's a musical. Hmm…' Rajendra considered the idea. 'Sounds interesting. Tell me a bit of the story.'

When Rawail proceeded to do so, and Rajendra, sensing the film's potential right away, stated, 'We will make the film.'

The very next morning, he went to meet music maestro Naushad.

'Naushad Saab, there's a film we are planning,' Rajendra told the music composer. 'It's set in Lucknow and music is its backbone. Only you can do it justice. After all, Lucknow is your home turf.'

Naushad nodded and asked, 'Who's the filmmaker?'

'Rawail Saab.'

'Oh, yaar, that man and me – we are poles apart!' Naushad sounded doubtful. 'He is volatile and I am of a quiet temperament. I am not sure I can work with him.'

'You don't have to work with anyone but me,' Rajendra hastened to reassure him. 'Please look upon it as *my* film.'

'Hmm...'

'I guarantee you that all will go well.'

As soon as Naushad gave his consent, Rajendra Kumar paid him the signing amount from his own pocket. Next, he zeroed in on the leading lady, Sadhana, who was clearly hesitant to sign on, as Rawail's last release, *Roop ki Rani Choron ka Raja* (1961) had flopped. But when she discussed the offer with filmmaker Hrishikesh Mukherjee, he advised her to go ahead and accept the film. His rationale was simple: Rajendra Kumar was *Mere Mehboob*'s leading man and his acumen for spotting potentially successful films had been proved, time and again.

Soon after, *Mere Mehboob* went on the floors.

The film released in January 1963. Apart from the lead pair, Rajendra Kumar and Sadhana, it starred Ashok Kumar, Nimmi, Pran, Johnny Walker and Ameeta. With its immaculate casting, the film showcased a whole new world of vintage romance, peppered with beautiful romantic songs. Staying true to its culture and etiquette, *Mere Mehboob* brought old Lucknow alive in the depiction of its attire and customs, its refined diction and manners.

Born and bred in an affluent Urdu-speaking family, a sherwani-clad Rajendra Kumar came into his own as Anwar, the dashing aristocrat, with his regal and controlled performance in *Mere Mehboob*. So believable was he in the deeply romantic scenes and song sequences featured in the film that the audience came away totally smitten by him. Anwar was just as taken with the young Husna, played by a radiantly beautiful Sadhana, right from the film's opening scene when his eyes met her luminous ones. *Such a lovely young woman! How can a man not feel romantic in her presence*, the actor would muse as his hands fleetingly caressed his co-star's. His reflections helped lend such depth and conviction to his depiction of the thrill of first love that it stirred every member of the audience.

The film's story then moved to Lucknow's University Hall, where Anwar was seen searching for the face behind the veil as he sang, '*Mere mehboob, tujhe meri mohabbat ki kasam...* (My beloved, swear on my love that...)' Finally, when Husna did remove her veil, Anwar Miyan was heard whispering in wonder, '*Subhanallah!*', revelling, it seemed, in the perfection of God's creation.

What followed was sheer magic – with repartee couched in poetry, Shakeel Badayuni's inspired lyrics and music maestro Naushad's compositions. Particularly memorable among the latter were '*Ae husn zara jaag, tujhe ishq jagaaye* (Rise, O beauty, awaken so that love can stir you)', '*Tere pyar mein dildar* (Lost in your love)' and '*Mere mehboob mein kya nahin* (There is no quality that my beloved does not possess)'.

*Mere Mehboob*, with its leisurely but compact plot, was declared a superhit at the box office, catapulting it to the Number One position in 1963.

*Mere Mehboob* was right up my sleeve. Full of Lucknowi *tehzeeb* and *adaa* and the delicate beauty of Sadhana living in purdah... One couldn't expect well-bred women of those times and from those families to frolic in public. I loved every aspect of the film and identified with it completely, having studied in Urdu-, Persian- and English-

*With Sadhana in* Mere Mehboob

medium educational institutions – at both school and college level. As for Hindi, I had only picked it up in India after crossing over during the partition. Even now, I cannot read and write Hindi that well, but I am fluent in Urdu. *Mere Mehboob* had such an impact on the audience that following its release, lakhs of Muslim families sent me letters, asking for my real name. They addressed me as 'Anwar Miyan'. They believed that I was a Muslim and that, like Yusub Saab [whose screen name was Dilip Kumar], I had adopted a Hindu screen name. I, of course, corrected them. My leading lady Sadhana was one of the most beautiful women I'd ever met. We became very close while filming *Mere Mehboob* and would work in many more movies together. Many people suspected us to be lovers and although I accept that I loved Sadhana, it does not mean that we shared a physical relationship. Ours was a platonic love. We liked and respected each other. Giving respect is love too.

*Rajendra Kumar Tuli*

Shortly after *Mere Mehboob*, writer-director C.V. Sridhar's melodramatic *Dil Ek Mandir* released on 18 January 1963. Despite Rajendra Kumar having turned down the offer to play the leading man in the director's previous film, *Nazrana*, Sridhar had approached him with a second proposal to play one of the main male leads in *Dil Ek Mandir*. The occasion on which the two men first met was a party in Vijay Gardens, Madras, organized by director and producer S. Krishnamurthy to honour Raj Kapoor and celebrate the success of *Jis Desh Mein Ganga Behti Hai*.

Sridharji, with drink in hand, came to me and said, 'I heard that you had not liked my story *Nazrana*.' 'I liked

> the story,' I told him, 'but not the character I was supposed to play in the film.' He then said that he had a good script for me. The very next day, we met in my hotel room and he narrated the story of *Dil Ek Mandir*. I told him instantly, 'You *must* make the film, Sridharji. I am not an astrologer, but the story is brilliant!' He said, 'Okay, then I will first make this movie in Tamil and with newcomers. If that film does well, I will also make it in Hindi.'
>
> *Rajendra Kumar Tuli*

Sridhar completed the Tamil version of the movie in one month, before coming back to Rajendra Kumar.

'We have organized a trial at AVM Studio for you,' the director told him.

After pack-up that evening, the jubilee star, along with Nargis Dutt, watched the trial of the Tamil film *Ninjal Ur Aliyam* (Every Heart Is a Temple).

As soon as the screening ended, Rajendra stood up and declared, 'It is such a good film! You needn't wait for its release to gauge public response. Just go ahead and make the Hindi version.'

Animated discussions followed and the director and star decided to cast Meena Kumari and Raaj Kumar for the other leading roles in the film.

> I recalled that the last time I had met Raaj Kumar, he'd said, '*Jaani, hamaara bhi khayaal rakha karo*. Do keep me in mind too.' And I had promised him I would. I called him for *Dil Ek Mandir* and asked him what he'd charge. 'Arre, *jaani, kuch bhi dila do, yaar*. Role *bahut accha hai*. My dear friend, any amount will do. The role is superb,' he said. 'Okay,' I told him. 'I had planned on seventy-five thousand [rupees] for you.' He was fine with it. In *Dil Ek Mandir*, I was the highest paid actor. According to my

contract, I was to be paid four lakhs, while Meena Kumari had an agreement for two and a quarter lakhs.

*Rajendra Kumar Tuli*

Before the film went on the floors, however, Nargis Dutt met up with Sridhar and offered to co-produce *Dil Ek Mandir* with him.

'Give Rajinderji whatever role he desires,' she told him, 'but the other role, my husband will play.'

Really tempted by the offer, the director met Rajendra Kumar that very evening to discuss it with him.

'No, Sri, we can't possibly do that,' the actor told him firmly. 'We have already promised the role to Raaj Kumar. Wouldn't be fair to him, would it?'

The outcome of this interchange was that Raaj Kumar went on to play the second lead, as had initially been agreed on. The decision left no room for regret whatsoever, with the actor giving one of the most moving and memorable performances of his career.

In *Dil Ek Mandir*, Rajendra played a melancholy doctor who chooses to live in the past. Raaj Kumar was cast in the role of his patient whose terminal illness fails to crush his spirit, even as he seeks, in the face of imminent death, to secure a stable future for his devoted wife, a role Meena Kumari excelled in.

While Rajendra Kumar stayed true to his image of a morally upright, tragic martyr in the film, Raaj Kumar introduced a touch of lightness to the ambience of desolation hanging over it. Along with the 'jubilee star' and Meena Kumari, he stole the hearts of the audience. The unforgettable songs composed by the Shankar–Jaikishan duo, particularly '*Yaad na jaaye beete dino ki* (The memories of the past live on)', '*Ruk ja, raat!* (O night, don't end!)', '*Hum tere pyar mein saara aalam kho baithe* (Steeped in my love for you, I have lost my bearings)' and the

*With music composer Jaikishan, Pallavi, his wife, and Shukla*

title track, '*Dil ek mandir hai* (The heart is a sacred space)', accomplished the rest.

Declared a hit, *Dil Ek Mandir* was the only movie to be reviewed by a star of Dilip Kumar's stature. He was generous in his praise as he described the performances of Rajendra Kumar, Meena Kumari and Raaj Kumar. But despite it all, the critical acclaim from others was reserved for Rajendra's male co-actor. Raaj Kumar received the Best Supporting Actor Filmfare Award for his portrayal of Ram, the doomed man with an indomitable spirit.

*I don't need awards and rewards. Yusuf Saab's appreciation is the greatest honour for me*, Rajendra told himself. But he did realize that it was imperative for him to take a break from the morbidity and melodrama he had been steeped in while shooting for *Dil Ek Mandir*. Thankfully, he would get that much-needed break while working in his forthcoming film, *Akeli Mat Jaiyo*, with Meena Kumari as his leading lady once again.

A light-hearted romance, the film released on 19 April 1963 and was a refreshing departure from *Dil Ek Mandir*. In the film, Meena Kumari, in a coquettish avatar, played a working girl who falls in love with a handsome stranger – Rajendra Kumar at his flirtatious best.

Rajendra's next release was *Humrahi*, directed by T. Prakash Rao who'd started his career as an assistant to director L.V. Prasad. This 1963 release turned out to be yet another hit for the jubilee star. Moving away from his serious image, Rajendra played a flamboyant philanderer who enjoys life, love and women, fantasizing about Jamuna as she lures him from bedroom to garden with the song: '*Mujhko apne gale laga lo* (Take me in your arms)'.

Later in the film, she laments, '*Man re, tu hi bata kya gaoon* (O my heart, tell me what I should sing)'. In *Humrahi*, O.P. Ralhan too was seen in a small role, thanks to his famous brother-in-law Rajendra Kumar's influence.

Illuminated though he was by the glow of stardom, Rajendra also had to play diverse real-life roles: that of the loving husband, the protective father, the dependable son and the responsible older brother. Being morally upright and at the same time sensitive and empathetic, the actor hadn't forgotten the daily battles he had had to wage just to get a foothold in the glamorous world of movies. He understood only too well how difficult it was for newcomers to make their way in the industry and went out of his way to help his relatives, friends and others who approached him for work.

Back in the late 1950s, director O.P. Ralhan had been among Rajendra's many friends who had survived by taking up small roles in a few films. Then, in 1958, his determination had paid off: he'd been signed on to direct *Mujrim*, with the main lead Shammi Kapoor in a Westernized espionage-agent kind of avatar. Although the film did release, it couldn't do much to further the director's career and he'd had to fall back on acting in minor roles again. It was around this time that he had taken to visiting the jubilee star regularly at his home, hoping that his friend would help him get more meaningful work.

'Yaar, *tu* star *ban gaya hai.* You've become a star, old chap. Get me something too, won't you?' he'd say in his characteristically nasal voice.

In those days, the Tulis were living in Dimple, their Carter Road home. Rajendra's mother, Vidyawanti, who was living with his family at the time, constantly fretted over her youngest daughter Manorama's single status and reminded her son every day to look for a bridegroom for his sister.

'Find a suitable boy for Manorama, Rajinder,' she urged him. 'She is the same age as Shukla. She should have been married by now and become a mother too.'

'I'll see what can be done,' Rajendra murmured absent-mindedly.

But the thought lingered at the back of his mind all day.

That evening, when he returned home, he found the solution staring at him in the face: there was O.P. Ralhan, who had dropped in to see him as usual. It struck Rajendra right away that here was an eligible bachelor, known to the family, who seemed a decent enough human being.

Without further ado, Manorama Tuli and O.P. Ralhan were married in a simple ceremony held at Dimple.

From then on, Rajendra Kumar would take full responsibility for the upkeep of the newly-weds and send his sister money for her household expenses every month. This arrangement worked well for some time.

Then, one day, the practical Shukla said to her husband, 'I know you love your sister and want her to be happy. But if you continue to pay for their expenses, Ralhan may get used to a life of ease and lose the incentive to earn a living. I think it would be better if you got him some work, instead.'

*At younger sister Manorama's wedding, 1959, with Bunty, his leading ladies, Shyama, Nargis and Ameeta, and others*

'I already have,' Rajendra told her. 'He is working in my film *Humrahi*.'

'Yes, as an actor, but he wants to direct. How far will these trivial roles take him? Making a film is a long-term investment and can bring him long-term profits. Help him with that.'

'Sounds sensible,' Rajendra murmured.

Then he called up Ralhan. 'You should make a film,' he suggested.

'That is my dream and my goal, Bhai Saab!'

'Then do it. I will star in it.'

'That's a wonderful idea! With Rajendra Kumar on board, financiers will fall over each other to produce the film. Thank you, Papaji!'

'There's no need to thank me or even pay me a fee for acting in your film. Just go ahead and direct the film!'

And direct he did. The film *Gehra Daag* went into production and Ralhan emerged as a producer and director to watch out for.

In the film, Mala Sinha played the female lead opposite Rajendra Kumar and a cute, perky Mumtaz was cast in the role of the hero's sister. *Gehra Daag* was a romantic crime drama in which Shanker, played by Rajendra Kumar, kills a man to defend his sister's honour and spends the next ten years of his life in prison. The film's opening scene shows him grasping the bars of his prison cell as tears flow out of his eyes and the background score rises to a crescendo, with the wailing of violins highlighting the pathos of his plight. That sets the mood for the rest of the film, where the then thirty-six-year-old jubilee star slips quite easily into the role of a college student and emerges, once again, as a supremely emotive actor. In this film, Rajendra Kumar also seems to have come to terms with dancing, which was an indispensable part of his films. Despite his awkwardness, he manages to go through the motions in the song-and-dance sequences with Mala Sinha, a *gamcha* slung around his neck, one of the duets being '*Tumhe paake hum ne jahan paa liya hai* (Now that I have you, I possess the entire world)'.

*Gehra Daag* released in 1963 at Bombay's Eros Cinema, a rare event at the time, as the cinema hall was known for exclusively screening English films. Ralhan was on cloud nine and blithely announced to the media that he would, henceforth, produce only colour films. *Gehra Daag* was a moderate box-office success, but word got around that it had earned more than a crore of rupees on an investment of just a few lakhs.

The birth of Rajendra and Shukla's third child and second daughter a year earlier had added to the jubilee star's sense of fulfilment and inspired him to work even harder. *After all,* he had told himself, *I am responsible for my immediate family and the extended one, as well as for the many staff members I've employed.*

For Rajendra, who had spent his early years in the lap of luxury and could well have emulated his father's flamboyant

*With Mala Sinha in a scene from* Gehra Daag *(courtesy Kamat Photo Studio)*

ways in Sialkot, whiling away time in self-indulgent pursuits was not an option that appealed to him. He eschewed the chosen pastimes of some of his fellow actors who splurged on entertainment and gambling. What he did give precedence to was a very comfortable lifestyle shared with his wife and children and, whenever he could get away from his work commitments, quality time reserved for exploring the world in their company.

# 13

# When It Rains, It Pours

People said I was tough to understand, that I was hard-headed and business-minded. But if I was tough to understand, why, then, did the same producers and directors want to work with me repeatedly? Because of my rapport with them. My ambition was to work with all the top filmmakers in the industry and I did. Small producers never dared to approach me. There was a commercial angle to my thinking: if I worked with big filmmakers who would be making a film not merely for me, but for themselves and their own prestige, and the film was good, I reasoned that by being in the same film my performance would automatically be seen in a favourable light. I was not ready to take any risks at all with my career. But I was not after money. I was after a big, solid career, which I could build only through [working with] good filmmakers. Producer Sashadhar Mukherjee [father of yesteryear actor Joy Mukherjee] had once asked me, 'How do you choose films?' 'Very simple!' I'd told him. 'If it touches my heart, I do it. Otherwise, I don't.' *Phir aise hi, naam aur daam aage badhta gaya.* And, in this manner, my fame and worth continued to grow.

*Rajendra Kumar Tuli*

The first day of 1964 dawned with a new film and a fresh chapter in the jubilee star's life. *Ayee Milan ki Bela*, directed by Mohan Kumar, released on that day.

Saira Banu, a London-educated beauty queen and daughter of another actor with stunning looks – Naseem Banu – was the film's leading lady, while Dharmendra, then a young actor on the rise, played the second lead. Being director Mohan Kumar's first choice for the role, this exceptionally handsome young man was given an important part in the film with leading man Rajendra Kumar's complete approval.

Although he had been cast in the hero's role in his last film, *Anpadh*, opposite Mala Sinha, the very charming Dharmendra took up the challenge of playing a secondary character with shades of grey in *Ayee Milan ki Bela*, even though the script dictated that he would get beaten up by the hero Rajendra Kumar in the climax. Director Mohan Kumar had the two Punjabi male leads polishing off glassfuls of lassi and fighting over the elegant young woman played by Saira Banu.

*With Dev Anand and Saira Banu at the silver jubilee celebration of the blockbuster hit* Ayee Milan ki Bela

Set against the backdrop of Kashmir, a place of serene beauty in those days, *Ayee Milan ki Bela,* a colour movie, was a sensory treat for the audience. Lending emotional heft to the love story were Shankar and Jaikishan's unforgettable musical compositions, with '*Tumhein aur kya doon main dil ke sivaay?* (What can I give you, other than my heart?)', '*Main pyar ka deewana* (I'm in love with love)' and '*O sanam, tere ho gaye hum* (O my beloved, I am yours)', among them. With so much going for it, the movie was a superhit at the box office.

Riding high on its success, Rajendra Kumar signed up for *Zindagi*, directed by Ramanand Sagar.

> Rajendra Kumar was a big name down south. He was Number One, as was Gemini [Studios]. My father [Ramanand Sagar] was one of the pillars of Gemini Studios and its head, Mr S.S. Vasan, was his guru in all aspects of filmmaking. Vasan decided to cast the jubilee star in *Zindagi*, his next production. Vasan and Papaji [Ramanand Sagar] wanted to keep it a secret, however, as in those days, the moment you met a star, gossipmongers would talk about Rajendra Kumar being in Ramanand Sagar's next [production], adversely affecting the signing on of stars, their rivals, other cast members, the choice of distributors, signing amounts and so on. So in keeping with the jubilee star's status, Papaji booked the beautiful, domed presidential suite at the Taj Hotel. That's where Ramanand Sagar met Rajendra Kumar for the first time. It was a historic meeting and *Zindagi* became a super hit. The film made Papaji the star of the Hindi film industry. *Zindagi* was based on the Ramayana. In the same manner that Sita was compelled to live in exile, in *Zindagi* Vyjayanthimala, cast as the wife of the man portrayed by Rajendra Kumar, is forced to spend the night in the house of another man, played by Raaj Kumar, because of riots breaking out in the city. And a

murder takes place... *Zindagi* was a fantastic drama. So much tension in the film! And Rajendra Kumar was perfect for the role.

*Prem Sagar*

As *Zindagi* played to a receptive audience over twenty-five weeks to achieve silver-jubilee status, 1964 proved to be yet another remarkable year in Rajendra Kumar's life. As they say, when it rains, it pours.

On 18 June, the same year, Raj Kapoor's magnum opus *Sangam* released at the refurbished Apsara Theatre in Bombay. First scripted in the late 1950s, *Sangam* was based on Inder Raj Anand's poignant tale of love, separation, jealousy and sacrifice. The film marked the entry of Raj Kapoor's cinema into the colour era and was the first Hindi film of such epic length, replete with on-location shoots in London, Venice, Paris and Switzerland. With the debonair, dignified Rajendra Kumar playing the role of Gopal, a radiantly beautiful and vivacious Vyjayanthimala in the role of Radha, a young woman torn between two friends with one of whom she is in love, and Raj Kapoor in the role of Sundar, a man who is both jovial and angst-ridden, loyal and insecure, loving and embittered, depending on his mood, *Sangam* became one of commercial Hindi cinema's most unforgettable films. Considered to be among Kapoor's most enduring works, the film presented a love triangle based on a complex psychological tale about childhood friends who grow up loving the same girl.

In the film, the adult Sundar, who has joined the Indian Air Force, confides in Gopal about his infatuation with Radha, who, in turn, is in love with her other friend. Gopal feels the same way about her, but decides to step aside for Sundar's sake, keeping his feelings for Radha well hidden from his friend.

In a twist of fate, Sundar's aircraft crashes during one of his flying missions and he is presumed dead. After mourning his death, Radha and Gopal inevitably draw close and end up confessing their love for each other. It is during this time that Gopal sends her an unsigned love letter. But in another ironic twist of fate, just as the two are contemplating marriage, Sundar, who had actually survived the plane crash, returns home. Once again, Gopal steps back, unwilling to stand in the way of his friend's happiness. Radha begs him to reveal the truth about her relationship with him to Sundar, but is unable to make any headway in the face of Gopal's obstinacy. Hurt, frustrated and angry, Radha gives in and weds Sundar. But their marital bliss is not fated to last; her husband accidentally discovers the secret unsigned love letter from Gopal that she has hidden away and is overcome with suspicion about her fidelity. Their marriage turns into a living hell and ends in a tragedy.

Helmed by director Raj Kapoor, with restrained performances by all three lead actors and meaningful, situation-appropriate songs by the Shankar–Jaikishan duo, *Sangam* turned out to be a blockbuster hit. Every song in the film, along with the film itself, seemed to resonate with references symbolic of the confluence of the rivers Ganga, Yamuna and Saraswati – whether it was Sundar pestering his beloved for an answer to his eternal question in the song '*Bol,* Radha, *bol, sangam hoga ki nahin* (Oh, tell me, Radha, do, if we'll ever become one)', or Gopal penning a love letter to the same woman as he sang, '*Yeh mera prem patra padh kar ke tum naaraaz na hona* (Let not my missive of love upset you)', or an agonized Radha giving expression to her feelings in '*O mere sanam* (Oh, my love!)' Shailendra's lyrics not only captured the dynamics of a man's love for a woman, but also the essence of humanity itself with the philosophical '*Yeh dharti hai insaanon ki/ Kuch aur nahin, insaan hai hum* (Earth is home to the human race and we are merely human)' and '*Har dil jo pyar karega/ Woh gaana*

*With Raj Kapoor and Vyjayanthimala during the shooting of* Sangam *at the Eiffel Tower in Paris*

*gaayega* (Every heart touched by love bursts into song)'. For the famous number '*Dost dost na raha* (A friend is no more a friend)', in particular, the manner in which Raj Kapoor enacted his feelings of anguished betrayal in the scene was so vividly real that it made his audience in the theatres squirm in their seats with a feeling of wrongdoing, much like the guilt-stricken, remorseful Gopal, sitting rigidly behind his friend Sundar, with the conflicted Radha forming the third point of the triangle. The way the song was picturized made the two lovers Gopal and Radha seem like traitors, not only in Sundar's eyes, but also in the eyes of the audience. Having scored with the audience on so many points, it was little surprise that *Sangam* not only went on to become a stupendous commercial success, but also earned enough acclaim to be considered a classic in the Indian film industry.

What a miraculous film *Sangam* was! A film reel of 19, 550 feet, just three lead characters, two intervals; and yet, no one in the audience could budge from his seat – so gripping was the film! For the Europe schedule in 1962, I was required for just a week. But I stayed on with Rajji for all twelve weeks. He just wouldn't let me leave. 'No, don't go,' he'd say. 'Alone, I feel lost.' And for the sake of our friendship, I did stay back. I'd go for the shoot every day to work with him, assist him in all departments, carrying camera batteries, sound machines, as he and everybody else did. We had no inhibitions, no airs that I was a star and he was the director. Everyone worked on every job. No one was a star. In Paris, we would go out every evening after work in a sleek luxury bus that picked up the whole crew after we'd changed and freshened up. We'd visit restaurants, clubs and bars. I recall that when Rajji recorded '*Dost dost na raha*', I wasn't there. I was shooting elsewhere. So when I heard the song for the first time, right before the shoot, I said to RK, 'It doesn't sound right. Song *galat hai*. It sounds contrived. How can you sing, "*Dost dost na raha*" to the very friend who has sacrificed his love for you? And the woman you loved, the woman who married you – you accuse her of being unfaithful, of creating a situation where "*Pyar pyar na raha,* where love is no longer love"? It's so wrong, so unfair!' Rajji responded by saying, 'The song is beautiful. Let me picturize it and then you'll see. I will make sure I justify its inclusion in the film.' Then for three days running, we shot the song, with Rajji playing the piano and lip-synching words reproaching his childhood friend for his betrayal, while I, in the role of Gopal, sat silently on a chair facing him, drink in hand, and Vyjayanthimala sat opposite me on another chair. Finally, on the third day, I got up and told Inder Raj, the writer, 'After the song ends, Gopal will speak, okay? I have a dialogue that I want to add to the scene.' Then I told my friend RK, '*Gaane ke baad* shot *lagaiye, main ek* dialogue *boloonga*. Once the song is over, set up the shot. I have a dialogue to add.' '*Kya* dialogue *bologey*, ji? Now what dialogue is that, pray?' he asked. '*Aap* shot *toh lagaayo*. Why don't you set up the shot first?' I insisted. 'Then you'll see.' Great filmmaker and good friend that he was, Rajji actually did set up the shot without further questions. As soon as the song ended, I stood up and delivered my lines, before walking out of the scene. I could hear Raj shouting [in frustration] at Inder Rajji, '*Dekho, Chacha, meri kiye karaye ki aisi ki taisi kar gaya!* Just look at the way he screwed up all my good work, Uncle!' I turned around and retorted, '*Yaar, tum jo teen din se gaana gaa gaa ke humari aisi ki taisi kar rahe the, uska kya?* What about the torture you put us through over the last three days, singing to your heart's content without pause? What of that, my friend?' That was typical of the banter we shared, [the banter that was a part of] our friendship.

*Rajendra Kumar Tuli*

However, in the final version of *Sangam*, while every important scene had the camera panning out to film the trio in a deliberate trilateral shot, every verse of '*Dost dost na raha*' was justified to perfection by the master filmmaker with a montage of Rajendra Kumar's romantic shots with Vyjayanthimala. And, yes, Raj Kapoor did allow his fellow actor to have the last word by retaining Rajendra's closing lines: '*Jo geetkar pe guzri, usne apne geet mein keh diya. Magar,* Sundar, *mere dost, kuch log aise bhi hote hain jin par guzarti hai, magar woh chup rehte hain.* Whatever suffering may have befallen the songwriter,

*With Raj Kapoor, trusted friend and colleague*

he is able to lay bare in his song and unburden himself. But, Sundar, my friend, there are people in this world who suffer just as much, but choose to remain silent.'

The moment those words were uttered by Rajendra Kumar in the role of Gopal, the audience in the theatres burst into applause and punctuated it with whistles of approval, thereby immortalizing the voice and the dialogue.

> Rajji's brilliance also shone through when he filmed the love song '*Yeh mera prem patra*' in a very modern style, comprising just one long shot – of us [Rajendra and Vyjayanthimala] walking through the garden and past the trees, with no filmy gimmicks – so poetic, so realistic, so close to life, so Raj Kapoor... He didn't like the running

around trees [that heroes and heroines of Hindi commercial cinema were, inevitably, made to do while singing duets]. His film moments were very natural. His films were, therefore, accepted by people from all walks of life. In '*Har dil jo pyar karega*', every shot he took was again a triangular composition. Sundar walks up to Radha, she to Gopal; and then, Gopal to Sundar. So symbolic was his direction and so technically sound!

*Rajendra Kumar Tuli*

Like *Sangam*, Rajendra Kumar's next project, *Arzoo*, was also based on a love triangle where, for the umpteenth time, he played the sacrificial lamb – yet again, for the sake of a friend.

I don't think we should evaluate others by the standards we set, as everyone has his own parameters, capabilities, ambitions and flaws. We should not look down on other actors or newcomers. Instead, we should look for and recognize their special attributes. If you like a quality in them, tell them directly; if you don't, just say that too. Back in 1962, when I was shooting for *Ayee Milan ki Bela* and for *Zindagi* in Madras, I had signed *Arzoo*, a film written by Ramanand Sagar that he was also supposed to direct. I asked him, 'Who are you planning to cast as the second lead?' He said, 'Dharmendra. Can you please talk to him? The two of you are shooting together [for *Ayee Milan ki Bela*], right?'

*Rajendra Kumar Tuli*

The next day, Rajendra Kumar called up Dharmendra.

'Sagar Saab is making his next film and wants to cast you in it,' he told the other actor. 'Sadhana is playing the female lead. It is a love triangle.'

But Dharmendra was reluctant to take up the role. 'Papaji,' he explained, 'after *Ayee Milan ki Bela*, I have signed lead roles in several films. If I take this up, I will be stuck with a side hero [second lead] image.'

'No problem,' Rajendra Kumar said in response. 'Don't do the film, then,' and ended the call by wishing him all the best.

Sagar, however, was quite disappointed. 'I especially wanted Dharmendra,' he said. 'Anyway, maybe Manoj [Kumar] will accept the role.'

'Manoj will never turn me down,' Rajendra declared confidently.

He was thinking of the time in 1961, when following the release of *Goonj Uthi Shehnai*, Vijay Bhatt, or 'Vijubhai', as Rajendra Kumar called him affectionately, had offered him the male lead in his next production, *Hariyali aur Rasta*. But tied up as he was with several commitments in the south, the jubilee star had sent a promising new actor in his place, who, he felt, would do justice to the role. Manoj Kumar subsequently became the hero of *Hariyali aur Rasta*. The film turned out to be a blockbuster hit, encouraging Vijubhai to cast its lead pair, once again, in *Himalay ki God Mein*. This film paved the way to great success for its leading man, the quiet, contemplative actor-writer now known to all as Manoj Kumar. When Rajendra asked him to work in *Arzoo*, Manoj Kumar, like Dharmendra, was already playing lead roles and wasn't keen on going down the 'side role' path again. Unable, however, to directly turn down a request from the man he had come to look upon as a mentor and an older brother, Manoj Kumar prevaricated for a few days, without giving an unequivocal reply.

The second lead in *Arzoo* finally went to the suave Feroz Khan.

*With Manoj Kumar*

Manoj *taal matol karta raha*. He continued to procrastinate. We were in a quandary now – to whom should we offer the role? And then in Madras I saw the rushes of T. Prakash Rao's *Bahurani* and this handsome boy Feroz Khan, who was working as a villain in the film [which had Guru Dutt and Mala Sinha paired together]. I liked Feroz. Moreover, my younger brother Naresh, who had begun producing films, was already working with him. I decided to cast Feroz in *Arzoo* and asked my brother to send him over to meet me.

*Rajendra Kumar Tuli*

Soon after, a hopeful Feroz arrived at Dimple, early one morning, to meet Rajendra Kumar.

'Will you work with us in *Arzoo*?' the senior actor asked him.

'I am grateful you thought of me, Bhai Saab,' the debonair young man smiled.

*With the flamboyant Feroz Khan*

'Good, then!' Rajendra said, happy with the arrangement. 'How much will you charge for the film?'

'I was paid forty thousand for my last film, so...'

'Okay,' Rajendra said decisively, 'we will give you forty-five... *Chalega?* Is that acceptable?'

No sooner had Feroz Khan nodded his acceptance than Rajendra asked Shukla to bring him the signing amount. A short while later, a beaming Feroz was striding out of Rajendra Kumar's home with the signing amount in his pocket and a big film in his kitty.

The deed accomplished, Rajendra called up Ramanand Sagar. 'I've found the second lead,' he announced. 'Signed and sealed.'

'Who is it?'

'Feroz Khan.'

'But... but he is still raw,' an apprehensive Sagar protested, 'and honestly, I haven't seen his films. I don't know if he will suit the role.'

'Yes, he will,' Rajendra Kumar insisted. 'Have faith.'

'All right, then...'

Despite Sagar's reservations, the film was made with the flamboyant Feroz Khan, who became a star after its release. With *Arzoo*, he earned his entry into the A-listers' club. But in the film's initial stages, after only a small part of the shooting had been completed, another issue cropped up. Sadhana developed an eye problem due to her thyroid condition. The producer panicked. Ramanand Sagar was in two minds. He wanted to replace the heroine with another actor.

But Rajendra discouraged him. 'Sagar Saab,' he said, 'don't worry. Sadhana will complete the movie.'

Ramanand Sagar's award-winning love story *Arzoo* dealt with the theme of how the physically challenged are marginalized by an uncaring society. Shot in the beautiful verdant valley of Srinagar, against the backdrop of a brilliant azure sky and breathtaking snow-capped mountains, the film features Rajendra Kumar as a ski champion who falls in love with the glamorous Sadhana and serenades her with the song '*Ae nargise mastana/ Bas itni shikayat hai* (Oh, maiden with the intoxicating eyes, I have but one complaint)', as she goes horseback riding. What follows is Lata Mangeshkar's mesmerizing rendition of '*Aji rooth kar ab kahan jaiyega/ Jahaan jaiyega humme paiyega* (Wherever you may go off in a sulk, you'll find me there with you)', where the two lovers exchange meaningful glances, their palpable chemistry leaving no viewer unmoved. The jubilee star, once again playing a character named Gopal, seemed totally enamoured by Usha, Sadhana's impish avatar in *Arzoo*. Later in the film, disguised as an old hakim (a practitioner of traditional medicine) out on a house call to see an indisposed Usha, he eulogizes the young woman he loves with '*Chhalke teri aankhon se sharab aur zyada/ Khilte rahe hoton ke gulab aur zyada* (Your eyes so intoxicating, your lips in bloom like roses)'. Then with the

*With Rafi and Dev Anand (courtesy* Mayapuri *magazine)*

*With Ramanand Sagar*

playful composition '*Jab ishq kahin ho jata hai* (Whenever love strikes)', the drama takes a turn towards the tragic. It rises to a crescendo as Gopal loses a leg in a serious car accident and moves out of Usha's life on the assumption that the woman who had declared that it was better to die than live with a physical handicap would now refuse to accept him as her life partner. Gopal's disappearance from Usha's life without an explanation convinces her that he has lost interest in her. Subsequently, his best friend, played by Feroz Khan, proposes to Usha. But she cannot forget Gopal, and her feelings are eloquently expressed in the song '*Bedardi balma, tujhko mera man yaad karta hai* (Oh, heartless love, my heart pines for you)'. Ultimately, however, the story ends with the hero and heroine being reunited, and *Arzoo*, released in 1965, going on to become a golden-jubilee hit.

It must be acknowledged that film stars of that era, including Rajendra Kumar, owed much of the success of their films to the music and songs that helped evoke moods, moments and memories in them and, therefore, to music composers like Shankar and Jaikishan, lyricists Shailendra and Hasrat Jaipuri and playback singers Mohammad Rafi and Lata Mangeshkar.

Papaji's [Ramanand Sagar] 1965 love story *Arzoo* took off from where the 1957 Cary Grant–Deborah Kerr starrer *An Affair to Remember* ended. Papaji was known for his deft handling of mother-and-son scenes and romantic moments. In the film, there is a scene where the lovers, played by Rajendra Kumar and Sadhana, stroll by Dal Lake in complete silence, even as their souls commune. Then to picturize the other song '*Ae phoolon ki rani, baharon ki malika*. O queen of flowers, goddess of spring', Ramanand Sagar wanted poppies blooming in the background. But these flowers only bloomed in

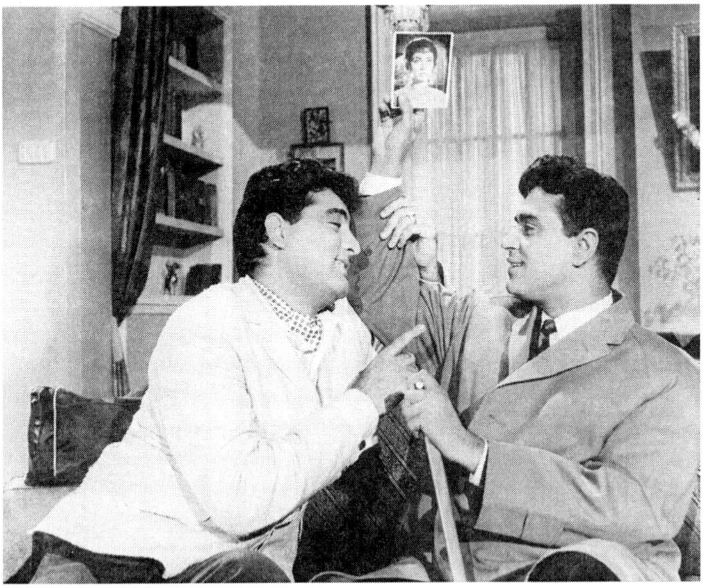

*Stills from* Arzoo *(courtesy Ramanand Sagar)*

season. Undeterred, he arranged for wagonfuls of flowers [to be brought] from Japan and China. So beautiful and real did the valley appear that the then chief minister of Kashmir who visited the sets was taken aback when he saw the unseasonal flowers blossoming on the shores of the lake. Finally, while shooting the climax scene, the crew was put up in Kufri to report the level of snow every day. Rajendra Kumar and Sadhana too were kept on hold. Papaji had said to them, 'I will give you three hours' notice before we shoot.' And when he finally did ring them up, they rushed to the location. But as soon as they landed in Kufri, it snowed so much that they couldn't go outdoors and were confined to their hotel for the next three or four days. And those were the number of days the stars had committed for this particular shoot. On the third day, with no solution in sight, Papaji went to them and said, 'Here are your tickets. I cannot detain you any longer when we can't shoot. I love you for the patience you have shown and for your dedication. I know both of you are very busy stars, but I need to say that this kind of snowfall is a once-in-a-lifetime occurrence. And the scene we are supposed to shoot is a destiny-making one. If we lose it, we lose the impact of the climax. Yet...' What can I say about the spirit of filmmaking and the dedication of all involved? Both the stars decided to wait for one more day and, miraculously, the weather cleared the very next day! *Sangals* [anti-skid iron chains] were tied to the tyres of jeeps transporting the crew and actors through the deep snow and big casks of brandy were also taken to the location. The scene was finally shot and it became one of the highlights of the film. I truly feel that *Arzoo* was Ramanand Sagar's best work. It was also Rajendra Kumar, Sadhana and Shankar–Jaikishan's best film. So pure it was and filled with so much love!

*Prem Sagar*

# 14

# *L'Affaire Aman*

I never felt that so and so will come [enter the film industry] and [as a result] my career will [fizzle out]. In fact, I felt I should help newcomers, as I too had once been one and realized how much we hope that someone will be there to help us. By the grace of God, I was now in a position to do so. Mohan Kumar had started his own company and we began work on *Aman*, a film based on Dr Dwarkanath Kotnis, an Indian doctor who is remembered in China for his service during the Second Sino-Japanese War that was fought between 1937 and 1945. It carried a message condemning the use of the atom bomb. We thought of approaching Lord Bertrand Russell, the philosopher, to deliver his own message in the film against the use of nuclear bombs.

*Rajendra Kumar Tuli*

Although 1963 and 1964 belonged to the jubilee star, a different genre of films was beginning to capture the public imagination. Along with Rajendra Kumar's *Sangam* and *Zindagi*, 1964 and 1965 saw films like *Haqeeqat*, *Dosti*, *Rajkumar*, *Ziddi*, *Kashmir ki Kali* and the mystery *Woh Kaun Thi?*, along with the path-breaking *Guide*, ruling the box office.

Despite this new development, Rajendra Kumar's diary remained chock-a-block with dates committed to different films. Well known for his far-sightedness, he had anticipated the turn of the tide and had begun preparations, as early as in 1961, to take his success graph to a new level by being selective in accepting offers of films that came his way. Moreover, he was aware of the growing demand for newer actors like Manoj Kumar, Dharmendra and Shashi Kapoor, among others. Intense, good-looking and with the kind of sex appeal that drew hordes of female fans, this younger lot, with all the potential of a modern leading man, had entered the industry with confidence and determination. While their arrival posed a challenge to his own position, a seasoned Rajendra did not once falter or retreat. To be rewarded for one's efforts with success and fame was one thing; to hold on to them and work one's way through the fear of losing them was another, he told himself. Hard work, staying on top of things and continuously reinventing himself were indispensable for retaining his position, and retain it he would. He did so admirably, reigniting his creative passion with his new pet project, *Aman*, the ideation for which had begun in late 1965.

During a brainstorming session involving the film's creatives, Rajendra Kumar had come up with a suggestion.

'Mohan,' he said to the director, 'let's try and get Bertrand Russell in the opening scene.'

The other man laughed at the very idea. 'You're joking, right?' he said. 'Lord Russell is one of the greatest philosophers of our time and a famous member of Britain's anti-war brigade. Look at his stature and look at us – just ordinary film-industry people! How could we even dream of bridging the divide?'

'True!' Rajendra admitted. 'But he advocates nuclear disarmament. Our film *Aman* conveys the same message. No harm in asking him, is there?'

*With Saira Banu in a scene from* Aman *(courtesy Emkay Productions, and Mohan Kumar and family)*

So the next day, the two men composed a letter and mailed it to Lord Russell. To their surprise, they received a reply from the philosopher's secretary ten days later. 'Lord Russell,' said the letter, 'has agreed to appear in the film's opening scene. However, because of his age, he is unable to travel to India. If you could be so kind as to come and meet him here, he will be glad to give you an hour of his time.'

Elated by the news, Mohan Kumar, Rajendra Kumar and their crew left for England without delay and made their way to Porthmadog, earlier known as Port Madoc, the small coastal town in North Wales where Bertrand Russell lived.

The ailing Lord Russell received the Indian film star with great warmth and respect and so enjoyed the meeting and the shoot that he worked on the scene for all of four hours, instead of the allotted one. With the first schedule of the film completed successfully, the members of the crew were soon back to the bay and busy with preparations for their next shooting schedule in Japan, slated for early 1966.

But over the next few months, the film that was being made with the intention of rekindling the noble spirit and driving principles of Dr Dwarkanath Kotnis's peace mission ended up robbing Rajendra Kumar's wife of all sense of *aman* or peace in her own home. It shook the foundations of the family she had painstakingly built and nurtured with her love and care.

> I was not the jealous type. I used to accompany Miyan to every party he attended and had understood and accepted the film industry and its ways. I remember Ashok Kumar asking my husband during the shoot of *Kanoon*, 'You married?' to which he'd replied that he was. 'Remember one thing, then,' Ashok Kumar had advised him, 'whatever you do, wherever you go, come back home and eat dinner with your wife every night. She will never nag you.' It was sound advice.
>
> *Shukla Tuli*

Shukla was well aware of the ways of the film industry and had come to terms with them. She had noticed women openly flirting with her star husband. Some would even slip him personal notes, uncaring of her presence. But that, she had come to realize, was part and parcel of the business of films and she had accepted the fact the day she'd agreed to marry a man associated with the film industry. She knew of many star wives who were tied down by domestic duties at home, looking after their children and other family members, while their husbands lived it up elsewhere. And those who did accompany their husbands to social gatherings and events would often be under severe stress, because they tended to feel neglected and insignificant in the company of glamorous, attention-grabbing leading ladies and starlets. Astute and self-aware, Shukla had resolved to be different. She kept up her morale by reminding herself that she too was beautiful and that even though her husband might indulge in a bit of harmless flirting, at heart he was a loyal family man. It was a common saying in the industry, however, that the family could be a long way from the latest movie set.

*Aman*'s second schedule in Japan stretched over a period of thirty days that seemed magical and dreamlike to its stars. Filming in quaint, picturesque local villages, glitzy towns and locations surrounded by breathtakingly beautiful mountains, the film's leading man and leading lady were attracted to each other. Responsible family man that he was, Rajendra Kumar tried to resist his co-star's bewitching charm and avoid a romantic entanglement with her, but Saira Banu's proximity during their leisurely evening walks in the enchanting gardens of their hotel plunged him into confusion.

Back in Bombay, gossip magazines went into overdrive and rumours of a love affair gained momentum. Photographs of Rajendra Kumar and his beautiful leading lady appeared in various publications, accompanied by spiced-up reports of their alleged affair. Shukla could hardly pretend to be unaware of the developments. It was not as if she had never faced such rumours before. They tended to surface with every new film that her husband worked in. That was par for the course in the film industry. But this time the talks circulating around her seemed to overpower her sensibilities. The rumours refused to die down and a restlessness beset Shukla. Her head throbbed with the whispers, setting off speculation within her mind, the images in the newspapers haunting her ceaselessly. She felt utterly helpless.

To compound matters, Shukla's back problem had flared up again, confining her to bed. Her doctors had advised surgery, but she'd vehemently refused to go down that path, reasoning that operations performed in India at the time were yet to be foolproof and she couldn't take the risk; she needed to be around for her three small children. *What do I do*, she asked herself in desperation and initially resigned herself to the situation. *What will be, will be.*

Shukla, however, was a fighter and her indomitable spirit would not let her rest. She called up her husband in Japan and asked him point-blank, 'Are you having an affair?'

'What? No, Biwi. I...'

'These daily letters you send me,' she continued matter-of-factly, 'they reek of a guilty conscience.'

'So a man cannot miss his wife?' he countered with a laugh. 'Stop being so suspicious! It doesn't become you.'

*With Shukla at a function in 1960*

Somewhat mollified, Shukla reassured herself, *I know my husband well. He will be over it in no time. The actress Saira is new and very beautiful. These things happen. Ho jaata hai!*

A niggling doubt persisted, nonetheless. Determined to take the reins of her life back into her own hands, thereafter Shukla made it a point to accompany her husband to all parties, functions and events he was invited to, staying by his side at all times.

Meanwhile, in March the same year, the Rajendra Kumar–Vyjayanthimala starrer *Suraj* released. This film was, yet again, the jubilee star's brainchild, a concept of his that had begun to take form in Madras way back in 1961.

> Every film in those days was ours. We belonged to it as much as it belonged to us. Every film crew became a family. Therefore, when I signed a film, I became attached to it as much as the producer and the director did. I was completely involved in the choice of locations, the filmmaking process, the music, and so on. I was close to Naushad Saab and Shankar and Jaikishan. So I would often be a part of the musical sittings and recordings as well. I never interfered or forced my opinions on anyone, but did offer friendly suggestions which, fortunately, hit the bull's eye. This happened as well with my next film, *Suraj*. The idea of *Suraj* had originated back in 1961, when I was working in S.S. Vasan's *Gharana*. One day, when producer S. Krishnamurthy and I were sitting in the Savera Hotel in Madras, I was struck by a novel idea.
>
> *Rajendra Kumar Tuli*

'Krishnamurthy, yaar,' Rajendra had begun, '*kya tum aisi* film *banana chahte ho jisme tum khoob* paisa *kamao*?'

'Of course I do!' the producer replied. 'Who doesn't want to make a film that can bring in lots of money?'

'Then forget social films. Make an action film – a costume drama.'

Dumbstruck, Krishnamurthy had stared at the star for a moment, before replying, 'Saar! You are a melodrama star. How can you ride horses and fight with swords?'

'Because I haven't done so ever before,' the actor had replied. 'It will be a novelty. And, believe me, it will be a superhit. Just think: if I do not accept offers of similar movies in the future, your film will remain a long-term, guaranteed hit.'

'Hmm! Let's see,' Krishnamurthy had said non-committally and left for home in a contemplative state of mind.

By the next morning, he had arrived at a decision and called up the jubilee star. 'I agree with you,' he said. 'Let's do it!'

'Great! Cast Vyjayanthi as the female lead.'

'Why Vyjayanthi?'

'Because it will be a prince-and-princess story. And she is so graceful and regal-looking…and the best dancer. I will play the title role of Prince Suraj.'

'Okay!'

But Rajendra Kumar wasn't done as yet. The following day, he gave his producer another shock.

'Make it in colour,' he suggested. 'The trend's picking up fast and we shouldn't be left behind.'

'What, saar?' the producer said. 'Every day, you are coming up with new things! Colour is just too expensive.'

'Yes, it is,' the actor agreed, 'but you did say you wanted to make big money. So if you invest a lot of money in making the film, only then will the returns be huge, right?'

Unable to find fault with Rajendra's advice and reasoning, Krishnamurthy had given in. 'But it will take time to get the finances in order,' he had warned.

'No problem, sir!' Rajendra had assured him, having accomplished what he'd wanted to. 'Whenever you are ready.'

A couple of years later, the film finally took off and was completed. *Suraj,* produced by S. Krishnamurthy and T. Govindarajan and directed by T. Prakash Rao, released on 25 March 1966. As predicted by the jubilee star, it became a superhit and the second-highest grosser of the year.

In this entertaining masala movie, Rajendra Kumar playing Suraj, a Robin Hood-type prince, falls in love with an uninhibitedly sexy Vyjayanthimala in the role of Princess Anuradha. Witty repartee, sharply choreographed swordplay, breathtaking dances and Shankar and Jaikishan's catchy songs based on Shailendra and Hasrat Jaipuri's lyrics added spice to the story. Moreover, the twist in the tale, with Princess Anuradha switching roles with her companion Kalavati, played

*The glamorous superstar*

by Mumtaz, to keep tabs on the man she is to marry, heightened the tension in the plot.

The two gorgeous ladies appear on the screen in a royal chariot, singing, '*Titli udi* (Butterfly fly)', singer Sharda's debut song for a Bollywood film. Later, in keeping with the norms of romance in Indian films, the hero attempts to thaw a haughty yet alluring leading lady with '*Chehre pe giri zulfein, keh do toh hataa doon main* (Your tresses tumble about your face, I could move them back if you say so)' and then again, with '*Itna hai tumse pyaar mujhe* (So intense is my love for you)'. Finally, the princess relents and the prince launches into the chartbuster '*Baharon phool barsaao/ Mera mehboob aaya hai* (Rain down flowers, O spring/ For my beloved is here)'. Prince Suraj, showers her with poetic eloquence and the universe sprinkles the verdant woods with colourful blossoms. Peacocks cavort in pathways and elephants and rabbits play dodge with the sensuous and perky Vyjayanthimala, who then gracefully reclines in a beautiful floral hammock. '*Sajaayee hai jawan kaliyon ne ab ye sej ulphut ki* (Ripened buds decorate a bed of love they create)', the besotted lover sings, as he rocks the princess to slumber.

The musical maestros Shankar and Jaikishan round it off with '*Kaise samjhaoon/ Badi nasamajh ho* (How do I explain to one so innocent, so naive)' a song that lends significance to the face-off between the supreme dancer Vyjayanthimala and a regal Rajendra. Also in the film is the villain, played by Ajit, who revels in pursuing and lassoing village girls, along with supporting actors Johnny Walker, Lalita Pawar, Baby Neetu Singh, Jagirdar, David, Agha, Mukri, Mallika, Niranjan Sharma and a prancing horse named Bahadur. They added myriad flavours to this colourful south Indian romantic adventure.

A resounding success, *Suraj* also gave a second lease of life to actor Ajit's floundering career, a possibility that Rajendra Kumar had foreseen when he took the initiative of persuading the screen villain, whose career had lost steam by the mid-sixties, to accept the antagonist's role in the film. Indeed, once *Suraj* released, there was no looking back for Ajit.

With *Suraj*, Rajendra also reached the zenith of his career. But, despite the film's immense success, the star, who was by then nearly forty years old, realized that from now on the pressure to improve on his previous project, to constantly hit the mark and stay on top had doubled. He reminded himself that although he'd been nominated for awards for his screen performances in 1964, 1965 and 1966 and these film awards had always eluded him, he would keep doing good work till his last breath. Cinema was his first love.

He still had a string of films in his kitty, but remained alert to potentially profitable projects and sound investments.

It was also in 1966 that the star struck gold in another area of his life by acquiring a huge prime property in Pali Hill. To build a dream home for his family on the plot, he engaged the services of Jalgobai, a renowned Parsi architect known for his creative sense of design.

Rajendra Kumar had been on the lookout for land in Bombay, when his real-estate agent, Raj, called him one morning to inform him of a prime property up for sale in Bandra.

'Okay, let's go and see it,' the star told him.

They decided to go and check it out the following afternoon.

Dry leaves crackled beneath the star's designer shoes as he walked through the estate gates with the broker by his side. As a quaint stone-and-wood bungalow came into view, Rajendra stopped short. Nestling amid lush greenery, the house had wide verandas, with a short flight of stone steps leading up to the front door.

'It belongs to a Parsi family. It's probably one of their many holiday homes,' the broker explained. 'It's old, but well maintained.'

Coincidentally, Nargis Dutt arrived at that very moment to have a look at the house. It turned out that she too was looking to buy a home in Bandra.

'*Bahut sundar hai!* It's beautiful!' she exclaimed. 'And huge!'

Rajendra nodded in agreement. 'And so perfect!' he added. Then reverting to the nickname he'd given her when they were shooting for *Mother India*, he suggested, 'Mummy, *aap khareed lo*. Buy it.'

However, the lady laughed off the idea. 'It is beautiful, Ramu,' she remarked wistfully, addressing him by the name of the character he had played in *Mother India*. 'But you go ahead and buy it. *Tu lele. Tere bhai ke pas paise kahan hai...*? Where would your brother [her husband, Sunil Dutt, who played the role of Rajendra Kumar's renegade brother in *Mother India*] get that kind of money?'

With Nargis bowing out, the sale of the house was a done deal. Rajendra Kumar purchased the 1 acre land for a sum of ₹6 lakh. Work began on his new home soon after.

Rajendra then left for Darjeeling again to shoot for *Jhuk Gaya Aasman* with Saira Banu. Back in Bombay, an apprehensive Shukla tried to allay her doubts and suspicions by keeping herself busy with the architectural design of her new bungalow. She also found solace in the company of her children and in her newfound spirituality.

By the time summer arrived, Rajendra had returned from Darjeeling and the Tulis set about planning their annual holiday to Europe. Shukla invited music composer Jaikishan's family to accompany them.

'But Jai is terrified of flying,' his wife, Pallavi, told her. 'Otherwise, we would be accompanying you to Europe every year.'

'This time, we must go together,' Shukla insisted. 'Do one thing – tell Jai that with both families around he doesn't have to face his fear alone.'

She was hoping Jaikishan would agree, and he did.

*With Shukla and Bunty at the new bungalow*

It was the music composer's first time on an aircraft and his first international vacation. As the plane soared across the skies, a certain lightness of being descended on the vacationers, and their time in Europe during the months of July and August turned out to be wonderful for both families.

It was a vacation full of fun and frolic, especially for the star who had given himself a sabbatical from the demands of being a celebrity. In Europe, he was just another man, not the film star who was mobbed by fans back in India. Here, he was incognito. It gave him the freedom to visit places, roam

*With the family in Montmarte, Paris, on their first trip together to Europe*

the streets, stop for treats and food anywhere he wanted to, go shopping, visit the market, cook for his family and just be himself. These relaxed moments with his family brought him much joy. The holidays were also very significant and precious to Rajendra's children, who savoured every opportunity to experience the unknown facets of their father's life, that too in Europe. Swimming, playing, buying food from roadside carts and sightseeing with their father was a gift they cherished above everything else. It was all so wonderful!

But then suddenly, mid tour, Rajendra announced a change of plan. 'I must return to Bombay on 23 August,' he told his wife.

Taken aback by the absurdity of his demand, Shukla tried to reason with her husband. 'But our tickets are booked for the 24th,' she protested. 'It just doesn't make sense.'

'True,' he agreed. 'But I got the date changed.'

'*Theek hai...* Okay,' Shukla said, resigned, preferring to let the matter rest.

But she couldn't help wondering what could be so urgent that they had to hurry back home with just one day left of their vacation. *Must be important work,* she told herself.

The mystery was unveiled the moment they reached home. Shukla discovered that 23 August was Saira Banu's birthday. She had planned a big party and had insisted that her onscreen hero attend it.

'You have to come,' she had urged him.

Fairy lights and flower decorations welcomed Saira Banu's guests into her new bungalow in Pali Hill. It seemed as if the entire film industry had gathered that night to wish the beauty queen every happiness. Rose water was sprinked over the stars at the gates, even as flashbulbs went wild with the arrival of the stately Rajendra Kumar. The star made an entrance with Shukla walking tall beside him, holding her own amid the pomp and show of glamorous celebrities.

At the party that night, I would meet the pretty hostess, looking absolutely stunning in a brocade saree as she greeted her guests and accepted gifts and bouquets of flowers, while her extraordinarily beautiful mother, Naseem Banu, and grandmother Chamiyan Bai, also known as Shamshad Begum, stood beside her. Yusuf Miyan [actor Dilip Kumar] was there too and came over to greet me. He loved me as though I were his little sister. Way back, when we'd first moved into the Carter Road bungalow, his sisters would drop in almost every evening and we'd sit down to innumerable dinners and meetings, oftentimes, with the legendary Dilip Kumar himself. Our house had practically become their second home and they were like our own family.

*Shukla Tuli*

'Happy birthday,' Shukla managed to say with a smile, when Saira came forward to welcome her and Rajendra.

'Thank you,' the young actress replied, before enquiring, 'how was your trip to Europe?'

'Wonderful.'

'Which place did you like the best?'

'Switzerland!' Shukla replied.

'Oh! That's my favourite too,' Saira told her guest, her face breaking into a crinkly smile, her eyes, carefully made up with liner to lend it a dramatic fishtail shape, lighting up.

It was a wonderful party, but the unexpected occurred after most of the guests had left. And the morning after, a surprise awaited the film world.

'Dilip Kumar engaged to Saira Banu!' newspaper headlines screamed.

The dailies also alleged that Saira's mother, Naseem, for whom Dilip Kumar had apparently had a soft corner since her heyday, had urged him to rescue her daughter from her rumoured liaison with Rajendra Kumar, a married man. After much thought, Dilip Kumar had given in. And, on the very night following her birthday party, despite the twenty-two-year age difference between them, Dilip and Saira had exchanged engagement rings.

When news of the sudden engagement broke, we were all shocked. I wasn't sure what effect it had had on my husband, but I was there for him if he needed me.

My husband, a film star, who had innumerable women chasing him, had shown great resilience and stood by his family, refusing to give in to a moment of weakness. I knew he loved me and so there I was, ready to support him, come what may. From then on, I would accompany Rajinderji to Darjeeling for the final schedule of *Jhuk Gaya Aasman*.

Both Saira and Yusuf Saab were there. Saira's mother was there too and prepared her special keema [minced meat] dish for everyone, as she had done earlier, from what I'd heard. *Jhuk Gaya Aasman* marked the end of my husband's screen pairing with Saira Banu.

*Shukla Tuli*

The truth was that Saira and I had become very good friends. She and her mother would also drop in at our place. My wife really liked Saira a lot. But another truth is that all the stars of those times were in love with the 'beauty queen', as Saira was known. We worked together and our films were hits. That doesn't mean that we had an illicit affair. Yes, there was some truth to the rumours about us, but Saira was a lovely girl and we liked each other a lot. Her mother too approved of me. I often told both mother and daughter about how I prayed that Saira would find a worthy life partner with whom she could be happy. And see, my wish came true; she married the legend of Indian films, Dilip Kumar. It's also true that if I had been single, I would have been with Saira. But why dwell on what could have happened and would have happened, the ifs and buts? What is present is the reality; the possibilities were mere dreams. Can't live off dreams, right? Today, Dilip and Saira are close friends and often drop in for dinner at our place.

*Rajendra Kumar Tuli*

# 15

# A Falling Star

*Aman* released in May 1967. It was a very good film, but it didn't run. For the Indian audience, the film was far ahead of its time. It enjoyed success mostly in Iran, Lebanon, Egypt and so on. Iranians would rush towards me, exclaiming, 'Aga Kumar, *yallah yallah! Aman, yallah yallah!*' It was such an honour for us to have Lord Bertrand Russell in our film, but the funny part was that the Indian audience neither knew who he was nor understood the value of his message and appearance. They thought, '*Pata nahin kaunsa buddha kahan se pakad layein hai?* Who knows where they picked up some old man and brought him here.' *Aman* is the only feature film that Lord Bertrand Russell appeared in. It was brilliant. The climax of the film was shot in Delhi. It was a funeral-procession scene, an *arthi* scene for which we had placed a small advertisement in the newspaper, stating that fans who wanted to witness and be a part of the scene should come to India Gate with flowers. Next day, millions of people arrived, showering the *arthi* with flowers, while the song '*Aman ka farishta*' (Angel of Peace) played in the background. *Halla ho gaya!* Pandemonium reigned. Even Madam [Indira] Gandhi couldn't pass through because of the surging crowds. She asked, 'What's happening?' A

> film shoot, she was told. From that day on, she banned shooting on Rajpath. When the film released, people thought [deceased Prime Minister Lal Bahadur] Shastriji *ki arthi ka* stock shot *tha*, but it wasn't.
>
> *Rajendra Kumar Tuli*

If 1966 was a tumultuous year in the life of the jubilee star, 1967 didn't augur well for him either. In this decade that saw the production and release of largely fun movies in which frivolity and light-hearted entertainment were finding a wide audience, Rajendra Kumar's cherished *Aman* was a departure from the norm.

Releasing in May 1967, the movie began with the bombing of Rangoon (now Yangon) before moving to the scene of a bustling London morning by the Thames and it was in beautiful, picturesque Japan that the story reached its climax. Thereafter, what was to have been a tribute to Dr Kotnis's life and a vehicle to create awareness of the devastating consequences of using the atom bomb on a country and its people turned primarily into a love story.

Enacting the role of a doctor in the film, Rajendra Kumar volunteers to help survivors deal with the horrors of radiation in the aftermath of the bombing of Hiroshima and Nagasaki. In Japan, he runs into a local woman, Meloda (played by Saira Banu), at a Buddhist temple where visitors are invited to randomly choose folded slips of paper and read what is already written on them – apparently, the course of their own destiny. The to-be lovers who are fated to meet coincidentally pick up the same folded slip. The message on it reads: 'You will meet your soulmate today in the guise of a stranger.'

The beautiful and vivacious Meloda woos the studious Indian doctor with a song and a bouquet of flowers, making it near impossible for him to remain unaffected by her naive flirtations. '*Aisuru, aisuru, mera watan* Japan (I love, I love my homeland, Japan),' she croons, leading the doctor up the garden path to explore love in this beautiful mountainous country. In the film, for the first time ever, Saira Banu herself sang a few lines with Mohammad Rafi, the playback for Rajendra Kumar, whispering sensual nothings in the song '*Aaj ki raat/ Yeh kaisi raat*... (This night – such a night...)'.

Other than featuring Lord Bertrand Russell in a special appearance, *Aman* presented other firsts too: ghazal maestro Jagjit Singh in a rare acting role and Naseeruddin Shah, making his debut as an extra.

Although critics rated Rajendra Kumar's performance, especially in the father-and-son showdown scene with Balraj Sahni, as one of his finest, the film failed at the box office. It remained just another film that the jubilee star had featured in.

The other Rajendra Kumar release of 1967 was *Palki*. Here, the star essayed the role of a morose, dejected poet who lives in Lucknow and is in love with his neighbour Mehrunisa, played by Waheeda Rehman. Their secret rendezvous on the terrace leads to the soulful, romantic '*Dil e betaab ko seene se lagana hoga* (I need to embrace the heart's restless pace)', before the lovers unite with another lovely track: '*Kal raat zindagi se mulaqat ho gayi* (It was last night that I met life itself)'. Finally comes the famous qawwali '*Main idhar jaoon ya udhar jaoon?* (Where do I go – here or there?)' Despite the film's evocative and unforgettable music, *Palki* proved to be a damp squib at the box office.

Rajendra Kumar, however, was a fighter. Not easily deterred, he still had several aces up his sleeve to get him through the era of changing cinematic tastes, shifting perspectives on star allure and the very definition of stardom. Moreover, his new home in Bandra was waiting to be built and work on the property was in full swing.

But even 1968 proved to be a lukewarm year for the jubilee star's career. It opened with the C.V. Sridhar-directed *Saathi*, starring Rajendra Kumar, Vyjayanthimala and Simi Garewal. The film was only moderately successful, despite brilliant performances by its lead actors and outstanding musical compositions by Naushad, who created magic by fusing intensified ragas with Western orchestration in '*Yeh kaun aaya?/ Roshan ho gayi mehfil kiske naam se?* (Who is this man, whose very presence has illuminated the occasion)', '*Mere jivan saathi, kali thi main toh pyaasi* (Oh, my life's companion; a mere parched bud, I await)', '*Mera pyaar bhi tu hai/ Yeh bahaar bhi tu hai* (You are my springtime, my love sublime)', '*Husne jaana idhar aa, aina hoon main tera* (My beautiful life, come to me, your mirror I will be)' and '*Jo chala gaya usey bhool ja* (Forget the one who has departed)'.

*Jhuk Gaya Aasman* released next in December 1968. It was the last film that Rajendra Kumar and Saira Banu would co-star in. Directed by Lekh Tandon, with music composed by the Shankar–Jaikishan duo, its story was borrowed from Hollywood film *Here Comes Mr Jordan* and featured Rajendranath and Prem Chopra in supporting roles. Playing a double role in *Jhuk Gaya Aasman*, Rajendra is both Sanjay and his evil doppelgänger, Tarun. The former dies in place of the latter. But as soon as the Death Angel realizes his tragic error, he leads Sanjay back to earth to win back Priya, the love of his life, played by Saira Banu.

Early in the film, the pretty heroine is seen pottering around in a towel and frolicking in the bathtub, singing '*Unse milee nazar, ke mere hosh udd gaye* (The moment our eyes met, my senses left my being)'. Subsequently, she appears dressed in a leather jacket and fitted pants to tease and tantalize the hero, until he is forced to pull her into his arms in the pouring rain. This sizzling chemistry between the lovers is mostly apparent in the segments of the film that were shot before Saira Banu's engagement to Dilip Kumar, and culminates in the scene – ironically, a forerunner of future off-screen developments between the leading man and his beautiful co-star – where a distressed Sanjay asks his lady love, 'So you have decided to marry someone else?'

'Yes,' she chirps. 'Do come to enjoy the sweets.'

Subsequently, the impact of Saira's revised status as Dilip Kumar's fiancée would become apparent during the second shooting schedule, as she turned up conservatively dressed, with headscarf in place, and maintained a safe distance from her leading man.

*Jhuk Gaya Aasman* was not alone in its average performance at the box office. Lost amid the changing genres of films and the rise to prominence of the fresher, younger lot of actors, even Dilip Kumar's 1968 films *Aadmi* and *Sanghursh* proved to be duds. Both the highest paid actors of the time, also considered Naushad's lucky mascots, the two Kumars – Dilip and Rajendra – were on their way down, while the music maestro was fighting his own battle to strike a balance between the growing Westernization of melody in films and the preservation of Indian ragas.

The winds of inevitable change were bringing new ideas, technology, stars, filmmakers and scriptwriters into the industry. New films had begun to be made in response to the evolving demands of an audience looking beyond the fare that had been available so far. And leading this new wave in 1968 was hunky he-man Dharmendra with his superhit films: *Ankhen*, co-starring Mala Sinha; *Shikar*, with Asha Parekh as his leading lady; *Izzat*, where he was paired opposite two leading ladies, Tanuja and Jayalalithaa, a star of south Indian films who would, many decades later, earn adoration from the masses as a political leader and chief minister of Tamil Nadu, and *Mere Humdum Mere Dost*, co-starring yet another pair of leading ladies, Sharmila Tagore and Mumtaz. In close pursuit were other new-age heroes, like the charming Shashi Kapoor, who rocked the scene with *Haseena Maan Jayegi*, with Babita was his leading lady, and *Kanyadaan*, co-starring Asha Parekh; and Manoj Kumar, whose brooding persona won many hearts and who would score big with *Neel Kamal* opposite Waheeda Rehman. There were other contenders like the immensely talented Sunil Dutt, Mehmood, the comedian par excellence, and the multi-faceted Kishore Kumar in the all-time favourite musical comedy *Padosan*, in which Saira Banu was the heroine. Children's films like *Do Kaliyan*, with Biswajeet cast opposite Mala Sinha; *Brahmachari*, with Shammi Kapoor and filmmaker V. Shantaram's daughter Rajshree as the main leads; and the Mehmood–Om Prakash–Pran starrer *Sadhu aur Shaitaan* too drew cinegoers of all ages to the theatres. It was a full house in 1968.

The following year was no different. Films released in 1969 saw a dramatic transformation of the onscreen scenario: the familiar trope of the young widowed mother in a shabby home working as a seamstress to earn a living had been cast aside; in its place were sultry vamps with glossy pouts and bouffant hairdos, glitzy dens, concealed doors, blinking red lights, transmitter watches and reverse revolvers. Romantic mysteries and espionage movies, pepped up with racy music, had begun to rule the box office and proved to be just the kind of fun entertainment the new generations were looking for. But, despite the deluge, a never-say-die Rajendra Kumar decided, as always, to swim with the tide. *This is no time to question or argue*, he told himself and gave the nod for the ultra-modern *Talash*, following it up with another spy thriller, *Shatranj*. Both films released in 1969.

*Talash*, a romantic mystery produced and directed by O.P. Ralhan, starred Rajendra Kumar as Raj Kumar, Sharmila Tagore playing two characters in a double role as Gauri and Madhu, along with Balraj Sahni and Ralhan himself. A production featuring swanky office spaces, glitzy pubs, lots of red top-down convertibles, extensive wardrobes and luxurious farmhouses, the film was one of the first to be publicized as having a budget of ₹1 crore. In *Talash*, Ralhan hogged as much footage as the hero, both playing fresh graduates who head for the snow-capped hills to celebrate their academic success that will clear the path for their careers. At their holiday destination, the hero falls for the petite and pretty village belle Gauri, a role that called upon Sharmila Tagore, clad in a ghaghra-choli (traditional Indian rural attire), cavorts barefoot around snow-covered meadows and sings the romantic duet '*Palkon ke peechhe se kya tumne keh dala?* (What is it that your eyes try to tell me?)' with her onscreen beloved. Later, she switches to a tribal dance, singing '*Aaj kojjuneli raat ma, dharti par hai aasman* (The light of the full moon tonight has brought the skies to the earth to unite)'.

On a parallel track, Ralhan falls for the sexy cabaret dancer Helen as she gyrates to the scintillating composition '*Karle pyaar, karle.* (Love me, oh love me)', clad in bright pink feathers and a shimmery bikini-style costume. But the twist in the tale surfaces when, back in the city, Raj discovers that his boss's daughter Madhu is a Gauri lookalike, but for her blond hair and sea-green eyes. Thereafter commences the quest – '*talash*' – to discover the true identity of the girl, with a supreme rendition of the song '*Tere naina talash karen jise/ Woh hai tujhi mein kahin* (The one whom your eyes seek lies within you)', by Manna Dey, befuddling the hero still further. Rushing back and forth from city to the hills to find out if there are, indeed, two women who look identical, Raj's confusion deepens when he comes upon Gauri, on the one hand, blowing on a coal stove inside a hut as she sings, '*Khayi hai re humne kasam* (We've taken an oath)', and her lookalike Madhu, on the other, alluring in sexy nighties and gowns, enticing him into her enormous bedroom with '*Kitni akeli, kitni tanhaa si lagi/ Unse mil ke main* (So alone, so bereft did I feel on meeting my love)'.

Intriguing though its storyline seemed and despite the myriad melodious compositions by the maestro S.D. Burman, *Talash* was billed in 1969 as merely an above-average movie. Moreover, Rajendra Kumar's fine performance notwithstanding, the film made it clear that he could, perhaps, no longer get away with playing a young man straight out of college.

In the same year, his next film, *Shatranj*, released.

Inspired by the blockbuster success of spy formula films like Dharmendra's *Ankhen* in 1968, and newcomer Jeetendra's desi-Bond act in *Farz* the previous year, the jubilee star too jumped on the suspense bandwagon with N.N. Sippy's *Shatranj*, directed by S.S. Vasan, a Rajendra loyalist. Although more of an entertainer than a whodunnit, *Shatranj* was loaded with comrades Ping, Chang and Shin Cho, flashing Buddhas, consoles of strobe lights, wall clocks, rotating walls, dungeons, electrocution apparatus, face masks, glitzy radios and much more. Adding to the gimmicky visual excess were Rajendra Kumar with squinty eyes and a Fu Manchu moustache, Shashikala in a blond wig and blue contact lenses, blowing smoke rings vamp-style, and Waheeda Rehman in bouffant hairdos and tightly wrapped sarees.

The film opens with Rajendra Kumar playing Jai, a secret agent dressed à la Jeetendra in a yellow T-shirt and brief white shorts, surrounded, surprisingly, by children, instead of women, and singing, '*Aao, tumhe pyaar karna sikha doon* (Come, I'll teach you how to love)', while Achala Sachdev and Waheeda Rehman seemed to have later reprised their mother and daughter roles for *Prem Pujari* too. Both women travel abroad for a show where Waheeda, in the role of Meena, takes centre stage as she, along with the alluring Madhumati, dances on spectacularly mounted sets to the number '*Jungal mein mor nacha kisne dekha*? (Who saw the peacock in the jungle dance?)'

Comedy king Mehmood too is at his funniest in the film, whether he is frolicking with Shashikala or calling out, '*Yebaebi! Baktamma baktamma ikada potora*! (Baktamma darling, where are you off to?)' to a sexy Helen during a dance number. It was wildly entertaining and it truly seemed as if everybody in the cast was having loads of fun. *Shatranj* was commercially successful, but fell short of its makers' expectations. Moreover, it was not without its share of troubles. Perceived by some as an anti-China propaganda movie, it provoked violent protests from radical communist groups, causing it to be forcibly removed from theatres in some parts of the country.

The 1960s closed for the jubilee star with *Anjaana*, produced and directed by Mohan Kumar. The film began with a done-to-death scene depicting a glowing and youthful Raju (Rajendra Kumar), a garage mechanic, and his widowed mother (Nirupa Roy) living in a small town. One day, Raju meets the wealthy Rachna (Babita) and, following the usual, predictable misunderstandings, the two fall in love. During the film's making, the very young and already successful Babita, who was dating Raj Kapoor's son Randhir, would address Rajendra Kumar as 'uncle'. *Anjaana* did average business, despite the appeal of its young leading lady and wonderfully fresh musical compositions like '*Main rahi anjaana* (I am an aimless traveller)', '*Ki jaan chali jaaye, jiya nahin jaaye* (Even if I die, my love is immortal)' and '*Rimjhim ke geet sawan gaaye* (Monsoon sings the songs of rain)' by the talented upcoming music duo Laxmikant and Pyarelal. It seemed like another setback for the jubilee star.

During this period, Dharmendra was still ruling the roost, with Manoj Kumar, Feroz Khan, Sanjay Khan, Shashi Kapoor and Jeetendra hot on his heels. But even before these reigning and rising stars could consolidate their position for a long innings, the wheel of fortune slid into its final rotation of that decade and came up with a new talent who would eventually become not merely a sensation, but a phenomenon – Rajesh Khanna.

Few could have predicted Rajesh Khanna's meteoric rise. Having made his debut in 1966 with Chetan Anand's *Aakhri Khat* opposite a relative unknown like Indrani Mukherjee, he had found himself at a depressive low when all his films tanked at the box office. Furthermore, Khanna hadn't had a single release in 1968, other than a special appearance in a Kishore Kumar movie, although he did manage to sign a couple of films, one of them being Rajendra Kumar's *The Train*.

> We all saw how the greats like Chandra Mohan, Motilal et al ended up… They never bothered thinking about the future. I've watched them squander away their money and learnt from their mistakes. Right now, I have films in hand, but times are changing. I have to do something. I cannot let all my years of hard work and my successes bite the dust. Maybe, I could produce more films. *Jo* producer *banne ki baat thi*, producer *main* indirect *toh tha hi*. As far as turning producer was concerned, I was a behind-the-scenes producer, anyway. *Phir ek* company *banayi* – Rose Movies – *jisme mera* nephew or *mera beta* Bunty, *un dono ko* partner *banaya*. Then I founded a company – Rose Movies – where I brought in my nephew and my son Bunty as partners. *Jo woh samajh boojh thi woh kaam aa gayi*. The little knowledge that I had gained through my years of experience in the film industry came into good use. *The Train pehli* picture *thi jisme* Rajesh Khanna *ne naam kamaya. The Train* was the first film of Rajesh Khanna's that earned him recognition. We signed Kaka [as Rajesh Khanna was known in the industry] in 1968, much before he became a star.
>
> *Rajendra Kumar Tuli*

On that fortuitous day in 1968, Rajendra Kumar had decided to back his wife's talented cousin Ramesh Behl by setting up Rose Movies. *The Train*, their first production, had set the ball rolling. Bowing to the popularity of the thriller genre, Ravikant Nagaich, who'd debuted with the James Bond-inspired *Farz*, had been roped in to direct *The Train*. Nanda was cast as Rajesh Khanna's leading lady. As the film progressed, the lead actors also began shooting for B.R. Chopra's *Ittefaq*, an offbeat quickie made, primarily, to utilize the shooting sets readied for his big-budget but delayed film *Aadmi aur Insaan*. A songless film, *Ittefaq* was shot in twenty-eight days and hit the screens on 4 October 1969. The Yash Chopra-directed film was a superhit and brought its lead actor into the limelight. The film's outstanding success also served as a boost for Rajendra Kumar, who was happy to have foreseen

*In high spirits with Rajesh Khanna*

the potential in the talented Rajesh Khanna while he was still struggling to establish his career. But even the former jubilee star could not have anticipated the tornado of events that would be unleashed as his production *The Train* raced towards its release date.

*Aradhana*, directed by Shakti Samantha, hit the screens in September 1969, *Ittefaq* followed in October and in December, the same year, *Do Raaste* released. It was a hat-trick of superhits for the then unassuming actor. From that moment onwards, Rajesh Khanna was unstoppable.

Speaking of *The Train* and her leading man in the film, Nanda told the *Deccan Herald* (19 July 2009): 'Rajendra Kumar had signed me for *The Train* opposite Rajesh Khanna.

'The first shot was to be canned at a bus stop next to my bungalow and people in the neighbourhood asked me who my young co-star was.'

*With Shukla, Raaj Kumar, Raj Kapoor, Manoj Kumar and Rajesh Khanna at a function*

'Later, Yash Chopraji started *Ittefaq* as a quickie, [which would be] shot within a month, and I recommended Rajesh Khanna for the role.'

'*Ittefaq* released immediately after, *Aradhana* and then came *Do Raaste*; and after that, one more shot had to be taken at the same bus stop for *The Train*. This time, the entire lane was jammed with people wanting to see the new heartthrob!'

Stars and superstars would come and go, but Jubilee Kumar's career vehicle was still chugging on despite the inevitable. December 1969 saw the star busy on the sets of *Dharti,* a film for which Waheeda Rehman had been cast as the leading lady. As he read through his lines in the dressing room, his mind drifted to some scenes they'd shot earlier. He recalled how his director Sridhar had commented on his looks.

'Sir, you are looking fitter than ever,' Sri had observed. 'You don't look forty at all.'

Yet, as the jubilee star stood facing the mirror and studying his reflection, he was overcome by a sense of finality. *Forty! I feel like I have just begun,* he thought and laughed at his reflection. But at the very next moment he told himself that he should face the truth – and the truth was that he would have to buck up.

Another unavoidable reality was that Rajendra Kumar's film career was on the downswing, even as his younger brother Naresh's career was on the rise. Naresh Kumar Tuli, the supposed black sheep of the family, was the only one of the four brothers who had not been able to complete his education. He'd been around ten years old when the family had migrated to India from Sankhatra, Pakistan. There had been no money to spare at the time for Naresh's schooling. Finally, when the family was financially stable, Ranjit and Virender, the two youngest Tulis, had reaped the benefits. The three brothers had moved to Bombay in the late 1950s, after Naresh began working as an assistant director with H.S. Rawail. Then in 1966, the street-smart Naresh had turned producer, directing his first feature film, *Ek Sapera Ek Lootera*, starring Feroz Khan and Kumkum. His production banner was called Dimple Films, in keeping with the Tulis' firm belief that the name had brought luck to their family.

Through 1966 and 1967, Naresh made a few small-budget films, gradually climbing the ladder of success. His younger brother Ranjit also worked with him and, soon, his family, who'd almost written him off as a good-for-nothing, sat up and began taking notice of the determination with which the once-wayward boy was building his career.

*The superstar on set*

*With Naresh Kumar, brother, ally, close associate*

By 1968, Naresh Kumar was finally in a position to sign his jubilee star brother for his next film, *Ganwaar*, opposite Vyjayanthimala. Rajendra Kumar had, at the time, been shooting for Mohan Kumar's *Aap Aye Bahaar Ayee* with Sadhana. All day, Rajendra would shoot for Mohan and in the evenings, he would work on *Ganwaar*, a film that would release in 1970.

With his dates fully taken for 1969, the year drew to a close for the actor. All seemed well. Yet, the universal law that dictates that what goes up must come down was making its presence felt in tiny, subtle ways.

# 16

# Dimple and Luck Change Hands

Stardom, like youth, never lasts. If you don't look after your body, how will it support you later in life? You'll fall. I kept this in mind and kept myself fit. I also invested wisely. Gambling, playing cards and betting on racehorses – these were never my kind of interests. I hated those durbars where you were surrounded by chamchas [hangers-on and sycophants]. My wife enjoyed the kitty parties, but I didn't. Not that I've ever objected to them. Many of my friends would sit down for card sessions during Diwali, but not me. I just distributed hundred-rupee notes for luck, that's it! People called me a miser, but tell me, have you seen my bungalow? The way I live? I've always owned cars that people hadn't even heard of. Umpteen times, I've taken my kids on world tours – and on my account. But, yes, I don't squander money. Let them call me what they want.

*Rajendra Kumar Tuli*

With Shukla and Rajendra's impeccable taste guiding them and their determination to live in a normal, 'non-filmy' home uppermost in their minds, the charming English cottage set in the heart of the Pali Hill area gradually transformed into an elegant, sprawling bungalow. Named after their older daughter, 'Dimple', it was made of wood and stone and surrounded by a lush garden and vast wooded grounds. The pieces of Italian furniture chosen with care to go with the interiors were custom-made. Finally, after three years in the making, the Tuli home was ready, and in early 1969 the family moved in after having the mandatory yagna performed on the premises.

Dimple was a dream home in a big city like Bombay, but even as the stars in the sky above twinkled brighter than ever, the brilliance of the jubilee star's aura had begun to dim. Life would never be quite the same again.

In the world of Hindi cinema, the year 1970 offered unique, innovative films, coming up with another mixed bag, in which action and spy flicks ruled the roost. Although the Dev Anand–Hema Malini starrer *Johny Mera Naam* was the year's highest grosser, it was Rajesh Khanna who held sway with a string of superhits like *Sachaa Jhuta*, co-starring Mumtaz; *Aan Milo Sajna*, where Asha Parekh was his leading lady; *The Train*, with Nanda as his heroine; *Kati Patang*, in which Asha Parekh was cast opposite him once again; and *Safar*, co-starring Sharmila Tagore and Feroz Khan. Dharmendra too had several hits to his credit, with *Jeevan Mrityu*, opposite Raakhee; *Kab? Kyoon? Aur Kahan?* with Babita as his leading lady; and *Sharafat*, co-starring Hema Malini. So did Manoj Kumar, with *Purab aur Paschim*, with Saira Banu as the female lead. Chetan Anand's romantic epic *Heer Ranjha*, featuring Raaj Kumar and Priya Rajvansh, also proved to be a hit. By this time, a new kind of leading man had emerged, who could dance as well as act. Among this breed were 'Jumping Jack' Jeetendra in *Humjoli*, co-starring Leena Chandavarkar, Navin Nischol in *Sawan Bhadon*, with a sixteen-year-old Rekha making her debut as a leading lady in a Hindi film, and Shashi Kapoor, paired with Hema Malini, in *Abhinetri*.

In this crazy melee of dancing stars and their hit films, Tragedy King Dilip Kumar had but one release – *Gopi* – co-starring his wife Saira Banu. It made no waves at the box office. The showman Raj Kapoor too resurfaced with his magnum opus *Mera Naam Joker*, a film doomed to colossal failure despite the lavish scale on which it had been mounted.

However, the year dawned with glad tidings for the jubilee star. On 26 January 1970, the Government of India conferred the Padma Shri, the country's fourth-highest civilian award, on Rajendra Kumar.

Meanwhile, his career continued to stay afloat that year with four releases, three of which did average business.

*Dharti*, the first of those films, co-starred Waheeda Rehman and was directed by C.V. Sridhar. It released on 6 February 1970 and did well at the box office on the strength of melodious compositions like '*Khuda bhi aasman se/ Jab zameen par dekhta hoga* (When the Creator's gaze falls on the earth below)' and '*Yeh mausam bheega bheega hai* (It's a wet, wet season)'.

It was followed by Naresh Kumar's *Ganwaar*, starring his brother Rajendra and Vyjayanthimala, for whom the film would be her swan song. *Ganwaar* was akin to a home production and was presented by Rajendra Kumar. In fact, the star went out of his way to put in that extra bit of effort. Despite his fading career prospects, he still wielded enough clout to persuade Naushad to compose the film's music, though it is true that by the 1970s, the music maestro's career too was on the decline. In an era when image was paramount, the star even took the bold step of trying to break his own entrenched one of the suave and debonair Gopal, the popular onscreen character that had won him many fans by reinventing himself as a *ganwaar*, a country bumpkin, who rides into the fields on the back of an elephant, singing, '*Duniya hase, hasti rahe, main hoon*

*Receiving the prestigious Padma Shri award from then President of India V.V. Giri, in New Delhi*

*With his mother, Naresh, Raj Kapoor, Shukla and Krishna Raj Kapoor at the party to celebrate the Padma Shri award*

*With Shashikala...*

*With R.D. Burman, Rajesh Khanna and Feroz Khan...*

*With Rakhee...*

*...at a party to celebrate the Padma Shri award*

*ganwaar, mujhe sabse hai pyaar* (The world may taunt and make fun of me, but I am, indeed, a country bumpkin and I love one and all)'. Village yokel or not, as the film progresses, the *ganwaar* is seen to be quite adept at courting his lady love, played by Vyjayanthimala, who dances atop his chest while he caresses her milk-white feet and sings, '*Humse toh achchhi teri payal, gori, ke baar baar tera badan chume* (Your anklet is better off than I am, my fair one; it caresses your feet over and over again)'.

*Ganwaar* released on 17 April 1970 and did average business at the box office. On the other hand, *The Train*, which had hit the theatres just a week earlier, was declared a commercial success. It added another feather to the jubilee star's cap in his career as a producer. Yet, he couldn't stave off a gnawing sense of unease. But then, as is often the case in the unpredictable world of films, *Geet* released and, with its success, Rajendra Kumar was back in the game.

Directed by Ramanand Sagar, this action musical was yet another of the films that released in 1970. It starred Rajendra Kumar, Mala Sinha and Sujit Kumar, and its music was composed by Kalyanji and Anandji. Although *Geet* went on the floors in 1969, the inspiration for making a musical based on the life of an innocent shepherd boy had come to Sagar in the mid-1960s, while shooting in the hills for another film. To develop the story and get a flavour of the place, along with a sense of the characters' ethnic backgrounds, the director had subsequently taken off for Manali and spent two entire months there, writing and doing a recce of the valley. It was also during the script-writing process that Sagar would pen the famous line: '*Mere mitwa mere meet re*'. The director used his time in Kullu to fly around the area with a Sikh pilot friend in his Piper plane, looking for the perfect location for his film. It was this pilot who would help him zero in on Himachal's 'best-kept secret' – a hidden valley.

Once back in Bombay, Sagar met up with Rajendra Kumar and related the story of *Geet*, starting from the very first scene.

The actor was hooked. 'I will play Sarju,' he declared.

'That's good,' Sagar said in response. 'But what about your image?'

'I need to change it.'

'You've read my mind. You are my mountain flautist, my Sarju in *Geet*.'

> When *Geet* came into his life, Rajendra Kumar was looking for a change of image, a different look in which he had never been seen before. *Geet* was, therefore, a calculated gamble. Also, my father, Ramanand Sagar, never repeated the same subject in his films and believed in giving actors different images. Papaji discussed the concept of *Geet* with Rajendra Kumar. It involved a shepherd boy who becomes a sensation on stage.
>
> *Prem Sagar*

With the leading man on board, *Geet* went under production. The day soon arrived when the cast and crew were ready for the film's outdoor shoot. With no commercial flights to Manali operating in those days, Ramanand Sagar chartered a plane from Delhi to fly his team to Kullu's Bhuntar airport. Among the passengers were his lead actors Rajendra Kumar and Mala Sinha, her parents and other supporting-cast members, including Nasir Hussain, the actor who almost always played the role of a father in Hindi films, Tun Tun, the screen name for singer-actor Uma Devi Khatri, who was famous as Hindi cinema's first female comedienne, and Keshto Mukherjee, a comic actor invariably typecast as a dim-witted drunkard in films of that era. Leading the team was the director himself, with his three sons in tow.

The small aeroplane took off from Delhi at 3 p.m. in the afternoon. But what was to have been a mere one-hour-thirty-minute flight turned into a traumatic three hours in the air as the plane went around in circles, weaving its way past mountain ranges, with the pilot trying in vain to find the valley where he was supposed to make a landing. Disaster seemed imminent as all the pilot could do was take the only visible route in mist-shrouded terrain and steer the plane away from one rock face after another. All seemed lost as the plane, flying low, hurtled through an interlocking valley into unmapped territory. Meanwhile, with no signal from the flight deck, Chandigarh air traffic control had announced that the plane was missing. Not long afterwards, Kullu air traffic control declared that the plane had crashed and that jubilee star Rajendra Kumar and his leading lady Mala Sinha were dead.

*A keen traveller at heart*

That last half hour in the plane… I saw death on the faces of the people on board and in the way they reacted. While Mala cried, 'I will die with my whole family!', Nasir rebuked us. 'You youngsters!' he scolded. 'You don't know where we've landed! *Tumko mazak laga hai!* You think it's a joke!' I realize why [he was outraged]. Surprisingly, Rajendraji sat in absolute silence and only once did he speak. 'What a tragedy!' he said. 'I will die without my wife [beside me].' It was quite dramatic. The calmest of them all was my father. He had visited the hidden valley earlier without a map to guide him and was sure of where he wanted to go.

*Prem Sagar*

When the pilot announced that they had an emergency on hand and he was trying to find a spot where he could go in for a soft landing, Ramanand Sagar rushed to the cockpit and said, 'Show me how you've arrived at this point.'

The pilot, a Dutch national, was equipped with updated maps and hadn't ever heard of the hidden valley, but he complied with Sagar's request. However, when the director insisted that they turn the plane around, go back and find the valley, the pilot flatly refused.

'No, I can't,' he said. 'There is only the mountain back there. It's a dead end.'

'Trust me,' Sagar insisted, 'turn around!'

'Even if I wanted to, I couldn't. It's an impossible feat.'

'Just do it!'

'There's no place to turn around and nowhere to land! We are heading for disaster anyway…' the pilot muttered while attempting to manoeuvre a tight turnaround in the corridor between the narrow mountain walls on either side.

But he managed it, somehow, and the small plane was soon on its new flight path, retracing the route back to the point where it had started. Visible ahead of them were nothing but snow-covered mountains. They'd turned back to face a dead end.

'Now what?' the pilot asked gruffly.

Ramanand Sagar strapped himself into a jump seat and replied, 'When we reach the rock face, turn the aircraft to the left.'

'I can't do that. The plane will crash!' the pilot protested. 'There are only more mountains there.'

'I've been there before,' Sagar insisted. 'Please trust me.'

With great trepidation and no alternative, the pilot gave in, once again, to the director's demands. Meanwhile, in the cabin, the plane's celebrity passengers were gripping the edge of their seats in breathless anticipation of the worst, as one snow-capped mountain closed in on them, followed by another and yet another. Death seemed imminent and many in the aircraft squeezed their eyes shut, ready for the dreaded moment of collision.

But it never came. In the nick of time, the pilot managed to swing the plane around the mountain bend and the aircraft soared into open skies. The tense silence, filled with the dreaded anticipation that had hung over the passengers, was followed by sheer relief.

Without the slightest notion of where they were, Rajendra Kumar and his fellow passengers now cautiously peered out of their respective windows. And, lo and behold, a hidden valley emerged through the thick swirling mist and clouds, a visual paradise that left the passengers and crew gazing in wonder. Dusk was beginning to fall and far below them lights twinkled in miniature hill abodes. Smoke trails rose from their chimneys. It was dark by the time they approached Kullu airport.

'We made it!' The sense of relief was now shared unanimously in the cabin and accompanied by whoops of joy.

The shooting of *Geet* began soon after. Lots of locals would gather to watch the shoot. A Tibetan, in particular, would turn up every day with a pair of shepherd dogs in tow – a black female and a white male. Rajendraji loved dogs and adopted the black one. My father [Ramanand Sagar] took the white one. He named them Laila and Majnu, as that was going to be the title of his next film. The idea was to bring both to Bombay and share their pups [among friends who were dog lovers]. *Geet* turned out to be Rajendra Kumar's most beautiful film. He was already a big star, especially in south India, but only in Papaji's films was he actually presented like a star. During the making of *Geet*, I'd hit upon a novel publicity idea for the film. Rajendraji was such a huge name that we'd been in a quandary as to how we could introduce him in a novel way. The pahari flautist, we decided, was an avatar no one had ever seen him in. '*Geet*! A musical film. Coming soon!' the banners promised, with stills of Rajendra Kumar in various stages of playing the flute pasted on massive billboards in cities across India. First came [a shot of] Sarju's [the character played by the star in the film] back, then his profile in shadow, followed by a lit-up profile, and finally Rajendra Kumar facing the viewer and playing the flute. We designed the entire publicity for *Geet* based on this one idea that left people wondering who this actor could possibly be. It piqued public curiosity and built it up steadily.

*Prem Sagar*

*Geet* released on 10 July 1970.

In the film, a glamorous stage performer, played by Mala Sinha, falls in love with Sarju, a flute player from scenic Kullu. The choice for the hero's part was crucial, and Rajendra

*A still from* Geet

Kumar's honesty and innocence shone through his mature performance, rekindling the love the audience had always reserved for the star. The beautiful Kullu valley, along with *Geet*'s lilting musical compositions, like '*Jiske sapne hum roj aate rahe* (The one that I dream of everyday)', '*Tere naina kyon bhar aaye* (Why did your eyes well up?)', '*Bansuri banai ke* (After making the flute)' and especially the track '*Mere mitwa mere meet re* (My friend, my partner)' that played several times over in the film, contributed significantly to its appeal. As in the case of the Rajendra Kumar starrer *Goonj Uthi Shehnai*, where the *shehnai* had enjoyed an important role and proved to be a major draw at the box office, the flute featured prominently in *Geet*. Played by a talented senior musician named Hariprasad, it conveyed so wide a range of emotions – joy, despondency, love and longing – and became such a sensation that the Sultan of Morocco is reported to have imported several hundred such musical instruments from India. The film also gave flautist Hariprasad the recognition he deserved; in the years that followed, he would come to be known as Pandit Hariprasad Chaurasia.

Rajendra Kumar's final release of 1970 was *Mera Naam Joker*, one of Raj Kapoor's most ambitious and expensive projects, in which Rajendra played himself. Six years in the making, the film finally released on 18 December 1970. Kapoor had invested much of his personal fortune in the film's production and word was that he had mortgaged the family's assets to release the film. But its length and experimental plot turned out to be among the causes of its colossal failure. Based on the life of a circus clown, the film bombed at the box office and nearly drove the Kapoors to the brink of bankruptcy.

With *Mera Naam Joker*, another decade in the life of the jubilee star reached its culmination. From this point onwards began a phase in his life during which he would spend increasingly long periods of time at home with his family – and in solitude.

Within the grounds of his stately house, the rain had left the green badminton court gleaming among the tall trees and flowering shrubs where Rajendra Kumar and his children were enjoying a friendly game.

'Good game!' he called out to his son encouragingly.

'Yes, Papa,' Bunty agreed. 'Thankfully, we managed to get in a few rounds, because it looks like it will rain again.'

'Hmm… You kids run along now. I'm heading back inside,' Rajendra said, before walking off the court.

Smartly dressed in white shorts and a sports T-shirt, he strolled past the verdant thickets flourishing on the grounds of his home. His children skipped ahead of him, prancing down the muddy trails that led, no doubt, to the hiding places they had found for themselves while engaged in play.

A lusty monsoon wind now swept through the garden's dense foliage, bringing with it the unmistakable whiff of damp soil. *Gaon ki khushboo!* The fragrance of the countryside! Rajendra paused for a moment to gaze up at his home. The rust stone villa with its white windows and verandas and its green tiled roof stood out against the cloudy monsoon sky. The white garden chairs were set off by the bright green of the lawns.

'Bahadur!' Rajendra called out, settling himself on a cushioned chair as his man Friday appeared with fresh orange juice. *My life is full*, the actor mused, sipping from the chilled glass. He had so much to be grateful for. He had seen it all – the fans, their frenzied adulation. Yet, for him, work was worship. To do nothing at all and idle away his time did not become a man like him. New stars would come and go, but his fans were loyal and loved him immensely. *They deserve to see me in bigger and better roles*, he told himself. Still, all said and done, it hadn't been a bad year with *Ganwaar* and *Geet*, Rajendra smiled to himself. He had put in so many years of hard work and yet the imprudent media had attributed his success to his ownership of Dimple, his beautiful home on Carter Road, and were now blaming its sale for the downslide in his career. *They should realize that it's the people who live in these homes who make it lucky or unlucky*, he thought to himself.

It was another story that Rajesh Khanna's career had, indeed, soared after he bought the jubilee star's Carter Road bungalow.

Shukla had been furious with her husband for letting the house go. 'We didn't need the money,' she'd scolded him. 'Why, then, did you give it to him and that too for a measly three and a half lakhs?'

Rajendra chuckled now, thinking back to that evening in mid 1969 when the sale had taken place.

Ever since the signing of *The Train*, Ramesh Behl, Rajendra Kumar and the hero of their film, Rajesh Khanna, had often spent evenings together, discussing films and future projects over drinks. One night, after downing one too many, Khanna had broached the subject of buying a home in the suburbs.

'Papaji,' he'd begun, addressing Rajendra Kumar, 'your Carter Road bungalow lies vacant and I am looking to buy...'

*Deep in discussion with Shashi Kapoor at the first Dimple bungalow, which was later renamed 'Ashirwad'*

He had let the words trail off.

Khanna may well have believed that if he managed to buy the jubilee star's house, his success would rub off on him too.

Rajendra Kumar had initially turned down the suggestion.

'I don't really need to sell it,' he had explained to the younger actor. 'I'd rather keep both the properties.'

'Papaji, at least give it a thought,' Khanna had urged. 'Imagine, my life would change completely if I acquired your residence. It's the house of the biggest star of India, after all!'

'Hmm... I...'

'Your stardom is at its peak,' Khanna had persevered. 'Whereas I am just starting out...'

Moved by his repeated entreaties, the senior actor had finally given in.

'*Barkhurdar*...young man,' he'd said, 'if that's the case, Dimple is yours.'

The deal was struck there and then. In an emotionally vulnerable moment, Rajendra Kumar sold off his beloved home, for a sum not even close to its market value, and that too to be paid in instalments.

Then Khanna had gone a step further. 'Of course, I'm allowed to retain the lucky name, aren't I?' he'd asked, his eyes crinkling as his face creased into the famous Khanna smile.

But this was one request the former jubilee star had firmly turned down.

'No, that cannot happen,' he'd told the other man. 'You must change the name. Dimple is my daughter's name. We'd named the Carter Road bungalow after her and we've named our new home Dimple too. But you have my blessings for your new home. May it bring you immense luck and prosperity.'

A grateful Rajesh Khanna had touched his senior's feet in respect. He would rename his newly acquired home 'Ashirwad'.

Not long afterwards, three of his films released in 1969 in quick succession: *Aradhana* in September, *Ittefaq* the following month and *Do Raaste* in December. The rest is history. Staying true to its reputation as a harbinger of good fortune, Ashirwad would take Rajesh Khanna to the heights of stardom, fame and glory. At least, that was what many people believed, discounting the fact that Khanna, the man who seemed so aloof, so arrogant in person, could melt hearts the moment he smiled on screen. In fact, much like the jubilee star himself, the immensely talented Khanna could emote, laugh, sing, cry, love, express anger and die on screen, and do so with such conviction, aided by his drawling dialogue delivery and meaningful pauses, that not one person in the audience came away unmoved. Fans of the superstar were so enamoured of him that they kissed his car, lined up along roads and waited for hours outside his bungalow to catch a glimpse of him. As for the women, many sent him letters written in their own blood. And some even married his photograph!

Although Rajesh Khanna had forfeited the name Dimple, destiny would bring another Dimple into his life. Soon after acquiring his new home, he married the young Dimple Kapadia.

While Khanna's career was reaching phenomenal heights, for Rajendra Kumar fame was a devious seductress, bringing fortune, success and accolades in plenty when it suited her, but also breeding in the person she fleetingly favoured vanity and the constant pressure to remain in the limelight. Fame, a fickle mistress, had now turned her attention and charm on the newer lot of rising stars.

Interestingly, in Rajendra Kumar's case, his dwindling fortunes seemed to have coincided with his bungalow Dimple not only changing hands, but its name as well. The consequences of the decisions he took in 1970 would spill into the following year, altering the course of many a life.

# 17

# Grace under Pressure

> Even when I was a big star, I knew that the shop was not a permanent one. This is a game of youth that doesn't last forever – not for anyone. So I never allowed myself to bask in the glory of having it all. Nor was I distressed at the thought of my stardom fading away. As a youngster, I had seen for myself how easily misfortune could befall my family. I had made snap decisions all my life and didn't believe in wasting my hard-earned money. Rather, I saved for a rainy day. And by the grace of God that money is still intact.
>
> *Rajendra Kumar Tuli*

The year 1971 belonged, without doubt, to the romantic superstar Rajesh Khanna who topped the charts, once again, with a diverse range of movies. These were *Haathi Mere Saathi*, co-starring Tanuja and a loyal and endearing elephant; *Maryada*, where he was cast in a secondary role, with Raaj Kumar and Mala Sinha playing the leads; *Kati Patang*, where his leading lady was Asha Parekh; *Mehboob ki Mehndi*, which featured Leena Chandavarkar opposite him; and the unforgettable *Anand*. Meanwhile, Dharmendra was still holding his own with *Mera Gaon Mera Desh*, while the Kapoors rollicked in *Andaz* (where Shammi co-starred with Hema Malini and Rajesh Khanna), *Sharmilee* (in which Shashi was cast opposite Raakhee) and *Kal Aaj aur Kal* (which featured three generations of the family, from patriarch Prithviraj to grandson Randhir). Jeetendra too scored with the musical *Caravan* opposite Asha Parekh. From among the old-timers, Dev Anand reinvented himself with some engaging films, namely, *Hare Rama Hare Krishna*, where Mumtaz played his lady love but the real sensation was Miss Asia Pacific 1970, Zeenat Aman, cast in the role of his sister; *Gambler*, with Zaheeda and Shatrughan Sinha as Dev's co-stars; and *Tere Mere Sapne*, where, interestingly, his director-actor brother Vijay Anand also featured, alongside Mumtaz and Hema Malini.

As for Rajendra Kumar, he managed to make it through the year, riding on the shoulders of loyalists like Mohan Kumar, Ramanand Sagar and his own brother Naresh Kumar by working in their productions, although Mohan Kumar's *Aap Aye Bahaar Ayee* remained the actor's solo release in 1971.

In this film, the characters played by Rajendra Kumar and Sadhana sever their relationship because of mischief on the part of their 'good friend' Prem Chopra, while Rajendra Nath, named Whiskey in the film, introduces some comic relief. The film's compositions, be it the tragic and moving '*Mujhe teri mohabbat ka sahara* (I wish I had the support of your love)', the flirtatious '*Tumko bhi toh aisa hi kuchh hota* (You too must have felt as I do)' and '*Pooche jo koi mujhse bahar kaisi hoti hai* (If someone were to ask me "what is Spring?")', the title song '*Aap aye bahaar ayee* (You arrived, and springtime came with you)' or the dance duet '*Koyel kyon gaaye?* (Why does the cuckoo sing?)', with Laxmikant and Pyarelal's lilting music coupled with Anand Bakshi's heart-rending lyrics, brought the characters and their relationships alive, contributing to the film's success.

But with just one release that year it was becoming glaringly obvious to all that the former jubilee star's career in films was approaching pack-up time. Rajendra Kumar, however, continued to resist the inevitable and remained unwilling to acknowledge defeat. He kept mulling over ways to get past what he felt was a low phase in his career, brainstorming with himself and occasionally with his dwindling group of benefactors and well-wishers, a few of whom still dropped in to meet him at home from time to time.

At Dimple, the star's residence, the wall clock in the veranda showed 9.30 p.m. Rajendra Kumar sat alone in the garden, pulling at his pack of 555 cigarettes from force of habit. The house had quietened down. Stray beams of light streamed out through the children's bedroom windows. With a sigh, the star leaned back, blowing out smoke rings and watching them drift away, then merge into thin air. Lost in contemplation of these wisps of smoke, the actor recalled the time when his home had been the hub of creative discussions, meetings, money talk, costume and media preparations and many a get-together. An image of the producers, directors, actors and other film staff who would gather here came to mind. Once upon a time, his home had been abuzz with the many comings and goings of people who had regarded him as an indispensable part of their lives.

But tonight the well-manicured lawns of the bungalow were silent, desolate. As the former jubilee star poured himself a drink, all he could hear was a light breeze rustling through the branches of the trees around him. *It can't be over just like that,* he tried to convince himself. *It simply cannot! I live to act. That's who I am. Acting cannot be taken away from me.* But, as always, after a few moments of insecurity, his fighting spirit came to the fore. He reminded himself that he had three releases coming up and all of them were promising films.

*With Prithviraj Kapoor and Om Prakash*

*With J. Om Prakash, Krishna and Raj Kapoor, Mohan Kumar, Shukla and Dharmendra*

The year 1972 actually saw a total of five Rajendra Kumar releases, one with Ramanand Sagar, three with Naresh Kumar and one with Prakash Mehra.

The first to be released was Sagar's *Lalkar*, adapted from a Hindi novel the producer-director had written himself. The film starred Dharmendra, Rajendra Kumar, Mala Sinha and Kumkum in lead roles.

> By the time *Lalkar* was in the works, Rajendra Kumar's [career] graph had gone down. Papaji [Ramanand Sagar] had never ever deserted his friends and, therefore, decided to make a film with Rajinderji, but it would be a multi-starrer. I worked as the director of photography for *Lalkar* and managed the publicity, PR and marketing too. Dharmendra, very big at that time, was in the main lead, with Rajinderji playing the second role in the film.
>
> *Prem Sagar*

*An august gathering – with Pran, Dharmendra and Raj Kapoor*

*Lalkar*, a war film, had a shirtless Dharmendra playing a firebrand, a competent Rajendra Kumar playing his brother and some great music. It became one of the highest grossers of 1972. Apart from his other films awaiting release, *Lalkar* was virtually the former jubilee star's swan song as leading man.

Ironically, 1972 was proving to be another memorable year for the Hindi film industry, with Rajesh Khanna and Dharmendra consolidating their superstardom with back-to-back hits, like the former's *Amar Prem*, co-starring Sharmila Tagore, *Apna Desh* and *Dushman*, with Mumtaz as the female lead in both, and the onscreen he-man's *Raja Jani*, with Hema Malini as his heroine, and *Do Chor*, co-starring Tanuja. The year also witnessed the rise of a female superstar – Hema Malini – who'd already starred in several hit films, like *Bhai Ho To Aisa*, co-starring Jeetendra and Shatrughan Sinha, and *Raja Jani* and would essay a double role in *Seeta aur Geeta*, a heroine-oriented film, also featuring Dharmendra and Sanjeev Kumar. The film was a stupendous commercial success and fetched its leading lady the Filmfare Award. It also set the trend that year for films featuring lead actors in double roles, one of them being Naresh Kumar's *Gora aur Kala*.

In *Gora aur Kala*, the now forty-plus Rajendra Kumar played identical twins. One of them was cast opposite the 'Dream Girl' Hema Malini, while the other was paired with the sultry Rekha. The film brought up the issue of skin colour unfairly defining a person's character: the fair, rich sibling among the twins, a prince, no less, was synonymous with good, while the poor, dark, crippled brother was automatically identified with evil. And what a treat *Gora aur Kala* turned out to be, especially for Rajendra's fans, who were delighted to see their favourite hero romancing two young leading ladies while attempting to depict villainy with a comic touch. As always, Laxmikant and

*A scene from* Lalkar, *with Dharmendra*

Pyarelal's music played an important role in the popularity of *Gora aur Kala*. While the romantic '*Dheere dheere bol, koi sun na le* (Speak softly lest others overhear you)' and '*Ek na ek din yeh kahani banegi* (One of these days a story will unfold)' were picturized on Rajendra Kumar and Hema Malini, the numbers '*Ek gora ek kala* (One fair, the other dark)' and '*Ek toh mera mastana shabab* (Firstly, my intoxicating beauty)' were filmed on the hero and a seductive Rekha, the song sequences turning out to be a draw for cinegoers.

Next in line was Naresh Kumar's *Gaon Hamara Shaher Tumhara*, which released the same year. Here, Rajendra Kumar was paired, once again, with the much younger Rekha. Then came *Tangewala*, an action film directed, yet again, by Naresh Kumar, in which Mumtaz, another young actress, was cast opposite Rajendra. All these films did average business, except for the Rajendra Kumar's final release of 1972 – *Aan Baan* – with Raakhee as his leading lady. The actor had a feeling since the onset of *Aan Baan* that it would flop and, as anticipated by the star, the film was a huge flop, proving how sharp his business acumen continued to be despite the reverses he had suffered in his career.

> There were very few of my movies that didn't work. Most often, when I had a gut feeling that the film would work, it did. *Magar kuch picturein chuk jaati thi.* But certain films did fail to make it. *Jaise* Aan Baan *mere* career *ki sabse badi* flop *thi.* Like *Aan Baan,* the biggest flop of my career. The story that was narrated to me by director Prakash Mehra and the final picturization were poles apart. It was about two brothers, one evil and the other good. Pran was to play the evil sibling. But then, during the making of the film, Pran Saab *aur* Mehra *ka kya gathbandhan hua ki* they made Pran Saab's role sympathetic. Pran and Mehra seemed to have arrived at some kind of an understanding, as a result of which the villain's role acquired a sympathetic slant. During the making of the film itself, I had told producer Malik Chand Kochar that his film had been ruined. '*Tumhari yeh jo* picture *hai, kharaab ho gayi hai,*' I had cautioned him. '*Yeh nahin chalegi.* It won't run.' The film flopped. I also incurred financial losses. My agreement [for featuring as the leading man] had been for ten lakhs. My under-production payment being four lakhs, six was due on the film's completion. But when I realized that the film was not going as planned, I took a written undertaking from Malik Chand that until he paid me the full amount, he could not even release the film's trailer. As predicted, the distributors watched the film and refused to take it. Malik was terrified, wondering what to do. Then a Punjab distributor, Gurdeep Singh, liked the

> film and said, '*Main* release *karta hoon*. I'll release it.' Malik came over to tell me that Gurdeep was ready to distribute it, provided that I issued a letter stating that I had no objection to the release. 'Just give me that one letter, please,' he implored. He was an old man [in distress]; so I gave him the letter.
>
> *Rajendra Kumar Tuli*

*Aan Baan* finally released in Punjab and Malik took the film's entire team there for the promotions. But on the very first day it was screened, the movie flopped and, subsequently, all its other distributors refused delivery of the film, even at half the fee agreed on earlier.

Back in Bombay, a harried Malik came over to Rajendra's home once again.

'What do I do?' he asked the actor in desperation.

Staying aloof, the actor replied, 'Look, Malik Saab, you're the boss. It's for you to decide. All through the making of the film, I did not ask you for anything. I got paid only four lakhs for my work in the film. The balance payment of six lakhs is still pending.'

Without a word, the old man bent down, slipped off his shoe and held it up with the sole facing Rajendra. It had a huge hole at the centre.

'*Beta,* you received four lakhs,' the producer told him, 'but *main toh ek saal se ek joota bhi nahin khareed saka.* During the entire year, I have not been able to buy a new pair of shoes for myself!'

The pain in his voice touched the actor's heart.

'*Aap baith jaayiye,*' he said. 'Please sit down. I'll be right back.'

Rajendra Kumar then went into his study where he penned a note on his letterhead that read:

*Respected Kochar Saab,*
*I have completed your film. You don't owe me anything and I don't claim anything from you.*
*With love, regards and respect,*
*Rajendra Kumar*

When the actor handed the note to his film's producer, Malik Kochar couldn't hold back his tears.

'*Aisa bhi hota hai.* Such wonders actually happen,' he murmured, incredulous.

'Whether they do or not is unimportant,' Rajendra told him. 'Just put it out of your mind. *Bhool jaayiye.*'

*Aan Baan*, directed by Prakash Mehra, released in 1972 and vanished without a trace, leaving Rajendra Kumar with not a single release the following year.

Disillusionment set in. On the flip side, though, it made the star introspect increasingly, until one day Rajendra Kumar

*Swami Muktananda*

and his wife met Swami Muktananda via the actor's sister Manorama. Thereafter, with Swamiji's blessings, the Tuli family went through deep spiritual transformation. Eventually, when Swamiji visited their home, he blessed it too.

'This is my Ganeshpuri,' he said.

But even as 1973 proved to be a completely barren year for the former jubilee star, it wasn't all that different for the nation's reigning heart-throb.

The shifting sands of fame had begun to move treacherously beneath Rajesh Khanna's pedestal as he clung to his superstar title with just one hit in 1973 – *Daag*, which paired him with Sharmila Tagore and Raakhee, who would go on to win her first Filmfare Award for her performance in the film. While Khanna's position didn't seem quite as invincible as it had earlier, the steadfast Dharmendra's career continued to flourish through 1973, his box-office status rising with superhits like *Jugnu*, opposite Hema Malini; *Yaadon ki Baaraat*, co-starring Zeenat Aman; *Blackmail*, with Raakhee and Shatrughan Sinha; and *Loafer*, where Mumtaz was his leading lady. But then the year was about to bowl another googly, stumping the entire Hindi film industry.

Two distinctly different films hit Indian screens in 1973. They unleashed a storm so powerful that it threw the tried-and-tested Hindi film formulae into disarray.

One was the Raj Kapoor-directed blockbuster *Bobby*, a fresh, breezy, runaway romance that starred the good-looking and charismatic teenagers Rishi Kapoor and Dimple Kapadia in the lead. The youthful, modern and fun-filled *Bobby*, with its peppy, mood-appropriate music, succeeded in hammering the last nail in the coffin of the 'middle-aged hero playing a young, meritorious college student' template that had constituted the backbone of many a star-studded film in the past.

The second sensation of 1973 was *Zanjeer*, a volatile and intense crime action movie produced and directed by Prakash

Mehra that saw the emergence of a tall, lanky newcomer with unconventional looks – Amitabh Bachchan. His brooding eyes filled with angst and fire, Bachchan stormed onto the screen with a stellar performance in *Zanjeer* in which he was seen battling the many evils and adversaries spawned by a corrupt system. And it was with this role of a headstrong individual refusing to bow down to the injustice inherent in the status quo that Bachchan would become the famous angry young man of Indian cinema, thereby recreating film history and reinventing the very concept of an onscreen hero.

Although as different as chalk and cheese, *Bobby* and *Zanjeer* changed the very notion of what entertaining commercial cinema was all about and brought an eventful 1973 to a close.

Out for a stroll on the grounds of Dimple, his tall shadow sauntering alongside, Rajendra Kumar paused in mid stride, cupping his hand around the flame of his silver lighter. Inhaling the nicotine from his cigarette and enjoying the warm, comforting feeling it gave him, he resumed walking. Moths fluttered around the garden lamps and nocturnal insects chirped happily. An owl called in the distance. The actor, however, was absorbed in his own thoughts. *No films in hand,* he pondered, his handsome face flushed with the winter chill. *The year has ended. It's unbelievable. And yet, I am the jubilee star.* He drew deeply on the 555, expelling rings of smoke. *There is so much enthusiasm, so much passion within me, and there are so many stories! First thing tomorrow, I will call up all my industry friends. My dear film industry will respond. They will not turn me down.*

But for all his efforts and enthusiasm, what eventually landed in his kitty was a handful of special appearances in Punjabi films like *Dukh Bhanjan Tera Naam* and *Do Sher,* both with Dharmendra as his co-star, although in the second film, where the younger actor appeared in a song sequence and one scene, Rajendra Kumar played a central role as a dacoit. The films released in 1974. Thereafter, sleepwalking into 1975, Rajendra appeared in *Teri Meri Ik Jindri*, a Punjabi film made to launch Dharmendra's cousin Veerendra. What did perk up the jubilee star a bit, though, was the release of two of his Hindi films.

The first was the remake of a Telegu film, *Sunehra Sansar*, directed by Adurthi Subba Rao and helmed by women actors, with Mala Sinha playing Rajendra Kumar's wife and Hema Malini his former flame. In the publicity posters of *Sunehra Sansar*, superstar Hema Malini featured quite prominently. Though the film was not a commercial success, she was much appreciated in a rare negative role. This was followed by *Rani aur Lalpari*, a children's musical with a melee of stars, such as Rajendra Kumar, Asha Parekh, Jeetendra, Feroz Khan, Reena Roy, Neetu Singh and others.

The year ended with *Do Jasoos*, a film that chalked up average profits. Produced and directed by Naresh Kumar, the film starred Raj Kapoor and Rajendra Kumar. Playing bumbling detectives, they were mere caricatures of their former celebrated selves. The adulation they had once enjoyed, the fame and stardom that had been at their fingertips had all but faded away. Of the two stars who were used to fans screaming, 'Raj! Rajendra! We love you!', Rajendra Kumar was still taken aback when he overheard somebody remark, 'I saw that actor and he looks old.'

*I've seen it happening to others over and over again, and yet...* Rajendra brooded one night, allowing his despondent mood to get the better of him.

'Biwi,' he said, turning to his wife, 'I'm not worried about growing old. But there is so much more that I want to achieve. I also have to keep the money coming in. All my money is invested, but to maintain this lifestyle, we will need more.'

'Hmm...' Shukla murmured, her eyes moving around their spacious home as she listened to her husband voicing his ambitions and fears.

'Tonight, I need a few pegs of good Scotch,' Rajendra was saying, 'but I am worried about using up our Black Label stock.'

Shukla shook her head in exasperation. *Actors*, she thought to herself. *Always so dramatic!* But all she said was, 'Miyan, go ahead and drink to your satisfaction and leave the money management to me. We have enough.'

In the days that followed, a lethargic calm descended over Rajendra Kumar's life. But the underlying tension of having no work remained, surfacing ever so often. At times like these, he would feel helpless, broken. Lying in bed one night, Rajendra reflected that in the current scenario the world was backing away from him, disinclined to professionally engage with a star who, they all felt, was past his prime. He sighed, turning on his side. Like his fellow actors, he too had struggled constantly to ensure that he wouldn't lose track of his real identity – the human being that lay at the heart of his star persona. Now he was caught in a dilemma: what was real – the elevated status he had enjoyed earlier, the glorification he had revelled in, his decreasing relevance in the world of films, the growing obscurity he now faced? With a multitude of defeatist thoughts vying for space in his mind, the former star shut his eyes and fell into a troubled sleep.

The next day was a Saturday. Rajendra awoke, feeling surprisingly refreshed and charged. As part of his routine, he dressed in shorts and a striped T-shirt, ready to sweat it out on the courts with a game of tennis. Bounding down the staircase of his magnificent bungalow, he called out to Kaajal, his younger daughter, who always accompanied him to the club.

'I'm going for a run. Let me know when you are ready,' he told her, before jogging down the narrow paths that cut across the grounds of his house. A cow mooed, bringing a smile to his lips. *Imagine*, he reminded himself, *in Bombay city, in Pali Hill, on the grounds of my luxurious bungalow, I have a cow, six dogs, a monkey and deer*! Rajendra smiled to himself, waving back at his neighbour who stood at the back gate.

'How's the cow doing?' Mr Choraria asked.

'Choraria Saab! What a gift you send over every morning!' the actor responded. 'A cow of our own to milk!'

'Of course! Growing kids need fresh milk, don't they?' Choraria remarked with a smile.

By this time, Kaajal, a sports lover like her father, had come running down the stairs. Father and daughter left for the club. Rajendra Kumar truly enjoyed playing tennis, because it offered him a reprieve from the depressing thoughts that seemed to preoccupy him much of the time. But once back home, even as he sat down to a hearty breakfast, his vacillating mind went into overdrive again. *Perhaps I should call it a day. I am at peace*, he reasoned. But then, the workaholic in him raised its head. *No, I can't just sit at home all day doing nothing*, he told himself. *I have invested years in films and I am sure they will keep coming my way. Maybe not the choicest ones, but...* Stubbing out his third cigarette, he lit up afresh as the houseboy brought out a tray of fruits. *What an industry*, the actor reminisced, biting into a crisp apple. *It gave me so much and I too gave back wholeheartedly. I never played politics. On the contrary, I helped and advised many newcomers. Ramesh Behl lived with my family from the age of fourteen. It was for him that we started Rose Movies. And we signed Kaka* [Rajesh Khanna] *even before* Aradhana [released and the actor's fame and popularity peaked]. *Rose Movies also gave Daboo* [Randhir Kapoor] *a new lease of life with* Jawani Diwani, *which became such a huge success. And Manoj* [Kumar]... *He is as dear to me as my younger brother. He also lived with us, until he made it. I helped him too...*

'Chai.' Bahadur interrupted the flow of memories with a cup of tea and Rajendra Kumar accepted it absent-mindedly, still deep in introspection.

He recalled how it was through him that actor Manoj Kumar had finally got his break as a hero in H.S. Rawail's *Kanch ki Gudiya* opposite Sayeeda Khan. Rajendra had even recommended Rakesh Roshan for his debut role in *Ghar Ghar ki Kahani*. Then there were the filmmakers J. Om Prakash and Mohan Kumar. They had remained his dear friends.

The star sighed, still lost in the past, attempting to convince himself that his film-industry friendships had endured, despite the downward curve of his career graph. But a deep frown continued to furrow his brow.

Time ticked on. The trees in the garden cast long morning shadows over the solitary star as he sat in contemplative silence.

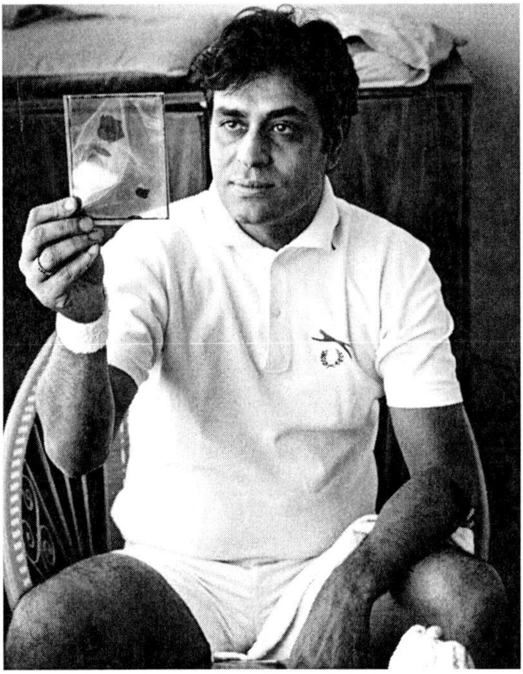

*Tennis time*

*I helped all those I could*, he pondered. *Where are they today?* Not that he had done it all to get something in return. God bless them! His relationships with them had been genuine, untainted by the expectation of gain – at least, on his part. Yet, the indifference with which a few in the film industry were now treating him was a fact of life; he would come to terms with it and sail through.

And so he did as, swept along by the tide of multi-starrers that came his way, he began accepting some of the character roles on offer. It was also in 1975 that Rajendra Kumar built Dimple Theatre, a very successful venture as the future proved, on the premises of his residential property.

*Mazdoor Zindabaad*, written and directed by Naresh Kumar, released in 1976. It was followed by *Shirdi ke Sai Baba* in 1977, a film written by Manoj Kumar and directed by his brother-in-law Ashok V. Bhushan. The Ravikant Nagaich-directed *Daku aur Mahatma* also released in 1977.

The following year witnessed a temporary upsurge in Rajendra Kumar's floundering career. His brother Naresh Kumar's action film *Sone ka Dil Lohe ke Haath* did average business, but then *Saajan Bina Suhagan*, featuring Rajendra Kumar opposite Nutan, released the same year. Produced and directed by Saawan Kumar Tak, the film was a success at the box office, with one of its songs – '*Madhuban khushboo deta hai* (The garden infuses all with its fragrance)' – becoming very popular.

The year 1979 saw the release of Rajat Rakshit-directed *Bin Phere Hum Tere*, with Asha Parekh as the leading lady, and *Aahutee*, a family drama directed, once again, by Ashok Bhushan, starring Shashi Kapoor, Parveen Babi, Rakesh Roshan, Zaheera and Rajendra Kumar. Composers Laxmikant and Pyarelal, working together with lyricist Anand Bakshi, created some unforgettable songs, namely, '*Jugani ek ladki ka naam hai* (Jugni is the name of a girl)', '*Kaash aisa hota, kaash aisa hota* (I wish it had happened this way)', '*Naukri sau ki hazaar ki/Keemat nahin hoti pyaar ki* (A job may be worth a hundred or a thousand but love has no price)' and '*Saathi mere saathi, rut aati jaati, kahe teri meri kahaani* (My love, the seasons come and go and they tell our story)'.

Several films featuring Rajendra Kumar in secondary roles released in 1980: *Oh Bewafaa*, another Saawan Kumar Tak film, with Anil Dhawan and Yogeeta Bali; *Dhan Daulat*, co-starring Rishi Kapoor, Neetu Singh and Mala Sinha; *Badla aur Balidan*, featuring Vinod Mehra, Moushumi Chatterjee and Asha Parekh; and finally, *Gunehgaar* with Rishi Kapoor, Parveen Babi and Asha Parekh yet again.

With more time on his hands, Rajendra began to focus simultaneously on Dimple Theatre. Editing and dubbing were among its many functions, and trial shows of several films, including those he was acting in, were often held there. But the most important fact was that Bunty (Kumar Gaurav) was now working in his debut film. Rajendra recalled the time when his son's decision to become an actor had taken him by surprise. It was back in 1978.

As was his evening routine, Rajendra Kumar sat out in his garden, ideating, creating and introspecting. *Change is the only constant and winter must give way to spring*, he reminded himself late one evening, as he stroked his pet Alsatian's head absent-mindedly. *To accept and to surrender is the way forward.* By then, dusk had begun to descend. A dry leaf fluttered down and settled on the grass near his feet. *Symbolic*, the former star thought, staring at it for a moment. Then he raised his eyes to the charcoal skies above. Venus, the evening star, was out, its glow steady and bright. *That's me*, the actor thought, *a star. No one should ever forget the jubilee star – Rajendra Kumar – ready to grow brand-new wings and fly again!*

'Papa, you're still up!' The garden gates had creaked open and his lanky son Gaurav was walking in.

*Kumar Gaurav, whose decision to join films took Rajendra Kumar by surprise (courtesy* Mayapuri *magazine)*

*With Kumar Gaurav and David Dhawan, 1988*

'Come, Bunty, sit with me for a while,' his father said. 'Tell me, your last year in college, is it going well?'

'Yes papa!'

'And how's work going? Are you enjoying being an assistant director?'

'Yes, it's cool.'

'It's been two years, right, since you began working with Rajji? That's quite a long time. You will soon be twenty-two years old. You should start planning ahead now.'

'Is this a serious discussion, Papa?' Gaurav smiled and pulled up a chair to sit facing his sombre father.

'Sure. It can be.'

'Papa, I want to become an actor like you.'

Although slightly taken aback, Rajendra was overwhelmed with a feeling of joy. 'Done!' he said enthusiastically. 'We'll begin work on it from tomorrow itself.'

'Wow! That fast?' Gaurav smiled, pushing back his chair.

'Yes, once the decision is made, we shouldn't waste any time.'

'All right, Papa.'

'Now go and get some sleep, son. Your dreams are about to materialize,' said the indulgent father, a faraway look in his eyes.

'Goodnight, Papa.'

'Goodnight, Bunty.'

A slow smile spread across Rajendra's face as he contemplated his son walking into the house. *There's my future*, he thought. *My son will take my legacy forward.*

The only imbalance in our father's life had become apparent when he was around fifty years old and his career was waning. Saddened by the turn of events, he would say, 'Now we will know who my true friends are. You just wait and watch; no one will drop in to see me now.' But when he was not working, Dad would go for his walks and play tennis. Besides, honours, awards and other event invites kept him happy. He loved to travel. And truly, wherever in the world he'd travel to, people recognized him and showered him with love. That was also a boost to his ego. He was worried about money, but then he turned producer and became successful again.

*Dimple Kumar Patel* and *Kaajal (Tulsi) Chellaram*

# 18

# Another Star in the Making

Bunty was an extremely shy child. During the *Kanoon* [a 1960 release directed by B.R. Chopra and starring Rajendra Kumar] days, when he was around five years old, he would visit BR's home with his father. They'd left at nine in the morning. At 2 p.m., I got a call from Mrs Chopra. 'What did you feed your son before he left home?' she asked. 'Why? Is something the matter?' I asked. '*Subah se* Papa *ke paas baitha hai, ek* word *nahin bola hai, na* toilet *gaya na kuch piya na khaya,*' she replied. 'Since the morning, he's been sitting beside his father. He has neither uttered a word nor eaten a morsel. He hasn't asked for water either. Nor has he been to the washroom. He hasn't budged from his seat.' As a child, Bunty was painfully shy and continued to be so, even while growing up.

*Shukla Tuli*

When his son was still a young boy, Rajendra Kumar would fret over him. *When will he get over his shyness,* he'd wonder. While he was out most of the time, shooting or on location, Bunty was forever in the company of his two younger sisters and his mother or with the maids. He was a film hero's son and yet he tended to clam up in the presence of others. *He has to learn; he has to toughen up*, his father fretted. And in this endeavour, Rajendra Kumar sent his twelve-year-old Kumar Gaurav off to boarding school – Bishop Cotton School in Simla (now Shimla). It was not an easy transition for the young boy, and heartbroken though his mother was at parting from him, she saw sense in the decision. However, so worried was she about her son having to fend for himself that every month she would land up at the hostel, until one day Bunty said, 'Ma, please don't come here so often. My friends tease me. They say, "Your mother lives here or what?"'

As it is, being an introvert, things had not been easy for him. It had taken him a few weeks to adjust to the new way of life. Seniors never missed the opportunity to waylay him and demand to know, 'Which film were you born in?'

'What?' Gaurav would mumble in confusion.

'In every film, your father gets married to a different girl. So which marriage were you born of?' they'd tease.

But Gaurav had hardly ever watched his father's movies, and among the few that he had seen, his father was always shedding tears. *What was the big deal, then*, he wondered, clueless about how famous his father really was.

The years went by in this manner and after completing his tenth standard, Gaurav returned to Bombay to further his education. From now on, the choice of college and the subjects he would select became a topic of discussion at dinner almost every night.

Rajendra Kumar asked his son, 'Colleges there are in plenty, but what do you want to graduate in? Commerce or science?'

'Honestly, Papa,' Gaurav replied, 'all I want to do is make movies. As for studying, I...'

This was the first time Rajendra Kumar had heard his son mention a career in the same film industry that he'd always scorned and, although happy, Rajendra replied in a noncholant manner. 'Bunty,' he explained, 'education is a must… As for films, they too involve a process of learning. And like I did, you should also start in the direction department. Decide whom you want to work with and let me know. Would you prefer Raj Uncle or Yash Uncle?'

'Raj Uncle, Papa!'

The very next day, Rajendra Kumar called up his friend and said, 'Our son wants to work in cinema and there is no one better than you to teach him.'

Raj Kapoor welcomed Bunty with open arms and the teenager became the youngest assistant director in the film *Satyam Shivam Sundaram*. He gave the clap and began his training.

Rajendra Kumar, the proud father, enthusiastically bought his teenage son a Volkswagen so that he could drive to work. But, after a couple of days, Gaurav returned home from work one evening and handed the car keys to his mother.

'I am the only AD who drives to work in a car,' he said. 'No one else has a car. So…'

From that day onwards, the family driver began to drop Gaurav at the Bandra station from where he would take the train and then a bus to R.K. Studios. Gaurav was paid ₹250 per month, of which he would give his mother ₹50. The rest, he would spend on food at the studio canteen: dal fry, *anda bhurji* and *paav* being the delicious staple items. With no special treatment meted out to him and none expected, Gaurav roughed it out like the others, travelling by local transport within the city and to outdoor locations like Hyderabad by bus with the light boys and the rest of the film crew. Son of a legendary star, the affluent Bunty put himself through his paces and came into his own, gradually emerging from the cocooned life he'd led until now. Watching his son evolve, Rajendra Kumar's heart was full, especially when Raj Kapoor called up to say, 'Bunty is a good boy, talented and very intelligent.'

Meanwhile, Gaurav was studying in Jai Hind College, Churchgate, while his younger sister Dimple joined St Xavier's College, in Marine Lines. Dimple's childhood friend Rima – Raj Kapoor's daughter – also became a part of her college group. It was the trend in those days for students to hop across colleges, meeting new girls and boys, and Kumar Gaurav took to hanging out with the Xavier's gang, watching films with them at the Metro theatre, frequenting restaurants and spending many an evening at Slip Disc, the newly opened discotheque. Others from the 1973–77 batch included Anil Kapoor, Sunita Kapoor (who later married Anil Kapoor) and Mazhar Khan. Although these outings and social interactions helped Kumar Gaurav open up to some extent, he remained a quiet, reserved person. But then, one fine day, a dramatic change came over the reserved teenager.

It was his sister Dimple who caught on, before anyone else.

> Raj Kapoor's kids were always in our home and we in theirs. Ever since she was a child, Rima had had a crush on Bunty. I knew my brother; he was so quiet and a complete introvert. Rima was the exact opposite, boisterous and headstrong. They were both so different. I wondered where this was heading.
>
> *Dimple Tuli Patel*

However, while Dimple remained undecided, things came to a head. It was a Saturday night and the gang of friends decided to party at 1900s, the newest hotspot at the Taj Hotel. It was from that night that Kumar Gaurav and Rima Kapoor began dating. Soon after their graduation in 1977, they got engaged with the blessings of both families. It was a lavish celebration, marking the future coming together of two prominent families of the Hindi film industry.

Meanwhile, *Satyam Shivam Sundaram* had been completed and was ready for release in 1978. Kumar Gaurav had worked on the film for more than two years as an assistant director to the greatest showman of the Indian film industry. What a learning it had been! Also, throughout the filming process, Gaurav had been surreptitiously practising Shashi Kapoor's dialogues, and had come to the conclusion that this was his true calling; this was what he wanted to do for the rest of his life – act!

A few days later, he shared his dreams of becoming an actor with his father. Rajendra Kumar couldn't have been happier. But his face remained impassive and he was silent for a few minutes. Then he said, 'Bunty, if you are sure you want to become an actor, then there is no stopping you. I know many producers and directors who will…'

At that very moment, Shukla walked into the room. Having overheard his words, she said, 'Really, Miyan? Tell me, who should make a film for your son? Rajji?'

'At least let me complete what I was saying, before you jump to conclusions!' Rajendra snapped. Then, turning back to his son, he continued, 'Where were we? Ah, yes! Although I know many people in the industry, I don't really need to go begging to producers and directors to give my son a chance to prove himself as an actor, because by the grace of God I can afford to launch him myself. I will make a film for you, son, but on one condition: you will have to go through a screen test like everybody else and then we shall see. If you look good on screen, deliver your dialogues and emote well, only then will I make a film for you. Otherwise, no.'

'Agreed!' was Gaurav's prompt reply.

After two years as an AD, Dad said, 'Enough. What do you want to do now?' 'Acting,' I replied. 'I want to become an actor.' Dad said to me, 'First thing is, you have to give a screen test. Screen test *mein pass hoga toh hi* film *banegi. Aise hi thoda* film *mil jaati hai.* Only if you pass the screen test will the film be made. Film offers don't come just like that.' At that time, [H.S. Rawail's son] Rahul Rawail was directing Dad and Rishi Kapoor in *Gunehgaar*. Rahul was older than me, but we had played together and were childhood buddies. Dad asked him to direct the film and he agreed. Rahul then arranged a screen test at R.K. Studios on the sets of *Duniya Meri Jeb Mein* [directed by Tinnu Anand and starring Shashi and Rishi Kapoor]. It was a Sunday. I shot a romantic scene with a senior actress and, although I was shy, like most shy actors I completely transformed myself in front of the camera. I opened up. Something happens to such actors and they suddenly blossom. Anyway, the scene went for development at our own Dimple Theatre and ten days later, my father, mother, Rahul and the cameraman Karmakar all got together to watch it. I didn't go in. I was pacing the pathway outside, shit-scared, waiting for the verdict. I hadn't seen the test myself. But as soon as I heard them coming out, I ran up to the house and plonked myself on the couch, feigning nonchalance. Dad was the first one to enter the living room, his face expressionless. But then suddenly, his voice boomed in the large hall. 'Champagne *lao*! Son, we are doing a film together!' That's how my journey in acting began. Soon after, I joined a six-month course with Roshan Taneja [the late founder of the Roshan Taneja School of Acting].

*Kumar Gaurav*

The Tulis were delighted. Not only had Bunty found love in his relationship with Rima and was engaged to her, but he was now also on the verge of professionally stepping into his father's shoes. As parents, Rajendra and Shukla wanted the best for their son. No wonder, then, that the veranda at Dimple was once again abuzz with brainstorming, ideation and the selection of writers, director and co-stars.

To direct their son's debut film, Rajendra and Shukla had first zeroed in on Manoj Kumar.

'Rajinderji, you've held him by his little finger and led him up the path to stardom,' Shukla reminded her husband, egging him on. 'Manoj will surely not turn you down.'

But when Rajendra asked his friend to direct the film that would star his son, Manoj Kumar's response was not quite what he had anticipated. 'Bhai Saab,' he said, 'I have my own company now and am busy with my own productions. How can I do justice to your film?'

Rajendra was aware of the fact that Manoj had already produced and directed two films by then and had a genuine reason for turning him down. Finally, Rahul Rawail was brought on board.

With his finger on the pulse of the youth, Rahul was the perfect choice for Gaurav's debut. *Everything happens for the best*, Rajendra told himself. *Bunty is an introvert, he might not have opened up in front of older directors. So it's best to let him work with younger people.*

Once the director had been decided on, the search for a suitable script began. Several writers put forth their ideas and their stories, but Shukla filtered out most of them, finally settling on the Mirza brothers. The latter had come up with the idea of a fresh love story, the only one to emerge after the blockbuster *Bobby*. But that too wasn't without its hiccups.

When Miyan finally okayed a script for Bunty, I demanded to hear it read out first. It was supposed to be Bunty's launch, but it had Rajendra Kumar and Shammi Kapoor playing dominant fathers, along with a policeman, a dacoit and Bunty and a new girl. The story revolved more around the two fathers and I was very upset. 'Are you making a film for yourself or for our son?' I asked my husband. We had an argument that day and it was in anger that I left for Shirdi. When I returned, I found the Mirza brothers, my brother-in-law Virender Tuli and my hubby sitting out on the veranda. Miyan ignored me, but turned to his younger brother and said, 'Tell your bhabi we have a new script. I've changed the story. She better hear it.' His tone seemed sarcastic. I had to sit down and listen to a reading of the script, because the writers were already there. But then, after hearing the narration of just two scenes, I said, 'I don't need to hear any more. This is the perfect movie for youngsters.'

*Shukla Tuli*

Subsequently, the creative frenzy involving the filmmaking process would take over and bring back the excitement that had lately gone missing from Rajendra Kumar's life. Meanwhile, seeds of ambition had also begun to take root in the young Gaurav. But along with the vision of his prospective fame and success arose many a doubt about his personal life. *I am going to become a film hero soon... My career is just beginning*, he mused. *And here I am, engaged to be married at such a young age. Why am I doing this*?

# 19

# Love Story: The Beginning and the End

We set up a company called Aryan Films and signed on the Mirza brothers to write *Love Story* – Bunty's debut film. Rahul Rawail was signed on to direct the film. At the time, Rahul, whom I looked upon with the same affection as I would my own son, was making his own film *Gunehgaar*, in which I was acting. We wanted a new girl [for *Love Story*] and Vijeta Pandit, younger sister of actor-singer Sulakshana Pandit, was chosen as the heroine. In fact, on the mahurat day itself, my distributor came running to me with an offer to buy the film and suggested, 'Sir, why don't you direct the film yourself? If you do, we are ready to pay you more money.' I turned down the idea. I said, 'No, Rahul is like my son. He is a good human being. Besides, Bunty won't be at ease working under my direction. I had wanted to bring in a friendly young director. Of course, I will always be there on the set, but behind the scenes, never interfering in their work. But I will definitely oversee the job being done.

*Rajendra Kumar Tuli*

It was one of the most exciting phases in the star's life. With renewed zest and vigour, he engaged in the process of filmmaking, determined to see his talented son reach the heights of stardom that he himself had attained and enjoyed. Rajendra Kumar was alive once again and he would leave no stone unturned to make this venture a success, with no cost spared.

> We shot for sixty-seven days non-stop in Kashmir. I was the first producer who had agreed to such a long stint of outdoor shooting and I loved it. Some people did turn up around this time to sign me up for their movies, but I turned them down, explaining that I was now a producer myself. Manmohan Desai wanted to cast me in *Desh Premi*, but I declined his offer. I was so involved in *Love Story* and I thoroughly enjoyed my involvement. It's another thing that Rahul, although a talented director, was so stubborn. I don't understand why, but he would demand many retakes, which for me was a waste of time and money. But I never intervened or stood in his way, because it was a question of my son's career. So we kept shooting.
>
> *Rajendra Kumar Tuli*

During this time, Rahul Rawail's *Gunehgaar* released in Calcutta, but was removed from theatres within a week. As a result, Rajendra Kumar had to forfeit his fee yet again. Nevertheless, he helped the young director bag his next film, *Biwi-O-Biwi*, under the R.K. banner. Keen at the time to boost his son Randhir's career, Raj Kapoor was on the lookout for a good project. When Rajendra recommended Rahul as director, Raj Kapoor signed him on for *Biwi-O-Biwi*. Meanwhile, Rahul continued filming *Love Story*, processing and editing the film in a Bombay lab as it progressed, along with editor David Dhawan.

When *Love Story* was almost complete, Rajendra Kumar asked Rahul to organize a preview of the edits at Dimple Theatre. The very next day, the Tulis and a few staff members watched the trial at their studio. Visibly excited, they waited with bated breath for Bunty to make his first-ever appearance on the screen. But the specially shot opening scene never came.

A shocked Gaurav asked his father, 'Papa, where are the intro sequences? You know the one I mean… Where I am flying a plane?'

Rajendra Kumar himself was so aghast at the scene's omission from the footage they had seen that he failed to reply. As the film rolled on and it became clear that a significant number of interesting and crucial scenes had been snipped out at the editing table, his angst and feelings of outrage heightened.

Two hours later, the lights came on in Dimple Theatre. A pensive Rajendra turned to his son and asked, 'The opening scene is the one we'd shot ourselves, isn't it, Bunty? And the other edited scenes – they were all my suggestions, right?' His voice was tightly controlled, lest his anger take over.

'There must be an explanation,' Shukla said, attempting to calm her husband down, though she herself was deeply upset. 'Miyan, it's okay!' she told him. 'We will…'

'Nothing is "okay"!' her husband snapped. 'This film is supposed to mark our son's launch. It was such a crucial shot; it was meant to be Bunty's introduction in the film and to our film industry… He is flying a plane in that scene. I conceived that scene and we shot it in Ludhiana's flying club. Do you know that Rahul came for just one day and left saying, "Sir, I have to go for the *Biwi-O-Biwi* shoot." I had urged him to stay, as we had managed to book the flying club and a plane too, but he bluntly turned down my request.'

'That's right, Ma!' Bunty confirmed. 'Papa and I, along with Radhuji [cinematographer of repute Radhu Karmakar], had to complete the shooting ourselves. How could Rahul do this? I can't believe that he actually edited out my opening scene.'

'I'll call him right now,' Rajendra decided, dialling Rahul Rawail's telephone number. 'He better have a good explanation for the blunder.'

When the director came on the line, Rajendra said, 'We saw the edits, but many of the scenes we'd shot are missing.'

'Those scenes were not required in the film,' came the audacious reply.

A muscle twitched in the star producer's jaw. In a dangerously low yet polite voice he said, 'Look, Mr Rahul Rawail, I liked those scenes very much. They have to be there.' When the director still refused to relent, Rajendra Kumar's anger got the better of him. 'Mr Rahul Rawail!' he thundered, 'I am the producer of the movie and *Love Story* will release with what *I* like, not with what *you* want!'

'If that is the case, why don't you complete the film yourself?' the director shot back.

'Okay. But do think it over,' Rajendra Kumar replied.

Even as he uttered those words, he couldn't get the image of a younger Rahul playing with his own children out of his mind.

But Rawail was implacable. 'I don't need to,' he retorted insolently.

With a sigh, Rajendra made one last attempt to give the young director a way out of the impasse. He was also anxious to prevent the sabotage of his son's debut film.

'Son, that isn't the solution,' he told Rahul gently. 'If I wanted to make the film myself, I would have done so from the very beginning. Let's meet and discuss the matter like members of a family would.'

*Stills from* Love Story, *in which father and son shared screen space*

But that did not happen. What did happen was Rawail deciding to step down from the director's role he had been assigned. This conflict caused a delay Rajendra Kumar hadn't anticipated and set back the film's release by four months. The actor then proceeded to restore the deleted scenes that had been the bone of contention between him and Rawail and, with that job done, *Love Story* was complete.

Meanwhile, Gaurav, who had always shied away from controversy, had taken it upon himself to meet Rahul, one of his childhood playmates, and try talking him out of his stubborn stance.

'Why are you leaving the movie?' he asked. 'You've made the film.'

But, having failed to make any headway, he left it at that. Besides, at this point, he had troubles of a different kind to deal with. Events that had occurred while filming *Love Story* had shaken the foundations of his personal life. He was exhilarated, bewildered and conflicted at the same time.

Thrown together, day in and day out, Kumar Gaurav had fallen in love with his first-ever leading lady, the petite Vijeta Pandit, also known as Pinky. Yet, he was engaged to be married to Rima Kapoor.

> Vijeta was like a naive little doll and Bunty her Professor Higgins [from the popular musical *My Fair Lady*, where Professor Henry Higgins mentors, trains and transforms a working-class waif without social graces into a poised, sophisticated lady]. She would ask him questions in a nasal, baby voice: '*Yeh* "jens" *kya hota hai*, Bunty?' And we sisters would explain to her that these were denim jeans. We helped her a lot, lending her our clothes and grooming her. Bunty fell for her innocence completely. He himself was a kid and saw in her this helpless, pretty girl who kind of hero-worshipped him. Also, she presented

> a complete contrast to the refined, confident and well-groomed Rima. The engagement [between Kumar Gaurav and Rima] was called off.
>
> *Dimple Tuli Patel*

The Kapoors and the Tulis were troubled and dismayed by the turn of events, especially in light of the fact that Raj Kapoor was a good friend of Rajendra Kumar's. For a few days, the mood in both homes was sombre. But then *Love Story* released, springing the biggest surprise ever on Rajendra Kumar's family. The film achieved blockbuster status, making Kumar Gaurav a star overnight.

Bunty and Vijeta's innocent real-life love and genuine chemistry seemed to have translated into convincing performances on screen. His chocolate-boy looks and her little-girl appeal, along with their obvious rapport, worked so well for the film that it drew cinegoers to the theatres again and again. And, just as Rajendra Kumar had predicted, the opening scene with Gaurav flying an aeroplane became etched in the audience's minds forever. An audible gasp would break through the silence in theatres as the audience first laid its eyes on the handsome Kumar Gaurav looking out of the small yellow aeroplane he was piloting. It was a defining moment. Subsequently, every second of the film would be a treat for the viewer, be it the freshness of its presentation, the acting skills of its cast, the comic situations with which the main narrative was interspersed, the brisk pacing, the engrossing dialogues and the smart direction. By captivating his audience the world over, Rahul Rawail had proved his worth as a director. Moreover, R.D. Burman's memorable compositions proved to be the film's pièce de résistance. '*Yeh ladki zara si deewani lagti hai* (This girl seems kind of crazy)', '*Yaad aa rahi hai.* (The memories come flooding back)', '*Kya gazab karte ho, ji*

(Your actions, they amaze me)' and the wonderfully playful '*Dekho maine dekha hai ek sapna* (Look, I've been dreaming this dream)' became smash hits. People of all ages, especially teenagers, fell in love with Kumar Gaurav. He was hailed as the next Rajesh Khanna.

The sun seemed to shine a little brighter on Dimple, the Tulis' Pali Hill home, and there was a new joie de vivre and buoyancy in their lives.

> I became a star overnight. Dad was thrilled. He said, 'From now on, I will make films exclusively with you.' Then he came up with the idea of *Lovers*, a remake of a film from the south. He sent me to Madras to watch the Tamil movie and to talk to Bharathiraja [the Tamil filmmaker P. Bharathiraja]. It was a good film, but I told Dad, 'We've already done one love story.' He said, 'Son, it's an award-winning film and I will make it.' 'All right,' I shrugged, 'you're the producer. Go ahead and make it.'
>
> *Kumar Gaurav*

While *Love Story* still retained its top position and continued to fill the box-office coffers, Rajendra Kumar, who was in Madras for a film shoot, had initiated his son's next project – *Lovers* – inspired by a very successful Tamil film he had seen at the urging of one of the distributors of *Love Story*. The film was *Alaigal Oivathillai*, directed by P. Bharathiraja.

'Make this film in Hindi with your son in the lead,' the distributor suggested. 'He'll be perfect for the role.'

'Maybe I will,' Rajendra Kumar responded.

The very next day, he organized a meeting with Bharathiraja.

'We would like to buy rights for *Alaigal Oivathillai*,' the actor began.

'Sir, this is such a coincidence,' a delighted Bharathiraja told him. 'I was also thinking of getting in touch with you to make the film in Hindi – but only with Kumar Gaurav as the hero. And, yes, I would like to direct the Hindi version too.'

'That's great! I will produce it and you will direct it,' a pleased Rajendra Kumar declared, concluding the deal.

Back in Bombay, Kumar Gaurav, who had been on a roll after *Love Story*, with producers vying to sign him on, had begun work on several films. For most of them, his leading ladies were pretty new entrants like Poonam Dhillon, Rati Agnihotri, Neelam and Padmini Kolhapure. His father's industry friends too had rushed in to sign up Kumar Gaurav as the hero in their forthcoming films. Too young to take responsible decisions, Gaurav had, nonetheless, experienced an inner resistance at first. There were many questions in his mind. *Why is Papa sending me to people of his own generation*, he wondered. *Why is everybody offering me the same stereotypical role?* His reserved and non-confrontational nature prevented him, however, from expressing his qualms.

*Launching* Lovers, *with Kishore Kumar, R.D. Burman and Amit Kumar*

His personal life too had hit a low point. His love story with his first leading lady had failed to stand the test of time, as Gaurav focussed on his career, and Vijeta, who had initially refused many film offers to be with him, went on to sign her next film *Mohabbat* which became a super hit. But it was all over between Bunty and Vijeta.

Gaurav's second film, *Teri Kasam*, released in 1982 and was moderately successful, although *Star*, a musical that released the same year, failed to make the cut. Still, the younger Tuli kept himself busy signing new projects. Then, the much-touted *Lovers* released in May 1983 and bombed at the box office.

> People said Dad interfered [in my film career]. He didn't really 'interfere', but he was quick to lose his temper [when there was disagreement over his ideas or resistance to his decisions] and I always shied away from conflict. So I kept quiet. It was just that I was signing so many films with people who belonged to Dad's age group. Like *Romance*, a film produced and directed by Ramanand Sagar. I remember sitting and listening to the narration of *Romance* and beginning to feel that the story sounded ancient [and not in sync with contemporary trends], but I had made a commitment and trusted that the older generation knew what it was doing. When the Mirza brothers and I sat with the director to discuss the scenes, Sagar Uncle began to suggest changes which I felt were really outdated. And I thought, *What's happening? The youthful flavour, the freshness is lost...*
>
> *Kumar Gaurav*

The youngster was right, because along with Sagar's film *Romance*, all the other films that he'd signed, like *Hum Hai Lajawab* and *All Rounder* with Mohan Kumar, among others, began to fail at the box office. Once hailed as the next superstar, the heart-throb of the nation who'd brought with him the whiff of a new romantic style of acting, Kumar Gaurav became the victim of his *Love Story* image. Unable to move out of its shadow, his stardom began to fade before it could rise to its highest point.

Significantly, around the same time, other star sons had begun to emerge and make their presence felt on the silver screen. All geared up to carry their family name forward, both Sanjay Dutt, with *Rocky* in 1981, and Sunny Deol, with *Betaab* in 1983, had been launched in what turned out to be highly successful films. And yet, like Gaurav, these young men, the progeny of famous actors, who sought to follow in their fathers' footsteps, instinctively understood the handicaps they would have to overcome: high public expectation, exposing them to merciless comparison with the achievements of their star parents, and the lack of drive and serious motivation that often came from being born to wealthy and influential families. Gaurav, like his celebrity offspring contemporaries, knew how difficult it was to get past these hurdles – especially, the complacency that came from being born to privilege and affluence and the problem of summoning and sustaining the level of commitment that had driven their parents to the heights of stardom. The star parents of these youngsters, who had struggled to achieve success, expected the same from them, though they were well aware of the inevitable pitfalls that came with success and the brickbats that accompanied failure.

Ironically, it was Rajendra Kumar who had technically paved the way for Generation X. Having done so, he couldn't help brooding over the reasons that had led his son's career to nosedive. Had they launched Bunty too soon? Was he not ready yet? Should he, Rajendra, have been more selective in his choice of roles for his son? Should he have just let the boy be? Maybe, he should... But no, Gaurav was, after all, Rajendra

Kumar's son and he was supremely talented. The audience had loved him once and they would surely come around again. Bunty could not possibly fail. Jogging through the vast grounds of his home in the rain, Rajendra's mind raced. But he could come up with no constructive solution.

In the years that followed, father and son made several attempts to find the right formula for a successful film, but the young man's career continued to slide. His family and friends and even the film industry were shocked at this cruel turn of fate. How could this have happened? One moment, a superstar and the next, a virtual nonentity! Like everyone else, Gaurav's mother, Shukla, was at a loss. She felt her son's pain more acutely than anyone else and found it hard to believe that this was what his future in films had come to. He had all the makings of a star – good looks, acting skills and lots of potential for growth. He *was* a star! So what had gone wrong? Fame and success had barely touched her Bunty before vanishing as though they had never come.

By the time 1985 dawned, Kumar Gaurav was left staring at a blank career canvas, although his personal life couldn't have been happier. He had forged a bond with Sanjay Dutt, who had been pitted against him by the media from the time both had appeared in their debut films. In reality, the two got along well. They were not just neighbours; their families had a shared history. As with Raj Kapoor's children, Gaurav, Dimple and Kaajal had also been friends with Sunil and Nargis Dutt's offspring Sanjay, Namrata and Priya. They often spent leisure time in each other's homes and partied together. The outcome of frequent socializing between like-minded young people would lead to Kumar Gaurav and Namrata falling in love with each other. Both families were delighted at this development and in 1984 Gaurav and Namrata were married.

Meanwhile, Gaurav had met Mahesh Bhatt through Namrata's brother, Sanjay. And it was during their meeting that

*With Sanjay Dutt, Shukla, Sunil Dutt and the happy couple at the wedding of Kumar Gaurav and Namrata Dutt*

the seeds of the film *Janam* were sown. Gaurav had realized by now that these were the kind of films he felt an instant connect with and that he needed to diversify his range of films. His instincts were sound, for his understated performance in this film was hailed as his career's best. With *Janam*, he had found his salvation. The idea of making *Naam* emerged from his complete identification with the intense roles that Mahesh Bhatt had a talent for writing.

> I was on the lookout for different genres of films. I loved working with Mahesh Bhatt. I did four films with him, including *Naam*, which was initially titled *Hamesha*. In early 1981, Bhatt, inspired by the [1949] English film *The Third Man*, had come up with the basic storyline for a film about two brothers. Mahesh signed Sanjay [Dutt] and me for the film. Mukesh Bhatt wanted to produce it. But then Sanjay was sent to rehab in 1982 [to treat his drug addiction] and the film was forgotten. Meanwhile,

I had begun working with Mahesh Bhatt in *Aaj*, along with Smita Patil. But, unfortunately, Mahesh, who was, at the time, a Rajneesh [Bhagwan Shree Rajneesh or Osho] follower, left the film midway to go and stay at the ashram. In the meantime, Sanjay had returned and he had no work. So we decided to do something together. Mahesh too was back soon afterwards and I asked him what he planned to do about that film *Hamesha*. 'I don't have a producer,' he replied. I said, 'I'll ask Dad.' The first thing Dad said was: 'Mahesh Bhatt *kaun hai? Woh* Rajneeshi?' He was from the older generation. Mahesh was the second generation. And I was the last. So, once again, I felt I was up against a wall. 'Papa,' I finally urged my father, 'at least listen to the idea.' Dad liked the storyline, but he said, 'Not Sanjay Dutt. Take Kamal Haasan and Bunty. Kamal was to do my role and I, Sanjay's. But then I got married to Namrata Dutt, whom I'd been seeing for quite some time. Naturally, Sanjay, being a part of the family, now became a part of the film. Meanwhile, Salim Khan had come on board as writer. At his suggestion, Sanjay did my role and I his. I suggested the title *Naam*. Dad didn't like it and said, 'What do you mean "naam"?' So I said, '*Nahin rakhna hai toh nahin rakho*. If you don't want to go with that title, don't.' But then he agreed. Salim Uncle also said it's the perfect title. Dad's first reaction to any of my suggestions was always: 'No! You don't know how these things work.' Because he always saw me as his kid. '*Tumhe kya pata hai?* What do you know?' he'd say.

*Kumar Gaurav*

Bunty said, 'Mahesh Bhatt has a story' and suggested that I should produce *Naam* with him and Sanjay. I liked the narration and said okay. Thus began *Naam*. We completed the casting. Anupam Kher was also roped in

> by Bhatt. Soon, everything was in place – script, actors, crew, costumes and so on. We were ready with everything and Aryan Films was all set to leave the following week for the shoot in Hong Kong, when, out of the blue, Anupam decided to meet Salim [Khan] Saab to learn more about his role.
>
> *Rajendra Kumar Tuli*

When Salim Khan narrated Anupam's scenes in the film, the actor came straight to the point. He was clear that he did not like his role and backed out of the movie at the last minute.

That same evening, Mahesh Bhatt called up his producer with the news. 'Anupam's not ready to work in the movie. He's dropped out.'

'What!' Rajendra Kumar exclaimed. 'But we are to leave for the shoot next week and his clothes and all have already been made to size!'

'What can I do? It was his decision.'

'It was you who brought him in. So I thought...'

'True. But when the artiste does not want to do the role...'

A worried Rajendra Kumar went over to Salim Khan's home to discuss the matter and, hopefully, find a solution. What he did receive was news about a brilliant new actor who could take on the role for which Kher had originally been signed on.

'There is this stage actor who would be suitable for the role,' Salim suggested. 'His name is Paresh Rawal. He has recently worked in the film *Arjun*.'

'Hmm... I don't know him,' Rajendra murmured. 'What do you think of him?'

'I like him. He's good.'

'Okay, then. Please send him over to meet me.'

> The next morning, when Paresh Rawal came over to my office, I thought his face was too innocent for the role in which we were planning to cast him. But I needed an actor and Salim Saab had praised him a lot. So finally I sent him for fittings to my tailor master. In this way, Paresh became a part of *Naam*. I called my make-up man and asked him to make a French moustache and a beard for him. When we got to Hong Kong for the shoot, I got Paresh ready in my room with that French beard and make-up and then called Mahesh in to have a look. He was stunned to see Paresh in the new get-up, because we had managed to camouflage his innocence. We completed the movie. People liked Paresh's work and he became a star.
>
> *Rajendra Kumar Tuli*

*Naam* was a film Kumar Gaurav believed in. On its release in 1986, it left not a single person in the theatres unmoved or dry-eyed. It tugged at the heartstrings of cinegoers all over the world and made them weep without restraint, especially when the song '*Chitthi aayi hai* (A letter has arrived)' came on. Poignant and harrowing, *Naam* related the story of Janki and her two sons: Vicky, the wayward yet vulnerable loser – the role essayed by Sanjay Dutt – and Ravi, the upright and dependable older brother, the part nailed with absolute conviction by Kumar Gaurav. Both the young stars lived up to the demands of their parts, with honest, gripping performances. Nutan, Amrita Singh, Paresh Rawal and Poonam Dhillon made up the stellar cast of this unforgettable saga of love, duty and sacrifice. It was clear that director Mahesh Bhatt's instinctive understanding of the film's emotional quotient and his special talent for tapping into its core to enhance the story and make it resonate with the audience had paid off, as had the evocative songs and music composed by Laxmikant and Pyarelal.

*Naam* saw Kumar Gaurav's re-emergence as a fine actor and served as Sanjay Dutt's comeback movie, following the break he had taken for his rehab programme in the US. It was also a fact that through thick and thin, through his tumultuous youth and the trauma of the addictions that had taken hold of him in those years, Sanjay's brother-in-law Kumar Gaurav and his sisters Namrata and Priya Dutt had stood by him.

*Naam* turned out to be a blockbuster at the box office, playing for over a year at most Indian cinema halls. It also justified the veteran jubilee star's initial reluctance to pit Sanjay Dutt against his son in the film. Rajendra Kumar had wanted Gaurav to play Ravi in the film, as he had anticipated from the very outset that Sanjay's character might walk away with the accolades. And despite the restrained performance Gaurav had put up that is precisely what happened. The good guy he played in the film was overshadowed by Sanjay's character, a man with intriguing grey shades. It was Sanjay that *Naam* would thrust into the limelight, serving as a stepping stone to his stardom.

*Naam* also became a significant film in writer Salim Khan's life.

> I was engaged to write *Naam* on Rajendra Kumar's suggestion. At that time, Javed [Akhtar] and I had decided to end our partnership and work independently. I wasn't getting satisfying work very easily. One evening, Rajendraji dropped in for a visit with Mahesh Bhatt. '*Kya, Miyan, kya haal hai?*' he asked. Once they were seated out on the balcony of my home, he related Mahesh's storyline for a film. Mahesh already had the idea, but not the screenplay. '*Yeh toh ban hi nahin sakti,*' I said. '*Kyon nahin ban sakti?*' Rajendraji asked. 'The basic plot is faulty,' I pointed out. 'The boy whom the mother has reared herself, giving him

more attention and care than she has her own son – he kills her in the end? My sensibilities say that instead of killing her, he should save her and sacrifice himself, like Karna did in the Mahabharata.' Plot is the most important thing for success. RK [Rajendra Kumar] was a very sensible person and he instantly grasped my point and agreed. It was, therefore, with *Naam* that I would, at the age of fifty, see my name – Salim Khan – on screen again for the first time after my break-up with Javed. *Naam* was very important for Sanjay too, as he had just returned from rehab and was desperate for good work. This role was just right for him, and according to me it was not interchangeable.

*Salim Khan*

After the success of *Naam*, Rajendra Kumar decided to make *Jurrat* with Bunty. At the time, film dialogue and screenplay writer Inder Raj Anand's nephew Mukul was directing a movie called *Sultanat*, starring Dharmendra, Sunny Deol and Sridevi. Since the film was being edited at Dimple Theatre, Rajendra would often run into its young director. And every time they crossed paths Anand would say, 'Uncle, please give me a chance to direct your next production.'

The day finally arrived when Rajendra did, indeed, sign on Mukul Anand to direct his next film, paying him a substantial signing amount for it. But, soon after, Anand did the disappearing act. He began avoiding the producer, until one day an upset Rajendra managed to catch hold of him.

'What's happening with our movie?' he asked.

'I am working on it, Uncleji,' Anand replied.

A few days later, he brought over a couple of half-baked scripts for Rajendra Kumar to read. But before the latter could finalize any of them, Anand had bowed out of the project. He proposed a replacement, however.

'Uncle, why don't you sign up David, our editor?' he suggested. 'He has some good ideas and he has edited so many of your earlier films and productions.'

For some time now, David Dhawan had occupied a special place at Dimple Theatre and practically lived with the Tulis in their bungalow. Having always appreciated his work, Rajendra Kumar decided to follow up on Mukul Anand's suggestion. He signed Dhawan on to direct *Jurrat*, a film whose storyline was inspired by the American movie *The Untouchables*. Gaurav, however, was wary of this development. In his view, the film didn't belong to the genre Dhawan was at home with. He would be proved right when *Jurrat* released in 1989 and failed at the box office. The Tulis also suffered huge financial losses, amounting to around ₹60 lakh.

As for Kumar Gaurav, who had regained ground after the success of *Naam*, he was back to square one.

> For *Jurrat*, we shot a scene involving a boat and a helicopter in LA. Imagine, for just a two-day scene, Rajendraji flew us all to LA! It was here that he met the Hollywood writer-director Raju Patel. He liked him a lot and later got his daughter Dimple married to him.
>
> *David Dhawan*

In the same year, Kumar Gaurav also featured in *Goonj*, a 1989 film that was directed by Jalal Agha and focussed on Goa's local political scene. This too failed to make a mark at the box office. Following this setback, it wouldn't take very many years for Kumar Gaurav, once a celebrity who'd had to face more than his fair share of professional failures and the ego-busting humiliation that came with it, to become a distant memory in the minds of cinegoers. *We become so very vulnerable to the*

*Walking his daughter Dimple to the mandap for her wedding in 1989*

*personal evaluations of the public,* he would now have the leisure to reflect, *and it is they who seem to be in control of whether our stardom should last or not.*

In 1993, however, Gaurav did resurface briefly when his father tried for the last time to revive his career with *Phool.* Directed by filmmaker Singeetam Srinivasa Rao, it starred Gaurav opposite Madhuri Dixit, with Sunil Dutt and Rajendra Kumar making special appearances. Pitted against the blockbuster *Darr*, featuring Shah Rukh Khan, Sunny Deol and Juhi Chawla, and other hits of 1993, like the Meenakshi Seshadri–Sunny Deol starrer *Damini*, *Aaina*, with Jackie Shroff, Juhi Chawla and Amrita Singh in the lead, and *Aankhen*, with Govinda in a double role, *Phool* didn't stand a chance at the box office.

*Phool* was also the last of Rajendra Kumar's films, the others being Manoj Kumar's 1989 box-office disaster *Clerk*, where he had a special appearance, and *Insaaf ka Khoon* that released in 1991, with Asha Parekh cast opposite him. But *Phool*'s failure was the final blow for the former jubilee star. This was the point where he seems to have surrendered to the dictates of destiny, all the more so, perhaps, because he was also dealing with personal vicissitudes. In 1988, Rajendra Kumar lost his best friend, Raj Kapoor, who had died at the age of sixty-three from asthma-related complications. He had collapsed at an event where he was to receive the Dadasaheb Phalke Award and was taken for treatment to the All India Institute of Medical Sciences in Delhi. But he could not be revived. Rajendra missed him terribly and life would never again be the same for him.

While his father was struggling to come to terms with his professional failures and personal grief, Kumar Gaurav had completely withdrawn for some time from acting in films, with only two delayed releases seeing the light of day in 1996. Yet, with his personal life going great guns, he remained in a happy space. He and Namrata moved into their own apartment in Juhu, where they would spend a decade of contentment with their two daughters, Saachi and Siya. In 1999, Gaurav even made a few appearances in television series, before bowing out of show business altogether.

> One thing I've realized – that there are no relationships in the movie business. It's all about the movie. As long as you are doing a film together, you are bonding; you are best friends with everyone, like a family. Everyone is bro, sis, lover, friend and so on. But once the film's over, all that love is gone. So there are no permanent relationships in this industry and one shouldn't expect them either. Treat it just like any other job.
>
> *Kumar Gaurav*

People insist that Bunty's career didn't shape up too well because I was a very interfering father. But let me clear up one thing: I've never accepted or chosen any film for him or decided how much he'd charge, except for *Star*. This film was an exception, because I'd met [its screenplay writer and music director] Biddu abroad. But even while the film was being shot, I told Biddu that his script was not up to the mark and he should improve on it. I was proved right. In my opinion, Bunty's career went the way it did because of the wrong selection of films. But then, he never did ask for my opinion and I never thought it right to interfere [in his career]. He is such an introvert. As a father, it's my duty to do whatever I can for him. After all, we're living for our children.

*Rajendra Kumar* to *Santosh Sud,*
*for* Cineplot *in 1989*

# 20

# A Hero's Farewell

The truth is, I had never interfered in Bunty's decisions about his career. I'd say, 'Son, you are young. You must take your own decisions.' But once you set someone free, it becomes a bit difficult to get him back again. Bunty wanted to marry Namrata. So in 1984 we decided to get them married. After their wedding, they lived with us and their first child was born in our house. But then, I don't know what happened. He moved with his wife and daughter to his father-in-law's house. How many times I have told him, '*Beta*, please don't punish me like this.' He did not live with me for twelve years. As for me, I will only make films with him... That is, if I make them at all.

*Rajendra Kumar Tuli*

Dad wanted us to move back to his house. He repeatedly told Namrata, 'Come back. Such a big home and only the two of us here.' But I said, 'No way! I am not going. I need my space and my own place.' I'd want my kids to move out too [when they come of age] and make their own lives. But then Dad fell ill.

Although a wealthy father's son, I did do my bit in trying to establish myself, in going through the struggles of life.

> Maybe I was born with a silver spoon, but I threw that spoon away and tried to pick up my own. And if we talk of bread and butter, there was a time when I was living for ten years in a [two bedroom-hall-kitchen] flat in Juhu with my wife and two daughters. Dad wasn't supporting me then. I used to run my home on twenty thousand [rupees] a month. We managed with that twenty thousand and never asked our rich parents for money – and those were some of the best days of our married life. At that time, I was being offered roles like 'Jeetendra *ka chhota bhai ban jao, yeh ban jao, woh ban jao.* Play [actor] Jeetendra's younger brother. Play this, play that' – all bullshit! And even though I needed the money, I refused to do this kind of work. If I wasn't convinced [by the role] myself, how could I convince the audience? I had and still have the hunger for good work. But I don't need to do any old rubbish. Even today, if I like a role, I will do it.
>
> *Kumar Gaurav*

It had all begun in 1996 when Rajendra Kumar's youngest brother, Ranjit, passed away. Devastated by a younger sibling's death, Rajendra would often withdraw into himself, trying to figure out what could possibly have gone wrong. *Ranjit, I saved you as a child while crossing the border*, he would muse, reflecting on the near miracle that had saved his baby brother from almost certain death at the time, *and today, your journey has finally ended.* Ranjit had been a favourite with both Rajendra and Shukla and the loss affected them both.

Later in the year, however, the veteran actor made an effort to step out of his self-imposed hiatus by accepting a role in *Ek Tha Dil Ek Thi Dhadkan,* 1998, a Mirza brothers' film, also starring veteran actor Biswajeet, among others. Although it had been years since he'd faced the camera for a feature film, Rajendra Kumar had kept himself busy managing Dimple

Theatre with Bunty, delving occasionally into television and making guest appearances at special events. He'd maintained his fitness routine as well through regular walks on the Juhu beach with his friends Manoj Kumar and Mohan Kumar.

For the Mirza brothers' film, the actor had to fly down to Nainital. But a few days into filming, he came down with a fever that refused to subside or respond to the medication he had been prescribed. Rajendra Kumar travelled back to Delhi where he was admitted to the Escorts Group hospital. Diagnosed with pneumonia, he was put on a cocktail of antibiotics. But in spite of the best doctors attending to him, his immune system shut down.

Having received the news of Rajendra's illness, Shukla, accompanied by their son, Bunty, rushed to Delhi to bring her husband back home. When she saw him, however, she was shocked at how much weight he'd lost in a matter of days. He was almost unrecognizable.

Flying him back to Bombay, the Tulis admitted Rajendra to Breach Candy Hospital, where Dr Farokh E. Udwadia conducted various tests. The diagnosis was myelodysplasia, a rare type of blood cancer caused by a lack of healthy blood cells. The actor's blood count had dropped drastically and he would, therefore, need regular blood transfusions to survive. Dr Udwadia, however, advised supportive treatment at first, in the form of daily injections and drugs to help control the symptoms of the disease and increase the number of healthy blood cells.

It was a painful process and left the star incapacitated on most days. Even as the suffering continued Rajendra Kumar attempted various natural therapies.

Miyan used to smoke too much. His lungs were the problem. Doctors had warned him several times about his habit and advised him to stop smoking. He'd even had an angioplasty done a few years before his illness. Ritu [Kapoor Nanda] had taken him to the Escorts hospital. He was there for two weeks. They said it was a dengue-type illness. They called me and asked, 'What antibiotics is he allergic to?' I said, 'I am not sure.' Later at Breach Candy, they did a bone-marrow test and it was diagnosed that blood was not being produced in his body.

*Shukla Tuli*

Meanwhile, the Tulis' older daughter, Dimple, who was now married and lived in Los Angeles, came down to Bombay when she learnt of her father's illness. Her husband, Raju Patel, who was not simply the Tulis' son-in-law, but a great friend and admirer of Rajendra Kumar, had insisted that Dimple take her father back to America for medical treatment. To her surprise, Rajendra, who, like most tradition-bound Punjabis, believed that a man shouldn't be indebted in any way to his married daughter, because she was now a member of another family, agreed instantly. It was quite apparent that he was desperate for a cure and America offered hope.

In January 1997, Rajendra Kumar left for Los Angeles with Dimple. From the moment they landed in the US, he felt a renewed sense of hope. He knew it had been the right thing to do. Feeling more positive than he had in a long while, he enjoyed the ride as they drove down to his daughter's impressive home in Beverly Hills.

Without further delay, Dimple and Raju took Rajendra to UCLA (the University of California, Los Angeles) where the doctors put him through a battery of tests. After going through the results, they told the couple, 'Why are you torturing him? Transfuse blood just once a month and let him be happy for the rest of the time.' But they also warned that from the time the blood transfusions started, the patient would probably live for no more than two years, because the transfused blood was a foreign body and alien to the patient's system. Hit hard by their verdict, Dimple was close to tears and felt utterly helpless. But she couldn't afford to break down. She had to steel herself for the sake of her father who was waiting outside.

As soon as a sombre Dimple and Raju emerged from the doctors' clinic, Rajendra Kumar asked, much like a child would have, 'What did they say? Will I be well again?' His eyes, filled with expectation and hope, moved from one to the other.

'Yes, you will,' Dimple replied with conviction, and seeing her father's eyes light up instantly, she felt validated in raising her father's expectations. She believed that the moment of happiness her words had given her father was the only truth.

> The process of blood transfusion seemed like something out of sci-fi. One minute, my father would be lying there, scrunched up and bent over, as if deflated, and in the next instant, with the fresh blood being pumped into him, he'd gradually straighten out like an air-filled doll. Then he would be active, energetic and lively for twenty to twenty-five days, before he began to sag and flop down again, his body racked with pain. This happened every month, but in the interim, Dad was at his happiest. He fell in love with LA.
>
> *Dimple Tuli Patel*

> In LA, we'd walk the streets and so many people – Indians, Pakistanis and Iranians – would rush to meet him [Rajendra Kumar]. That made him so happy. *'Arre, mujhe pehchaan liya!'* he would exclaim. He was so grateful for the recognition. But as I remember, the worst part of his life was when he fell ill. He just couldn't take it. He, who'd been so proud of his fitness and his disciplined lifestyle,

couldn't accept that he had fallen ill. 'How could I?' he'd say. Also, he couldn't bear being dependent on anyone. And his appearance! For an actor to see his face swollen from steroids was terrifying. It broke him.

*Kaajal (Tulsi) Chellaram*

October 1997: For nine months, I've been in America for my treatment. My daughter Dimple (very rarely is someone blessed with a daughter like her) brought me here and she looks after me like a mother. And my son-in-law, my namesake, Rajendra Kumar Patel... God bless them both. Raju has been like my son. He's fulfilled many of my dreams. I had a dream of becoming the producer of an American film and he made that a reality. He made me co-producer of Walt Disney's *The Jungle Book*. All the shooting had taken place in India. So that way I have much to be grateful for. God does fulfil some of our dreams and it has always happened with me that in any calamity God stands with me till the end.

*Rajendra Kumar Tuli*

Rajendra's days in Los Angeles were filled with joy. Ensconced in Dimple's luxurious home, he would go for morning walks, read, cook and spend time with his grandson Karam. These activities brought him immense joy. He also looked forward to the evenings spent with his son-in-law and the latter's illustrious Hollywood guests.

At the time, Raju Patel was working on *The New Adventures of Pinocchio*, having already produced several films, beginning with the 1984 comedy *Bachelor Party*, starring Tom Hanks, followed by *The Jungle Book* in 1994, *The Adventures of Pinocchio* in 1996 and *The Second Jungle Book* the following year.

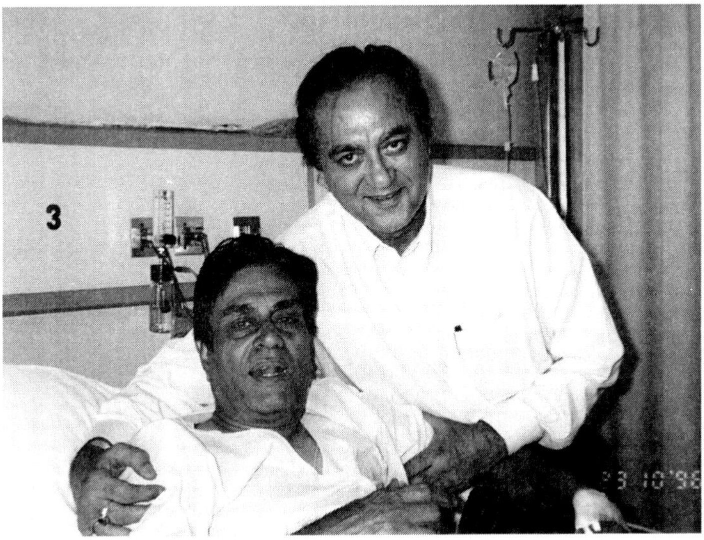

*With Sunil Dutt in 1996*

'Films follow me everywhere!' Rajendra would laugh, as fans greeted him on the streets, in restaurants, theatres and malls and asked for autographs and photographs, much to the amazement of his young grandson. Every so often, he had film personalities from India dropping in on him in Los Angeles. Sunil Dutt, in particular, who would travel to America regularly for events connected with New York's Memorial Sloan Kettering Cancer Center where his wife, Nargis, had once been admitted for treatment, was a frequent visitor.

Rajendra Kumar's connect with Dutt had begun with *Mother India*. It had been formalized when Gaurav married Namrata. It had intensified when Rajendra fervently campaigned for Dutt during the elections. The two legendary actors had also stood by each other when their families were going through harrowing times, particularly when Sanjay Dutt's problem with drug addiction and troubles with the law were making headlines. Now they were content to spend time in each other's company at Dimple's Beverly Hills home. Sunil Dutt even cooked his famous chicken for his ailing friend. Yet, there were days in Rajendra Kumar's life when the inevitable depletion of energy would set in at the end of every blood transfusion cycle, and there was no respite from the excruciating suffering that ensued. Although he had come to terms with the changes wrought by the disease, some days were so agonizingly painful that he'd tell Dimple in a defeated voice, 'I don't want to live like this, to suffer like this.'

> I was so worried for my father, but had to try to be happy. I'd just discovered that I was pregnant.
>
> *Dimple Tuli Patel*

In January 1998, when Dimple shared the news of her pregnancy with her ailing father, who'd already spent a year in Los Angeles by then, he decided to stay on until his grandchild's birth. Shukla, whose mobility had been hampered for quite some time by the acute spondylitis she suffered from, called from India and scolded her husband for delaying his return to Bombay. But he reasoned that since Dimple was expecting a baby and her mother-in-law was not present in the city, he would stay on 'till the baby is born'.

Finally, in October that year, following the birth of Dimple's second son, Amar, a reluctant Rajendra Kumar returned to India as deep down he had realized the futilty of the painful treatment that he was undergoing as also how difficult it would be for his daughter to look after her son, her newborn baby and her ailing father. Moreover, he felt the need to spend the rest of his days in his own country.

Back in Bombay, the blood transfusions continued. Every month, the star travelled to Breach Candy Hospital, accompanied by his son, Bunty. They'd stay overnight at the hospital and return home the next morning.

Dad went to LA to live with my sister Dimple and get medical treatment there. But after he returned home, he became bitter about life. He hadn't expected this to happen to him.

*Kumar Gaurav*

He had become very thin. My in-laws were living in Breach Candy. So on the days the blood transfusion took place, I was there with him first thing in the morning. He would say, '*Saal* 2000 *dekhunga ke nahin*? Will I get to see the year 2000 or not?'

*Kaajal (Tulsi) Chellaram*

The months flew by and Rajendra's health continued to seesaw, as did his mood. His plight naturally played havoc with his family's emotions. It was a heart-rending experience for them to now look at the man whose handsome features had once glowed with a healthy sheen. The former jubilee star had become painfully emaciated and weak and his complexion was now many shades darker, especially when his blood count fell drastically.

With time, the frequency of the blood transfusions increased and Rajendra had to be admitted to the hospital oftener and for longer periods of time, sometimes over nearly three days.

On 11 July 1999, the former star lay in his hospital bed, jotting down his thoughts in a small notebook. He'd been doing this for some time now and the language he had grown up with – Urdu – was the one he always turned to for the purpose. His writings dated January 1999 onwards had commenced with topical issues like the country, its politics and its religious mindset and moved on to thoughts on oneness and forgiveness, questioning his fate and his illness, and thereafter introspection and a preoccupation with the afterlife and rebirth. Many pages in the little book were especially dedicated to expressing love for his family and his wife, saluting her strength, her brilliant role as a mother and her inner beauty.

As the early morning sunlight streamed into his hospital room, his daughter Kaajal arrived. While Rajendra had his breakfast, father and daughter chatted for a bit. When he was done, he turned to Bahadur, the attendant who had been brought from the Tuli home to be with his master, and asked for water.

But when the man did his bidding and handed him the glass, it slipped out of Rajendra's grasp and fell to the floor with a crash. The former actor was shocked. 'Has my time come? Is this a sign?' he asked, expelling a deep sigh. But then noticing the stricken look on his daughter's face, he abruptly changed the topic. 'Today is Bunty's birthday,' he stated. 'I hope everyone's coming here?'

'Yes, I am sure they are,' Kaajal replied. 'And, anyway, we can celebrate it properly tomorrow.'

*With Kumar Gaurav*

With that, she kissed her father on the forehead and left. Dimple, who had arrived from Los Angeles a month earlier, was to take over in the afternoon. But she was down with viral fever that day and had asked her mother to visit Rajendra at the hospital in her place. Shukla rarely went to the hospital, because her severe back problems prevented her from travelling over a stretch of time without adequate intervals of rest. But that day was special; it was Gaurav's birthday. So, on Dimple's insistence, she did make it a point to visit her husband, as did Namrata and Sunil Dutt, along with a few other relatives. Only the birthday boy was missing.

When Bunty failed to arrive by late evening, Rajendra Kumar called up his son to wish him and said, 'Yaar, *tu aaya nahin*. You didn't turn up.'

'Dad, I was shooting,' Bunty explained. 'Couldn't disrupt the schedule. I'll come to the hospital straight after pack-up.'

'No, son. That's not necessary,' his father told him. 'Why don't you come tomorrow to pick me up?'

'Okay, Papa! I'll see you tomorrow, then.'

Now that Gaurav wouldn't be dropping by that evening, Shukla, along with Sunil and Namrata, who had been at the hospital with her all this while, decided to call it a day.

Bidding Rajendra goodbye, Sunil promised his ailing friend, 'I will come with Bunty tomorrow to take you home.'

Once his visitors had left and he was alone in his room, but for the presence of Bahadur, Rajendra went to sleep.

Gaurav was still busy shooting for *Chocolate* with Vivek Agnihotri at Natraj Studio when his father-in-law called him.

'Dad's okay,' he reassured him. 'Why don't you drop in at our place after the shoot? We'll open a bottle of wine.'

And so, after pack-up, Gaurav headed for Ajanta, Sunil Dutt's bungalow in Bandra, where he had a couple of glasses of wine. Then, exhausted after the day's work, he went to bed at 1.30 a.m.

The silence of the morning of 12 July was shattered at around 2 a.m. Phones trilled sharply in Dimple, the Tulis' bungalow, and then in Sunil Dutt's home.

'Calling from Breach Candy Hospital,' the unknown caller said. 'Mr Kumar suffered a massive heart attack. He is no more.'

# Epilogue

Rajendra Kumar's family had been looking forward to having him back home on 12 July, but that was not to be. The doctors at the hospital had tried to revive him, following his heart attack in the early hours, but their efforts were in vain. The former jubilee star seemed to have chosen that moment to depart.

Later, his body would be brought home as promised by his friend Sunil Dutt and his son, Kumar Gaurav.

When the funeral rites were being performed on the appointed day, members of the film fraternity, industrialists and politicians arrived in great numbers to pay their last respects. The narrow lane running past the Dimple grounds was soon chock-a-block with countless Rajendra Kumar fans.

It was a memorable and fitting send-off, a final salute to the talented, celebrated, larger-than-life movie star with admirers the world over. It was, above all, a moving farewell to the loyal family man, a man of great insight and dignity, who had been a friend to many.

Dad used to say, '*Koi nahin aayega*. No one will turn up.' But what a funeral! It was like a state funeral. Sunil Uncle did so much. And we were told, 'First, the public will see him. Then you all can.' After all, he was a public figure. People had climbed over the walls of our home to get a last glimpse and the media was all around.

*Kaajal (Tulsi) Chellaram*

Dad had a good life, but he missed his old friends – actors, directors and so on. He would say, 'Here I am, ready to sit and chat, eat and drink with friends for company, but nobody comes to meet me any more. Dad was an emotional person. He'd have been happy to know that everyone came to pay their last respects at his funeral. Sunil Dutt, my father-in-law, used to call Dad 'High Command'. He was with us all through this trying time in our lives.

*Kumar Gaurav*

In 2002, three years after the demise of the jubilee star, Sunil Dutt, along with then Maharashtra chief minister Vilasrao Deshmukh, inaugurated the Rajendra Kumar Chowk that leads to the jubilee star's home on Nargis Dutt Road.

Four years later, the actor's much-coveted property was given up to a builder for redevelopment. Its grounds, along with the palatial bungalow that stood on it, had lain bereft of its owner for some time now. While no one lived there any more, the stately home was occasionally let out for film shoots, including that of *Hum Kaun Hai*, starring Amitabh Bachchan and Dimple Kapadia. Only Dimple Theatre was still functional. The bungalow that had been a witness to the Tulis' lives has since been renamed. It is known as Seven on the Hill.

# Tribute

On returning from Rajendra Kumar's funeral, which he had gone to attend at the Santacruz crematorium, Pandit Razdan, a senior journalist, observed, 'The industry was there to pay its respects. Sunil Dutt, Amitabh and Jaya Bachchan, Feroz Khan, Rishi and Randhir Kapoor, Ramanand Sagar, B.R. Chopra, Lekh Tandon, Vijay Anand, Mrs Raj Kapoor, Surinder Kapoor and his wife, Manoj Kumar and his wife, Jackie Shroff – all of them were there. [Rajendra Kumar] had quite an innings, I must say. We all entered the industry in the 1950s and now it's time for us to go – almost all of us are in our seventies.'

Writer and journalist Lata Khubchandani wrote for Rediff.com: 'Success, by another name, would have been Rajendra Kumar, who passed away early this morning. He was eight days short of seventy-two and had been suffering for some time from cancer of the bone marrow, for which he was being treated in the US.

'Born in 1927, life for Rajendra Kumar was a long struggle – until he became so successful as to be known as Jubilee Kumar. Rumour has it that he was one of the richest stars in the industry, having made the most of his success and invested his money wisely. Yet, people remember the struggling Kumar and the successful one with equal warmth.'

Ramanand Sagar, who had made four films with the star (*Zindagi*, *Lalkar*, *Arzoo* and *Geet*), recalled, 'We were both strugglers, travelling by train, looking for work... Our bond goes back many years. He ruled the film industry for a decade and was known as Jubilee Kumar, because most of his films were silver jubilees. He was considered lucky because of that.'

Shammi Kapoor remembered Rajendra Kumar as 'a little senior to me; in fact, he was more my brother's associate. In his struggling days, he used to assist H.S. Rawail. Then he got [a role in] *Vachan*, opposite Geeta Bali, my wife – he played her brother in the film. We never got the chance to work together, but we were friends.'

When Hema Malini entered the industry with *Sapnon ka Saudagar*, Rajendra Kumar was still riding the wave of success. Though he was her senior by many years, they worked together in films like *Gora aur Kala* and *Sunehra Sansar*.

'As a child,' reminisced Hema, 'I was an absolute, diehard fan of his. And when Raj Saab [Raj Kapoor] introduced me to him during *Sapnon ka Saudagar*, I could not believe that I was meeting my hero.

'I was dying to work with him. And when I finally got the opportunity, it proved to be great fun. He never allowed me to feel that I was working with a big star, someone far senior to me. He used to joke around and make me feel comfortable. And he would speak to me in Tamil, because he was doing Tamil films at the time.

'After that, whenever we met, wherever we met, he would always sing, "*Dheere dheere bol, koyi sun na le* (Speak softly lest someone overhears you)." Even if we met on a flight, he would sing this song for me, until I started laughing.'

B.R. Chopra, with whom Rajendra Kumar did two of his classic films, *Dhool ka Phool* and *Kanoon*, said, 'There was a time when we met every week and compared notes. In fact, I met him just ten days ago and we spent two hours reliving old memories... How was I to know that the end would come so soon? Even though he was suffering from cancer, he seemed fine when I met him; he wasn't even in bed. He was sitting and talking with me. We'd been friends for long. I'm told the end came with a sort of heart attack. We have lost one of our finest friends.'

Mala Sinha, who co-starred with the jubilee star during his early days of struggle as a relative newcomer, said, 'I knew him from the days of the black-and-white era. We worked together in films like *Dhool ka Phool*, *Devar Bhabhi* and *Lalkar*. He used to be really lively on the sets. You never saw him in a grumpy mood. He'd sit with anyone – the cast, the crew, the technicians... He would eat with everyone, often pinching eatables from other plates.

'He was a very big star by the time we did *Geet*, but not once did I see any difference in his behaviour. He was still down-to-earth and co-operative. Even if the director asked for many retakes, he would oblige and never complain. He never made you feel that he knew everything. There was no trace of arrogance in him. To be a good artiste, you have to be a good human being and that is what he was. He was a good friend to me always.'

Mahendra Kapoor, who lent his voice to Rajendra Kumar on a number of occasions, recalled, 'In my days of struggle, I used to always travel by train. It was on one such trip to Goregaon that I met H.S. Rawail. I had always wanted to see a studio and he invited me to visit him at Famous, Tardeo. That was where I met Rajendra Kumar for the first time. He introduced me to Shyam, the hero of *Patanga*, and made me sing in his presence.

'I remember seeing Rajendra Kumar on the railway platform; he was on his way to hardcore success and people would chase him and call him "duplicate Dilip Kumar". I sang for him in

*Dhool ka Phool* and our combination clicked, especially in songs like "*Tere pyaar ka aasra chahta hoon*".

'I sang for him again in *Ganwaar* and *Sangam*. In fact, he took me in his car to meet Raj Kapoor and said that he wanted me to sing for him. Which is how I got the song "*Har dil jo pyar karega*" in *Sangam*. Before he fell ill, we used to meet regularly at Jogger's Park and exchange notes. But afterwards I didn't get to see him, since he was mostly in America. I will always remember him as a very bright and jovial person.'

A few weeks earlier, as Rajendra Kumar lay in the vast bedroom of his palatial suburban Mumbai bungalow, his body racked by a serious, debilitating illness, he apparently told his old friend and producer Mohan Kumar, '*Yeh chola mera chhurva do. Koi aur chola leke main kuch kaam toh karun.* Help me leave this body and be reborn in another one so that I can, at least, fulfil my purpose.'

For a man used to enviably good health – Mohan Kumar said that in their more than forty years of friendship, he couldn't remember Rajendra being indisposed even once – his prolonged illness was sheer torture. But he bore it with equanimity. 'I've enjoyed the years of glory,' he once remarked. 'Now this suffering is also mine to bear.'

At the star's heavily attended funeral, Mohan Kumar ran into Rishi Kapoor. Rishi remarked that Rajendra was probably with Raj Kapoor at that moment, enjoying a drink. 'And I could almost see them,' said Mohan, 'Raj and Rajendra, smiling, with stiff drinks in hand. Just like the old days. I was at peace.'

So, one would like to believe, was Rajendra Kumar.

# In His Own Words

## RAJENDRA KUMAR ON HIS MOVIES

### *Mother India* (1957)

The film works, even today, because it is *desh ki mitti ki.* It has a soul connection with the soil of our motherland. Hindustan *ki tareeq main woh hi ek* film *hai jo* art film *bhi aur* commercial film *bhi thi. Mother India* was the only film that could be classified both as an art film and a commercial success. No one has ever given the kind of performance that Nargis Dutt did in that film.

### *Goonj Uthi Shehnai* (1959)

Vijay Bhatt was a great director. I had watched his films as a child – *Ram Rajya* (1943), *Bharat Milap* (1942). For *Goonj*, I didn't learn to play the *shehnai*, but sat with Bismillah Saab [Bharat Ratna awardee Ustad Bismillah Khan] for all recordings, studying his mannerisms, his movements and body language, etcetera… Then I bought a dummy flute and practised the same mannerisms to the tunes [that would be played in the film]. Bismillah Khan Saab watched the trailer of the film at Prakash Studios.

I remember nervously asking him, 'How was I in the film?'

He had replied, '*Arre, aapko toh hum dekh hi nahin paye! Humne toh apne-aapko hi dekha.* I didn't even notice you in the film! All I saw was myself.'

That was a big compliment.

## *Kanoon* (1960)

Chopra Saab [director B.R. Chopra] made such a tight script – no songs, no frills – but he still managed to keep the audience rapt. I must have been very convincing in my role as a lawyer. So much so that one day, as I was coming out of Minerva [theatre] with Yash Chopra [the director's younger brother and a director in his own right], a stranger fell at my feet and begged me to take up his case.

## *Dil Ek Mandir* (1963)

[Director C.V.] Sridhar is like my brother. The film was made with such dedication and sincerity. We shot it in twenty-eight days flat, with no breaks. We ate, drank, lived, slept *Dil Ek Mandir*! That's why film *ka sur ek sa raha.* It was so in tune.

Meena Kumari was Hindustan *ki sabse naayaab*, the country's most unique, artiste, but she was an even better human being – soft, sensitive, with a heart of gold. *Dil mome sa tha…* Since day one, I would address her as 'Memsaab', as she was slightly older than me. She helped me a lot. If the shot was not okay, she'd murmur softly in my ear, '*Ek baar aur kar lete hain.* Let's go for a retake.'

Raaj Kumar was a very good friend and a very good actor. But people misunderstood him, as he was open about his feelings and spoke from the heart, without bothering about how others might react.

'*Jaani*,' he would say, '*hum to woh hi kahenge jo sach hai.* I will only speak the truth.'

### *Mere Mehboob* (1963)

*Mere Mehboob* was successful for its story, direction and, most importantly, its music. And, yes, because of Anwar Miyan and Husna.

Sadhana [the actress cast in the role of Husna] was my best friend. We addressed each other as 'Papen' [pal/buddy]. She was a bold woman and knew how to face life and enjoy it.

### *Sangam* (1964)

Raj Kapoor *ka zikr aata hai toh mere dil ke taar hil uthte hain aur unme ek dard sa uthta hai.* The mere mention of Raj Kapoor gives my heartstrings a painful wrench, because in my thirty years in the film industry, I had only one very close friend – RK. Our relationship went beyond films. We would make an effort to meet every single day. We shared so much. After he passed away, a big part of my life was snuffed out. I even stopped going out – for functions, parties and so on, because we'd always attended these events together. The Indian film industry will never get another RK.

### *Suraj* (1966)

I literally forced [producer S.] Krishnamurthy to make this film. He was shocked at my insistence. But he made crazy money. And I didn't do another film like it ever again, even though I got at least six similar offers. Even today, at any wedding I attend, the *bandwala*s begin playing '*Baharon phool barsao*' [a popular number from the film] the moment I enter.

### *Saathi* (1968)

I played a blind person in the film. I mentally trained myself to forget that I was able to see at all. The best thing about that film's story was that it was a love story about a man and his wife. Their romance begins only after their wedding.

### *Gora aur Kala* (1972)

I loved enacting the *kala*'s [dark-skinned person's] role. It took us three hours to get the make-up on.

It is a blessing that I got to play so many lives in one life; and the strange thing is people believed that I really was the characters I played in my films. They identified the characters with me and imagined they were me. Acting is a tough profession, an infinite art.

# In Their Own Words

In this chapter, I (Seema) have described my meetings with Rajendra Kumar's family and those in the film fraternity who knew him intimately. I am grateful to them all for regaling me with their precious memories and recollections, which have enriched this biography beyond measure.

## Shukla Tuli

It was in January 2018 that I first met Rajendra Kumar's wife, Shukla. Still elegant and yet so unassuming, she received me with warmth at her beautifully done up apartment in Bandra, Mumbai. It was quite apparent that she was eager to share her memories of her life with 'Rajinderji' – as she called him, Rajinder being the Punjabi pronunciation of Rajendra – her husband, the father of her three children and the reigning male star of sixties Bollywood. She spoke of him with pride and shared her memories of the home they had made together and their life as a film-industry couple.

Our bungalow [named after the Tulis' older daughter, Dimple] was made of stone and wood – not '*filmi*' at all; and it became the hallmark of good taste for other members of the film fraternity. [Film producer and director] J. Om Prakash, [director, producer and screenplay writer] Mohan Kumar – all of them attempted to model their homes on ours.

My husband, the star, never received his just due as an actor from the film industry. But the public adored him. In the 1960s, around six to seven theatres would be screening Rajinderji's films simultaneously. Being a movie buff, I would go to Bandra Talkies every week for the three o'clock show with either friends or relatives.

One evening, when Miyan [as she called her husband affectionately, preferring to use the Urdu term for a male spouse] returned from a shoot, he found us all sitting around having chai.

'So which movie did you all watch today?' he asked.

'None! Because every theatre is showing only Rajinder Kumar movies,' we replied. 'And, honestly, we are quite fed up, because at home we see you, and when we go to a cinema hall it's you all over again. What to do?'

It was a routine practice for me to watch the first trial show [as a preview was referred to in those days] of every one of my husband's films and offer my opinion, as I was very forthright.

So when the film *Aman* [with Rajendra Kumar and Saira Banu in the lead] was ready for release, Miyan suggested, 'Biwi, *jao, dekh lo*. Go watch it.'

I did. I also told him quite frankly that this film would never work. A doctor visits a war-torn country on which the atom bomb has been dropped. But in the entire film, all he is seen doing is romancing a girl and singing songs with her, that too seven to eight songs! I was proved right: the film flopped.

I was never my husband's fan; we were too close for that. But we did share a kind of rapport, akin to telepathy, a tuning. Rajinderji would call me his beloved – a complete woman. When I watched his movies, I didn't see my husband at all; I saw Rajinder Kumar, the actor.

Personally, my favourite hero was Rajji [Raj Kapoor], because he looked so romantic [in his films]. I preferred talented and intense actors like Dilip Kumar. But there again, I was too close to him to think of him as a star.

My husband was hot-tempered; only I could calm him down. Everyone else in the family was scared of him. He was very conservative. His brothers feared him and always asked me to talk to him on their behalf [when some issue needed to be resolved]. Even his heroines insisted that I alone could handle him.

Sadhana, who used to address him as Papa, would say, 'If anybody makes an inappropriate remark, Papa will rush to confront the person. And this is not just for me, but for every woman [who has been treated with disrespect in his presence].'

He simply couldn't bear to see anyone misbehaving with ladies. He would start bashing up anyone who did. Even when we were mobbed [in a crowd by the actor's fans] and fans banged their fists on our car windows, I had to restrain him from getting involved in brawls.

Rajinderji was quite a linguist, fluent in Gujarati, Marathi and Tamil too. He enjoyed working with the film industry in the south; they paid well and were organized. And he admired their straightforwardness, their cleanliness and their tradition of eating meals on banana leaves.

We often accompanied him on shoots to places like the Brindavan Gardens in Mysore and several others. Kashmir was a favourite holiday destination. The Oberoi Palace [in Srinagar] was like a second home.

In the early days of my husband's career, we were better acquainted with the families of producers and directors than those of actors. We would go for picnics to Bhushi Dam in Lonavla with J. Om Prakash, [actor] Manoj Kumar and their respective families.

Mrs Ira Roshan [mother of Rakesh Roshan and Hrithik Roshan's grandmother] was a very good friend. When Roshanji died, we helped them a lot. We got Guddu [Rakesh] an AD's job, and got his *rishta* done with J. Om Prakash's only daughter, the very beautiful Pinky.

## Kumar Gaurav

It was in May 2018 that I met Rajendra Kumar's son, the handsome Kumar Gaurav, in his home in the beautiful, self-contained apartment building Seven on the Hill on Pali Hill Road that had once been Dimple, Rajendra Kumar's bungalow.

Gaurav answered the door himself and ushered me into the plush sitting area. The passing years had been kind to him and he still retained the charm and good looks of 'Bunty' from *Love Story*. Seemingly content and at peace, Gaurav asked me to wait as he was busy with his gardener. But, within a few moments, he was ready to settle down for a chat.

My birth name was Manoj, but it was never used.

When I was born, my father was just beginning to establish himself. At that time, we lived in a small rented house. Then Dimple [his sister] was born and we shifted to our Carter Road bungalow. We had a very normal childhood and were not treated like [star children]. After school, I'd come straight home and would be in my room [for the rest of the day], making model planes. They were [the source of] my fascination – WWII aeroplanes! They still are. I still have the models. Sometimes, a friend or two would drop by and we'd play badminton, tennis or cricket, but all [our activities would take place] at home.

I was content at home. I was an aloof kid. Dad and I were poles apart. He was exuberant and outgoing, but I was an introvert. My favourite childhood memories are of our holidays abroad and the outdoor shoots.

I didn't like melodrama and crying in films. My hero was Johnny Walker. So I used to tell my dad, 'Why don't you act like him?'

He would laugh at me.

One day, I watched a film which had sword-fighting scenes and told my dad, 'That's the kind of film you should work in.'

Then he made *Suraj*. He said, 'I am doing this film only for you.'

He took me for the outdoor shoot. It was only me and Dad for those ten days. It was a wonderful time.

Whatever I learnt about films was from Mr Raj Kapoor. I remember the night Rajji came over to our house. He was high. 'I do only two things – make films and drink,' he said. 'So you can choose which you want to learn.'

The first love story following the release of *Bobby* was our *Love Story*. I was completely involved in the film. It was I who came up with the concept for the scene [featuring the song] '*Dekho maine dekha hai ek sapna*'. I had seen a film called *A Star Is Born*, in which the leading man takes the lady into the vast, empty wilderness and mimes out the idea of space. We narrated the idea to [music director, composer and singer] R.D. Burman and he suggested a song to go with it.

*Star* [where Kumar Gaurav was cast opposite Rati Agnihotri and Padmini Kolhapure] was a good movie, but people couldn't understand it.

When *Love Story* brought me superstardom, I was wary of people fawning over me. I was zapped when the success came – and zapped when it went. When Rajesh Khanna came, everybody [gravitated towards] him. So Rajendra Kumar was left out. Dad was an emotional person. He took it badly.

But Dad had a good life. If there were any affairs, I was unaware of them, because I was not at all involved in [matters relating to] the film industry. The only thing he hadn't expected was that his career and life would go so fast. He often mused, 'Here I am, ready to sit, chat, eat and drink and nobody comes to meet me any more.' He missed the old-timers, his brethren. People he'd helped turned their backs on him.

That's why I say when the movie is over, that family act on the movie set is over. No one is interested [in you any more]. They move on to the next [successful star].

I got married [to Namrata, Sunil and Nargis Dutt's older daughter] in December 1984. My father-in-law, Sunil Dutt, was an amazing man. He and Dad connected well after my wedding. We were family. Then Dad helped my pa-in-law a lot during the elections [when Sunil Dutt was contesting as a Congress candidate from the Mumbai North West constituency].

Before my marriage, Sanjay [Dutt] and I had become great friends. He would often stay over in my room, and then we did *Naam*.

One scene in *Naam* I can never forget – where I meet him in the cemetery in Hong Kong. We had permission to shoot for only three or four hours, but the chemistry between Sanjay and me was so brilliant that day that the scene was completed in minutes. [For those few moments] it became a real-life scene and we were just Sanjay and Bunty, not the film's characters. It just worked like – bam! No one expected it to be so poignant. I slap him and then I hold him and we cry.

I like to do intense roles.

[In those days] I had no friends in the film industry. I still don't. I was never a party guy.

I enjoy working in films, but not the fringe benefits, it brings and I wasn't after publicity, fame and so on. I just loved the job. For me, acting is more of [a feeling of] intensity from within. It was never about the look [the superficial aspects]. That's why I said *Kaante* [the actor's last Bollywood film, a crime thriller directed by Sanjay Gupta, where Kumar Gaurav was part of an ensemble cast] was a shit film. It was stylized but cut to cut – every scene edited in such an abrupt fashion – and, although slick, shot in LA, with lots of money spent and top stars, it had no story, no soul. I don't like such movies.

After Dad passed away, I managed Dimple Theatre. Then I thought of producing films, but with no good scripts I let it go. Anyway, to run after corporates for finances and so on was never my scene.

Today, I shuttle between Bombay and Goa. I have a home there too.

My daughters Saachi and Siya – neither of them were interested in acting. Saachi is married to Bilal Amrohi, the grandson of Kamal Amrohi, the film director. It wasn't a grand wedding. She married without my consent and I had told her then, 'Your life; your choices. If you ever need me, call and I will be there.'

But we are happy for her. Bilal is a nice person.

As for Siya, my younger daughter, she is very creative and intense, just like me. She is a writer and a trained designer.

## Dimple Kumar Patel

It was over lunch that I met up with Rajendra Kumar's two attractive daughters – Dimple Kumar Patel and Kaajal (Tulsi) Chellaram. I had met Dimple, the older of the two, earlier and noticed that despite the expressive eyes she had inherited from her father, she looked more like her pretty mother and liked to dress casually. She had been married to the late Raju Patel, a Hollywood producer and director, and is the mother of his two sons – Karam, a Los Angeles-based rapper, creative animator and audio engineer, and Amar, who is a student in Boston.

Getting to interact with Kaajal, however, was quite a feat, as she was busy travelling the world and also spending time at Baba Muktananda's ashram. Renamed Tulsi after her marriage to Hari Chellaram, the Bombay-based Kaajal looked athletic and stylish when I finally met her. I was surprised to see how closely she resembled her father.

Dad gave the best hugs. I was a little fan of his, in awe and completely enamoured of my father. He seemed larger than life.

My parents loved the good life and the good things in life. They made a striking couple, so stunning to look at and so stylish and well turned out.

My father was the only star [in the Hindi film industry] who paid for all holidays with his family from his own pocket. On our first Europe trip, when I was around ten years old, we took [film producers and directors] Rahul Rawail and Ramesh Behl along with us. We stayed in the best of hotels – all paid for by my dad. Dad took us to the Lido and the Moulin Rouge in Paris. He permitted us to have champagne and watch the [performers of the cabaret] dancing on tabletops.

When Dad's career began to decline, he started worrying about money, but then he was happy being invited for events like the Grand Marshal Parade in New York, being the personal guest of the President of Mauritius and travelling to his hometown in Pakistan. He travelled with Mom. He loved to travel and was willing to jump on a plane at the first opportunity. What kept him going in his later years was the recognition, appreciation and love he received the world over.

At my wedding, Dharmendra Uncle had said to my husband, Raju, '*Beti ke saath koi gadbad hui toh maar padegi.* Don't ever mess with our daughter or you'll get thrashed, for sure.'

My father spent the last days of his life with me in LA, but he insisted on paying for everything himself, from his travel to all his [medical] treatment bills. In fact, all he ever did was give, before he left us forever.

## Kaajal (Tulsi) Chellaram

I am the third Kumar. I was born in Elizabeth nursing home [St Elizabeth's Hospital, Mumbai]. My father was at the peak of his profession at that time. Dad loved cars and every month, we would have a new one. I would ask the drivers, '*Kaun laya?* Who brought it?' They would say it was Dad. He was very stylish too – he wore fantastic clothes and shoes.

He was a star and we were star kids, but he instilled a lot of discipline in our lives. Dad was a disciplinarian, very orthodox and very hot-tempered. His aura was such that one look from him and we were frozen [with fear]. Even our drivers would run away when he was angry. We were rich kids, but with our values in place. We all learnt to play one musical instrument. We all had our own nannies. But we were taught not to splurge.

At the same time, Dad was soft-hearted. He was so generous, so grateful [for all that he had received in life] and gracious. If he could give [film star] Rajesh Khanna our house for peanuts… Imagine! Who'd do that?

Many *filmi* sons [the sons of film personalities] had wanted to marry me, but I was least interested. And then Dad really screened each and everyone thoroughly.

Eventually, I married Hari Chellaram.

I was five when I was introduced to Baba Muktananda [who is her guru today] by my parents. Together, we sat on the floor with the guru to share a meal. It left a lifelong impact on me. When Dad first met Babaji, he felt so much at home. He knew that he had it all – and then to meet a spiritual master! It was the completion of his life cycle.

He was proud of his health [fitness levels] and often said, 'I am so disciplined. How did I fall ill?'

## Kamla Bhandari

> Rajendra Kumar's sister Kamla Bhandari spoke to me over the phone for barely five minutes. She came across as a person who was protective about her privacy. The few observations she shared were, therefore, precious, offering as they did insights into Rajendra Kumar as a young man and a much-loved sibling.

I don't remember much of Sankhatra [in Sialkot, Pakistan]. I was the youngest child. My brother Rajinder was quite naughty, but he was my mother's pet. He studied commerce in a Lahore college. He was one of the handsomest students in Lahore. So many girls liked him, but then ended up becoming his sisters [because he treated them like buddies, rather than romantic interests]. Later, I got married to Vasdev Bhandari and left for Uganda, East Africa.

Rajinder had to face many hardships after Partition and in Bombay as well. But Shukla, my Chhoti Ma [Rajinder's wife and Kamla's sister-in-law], was lucky for him. Today, I am living in Pali Hill with my family only because of my famous brother and my *bhabi*. She took care of our family with complete devotion. When I think of my brother Rajinder Kumar now, I can only remember his good deeds. Whoever met him would receive a warm hug, full of love.

## Virender Kumar Tuli

I was fortunate in being able to get in touch with Virender Kumar Tuli, Rajendra Kumar's younger brother, albeit over the phone. Having borne the consequences of some of his creative decisions and the impact on his life of certain decisions made by the family, Virenderji appeared to have withdrawn and become something of a recluse. His tone and words implied that his was a lonely existence. But, despite his apparent melancholy, the artiste and philosopher in him seemed very much alive and came to the fore as he spoke of his superstar brother.

Rajendra Kumar started as an assistant director with H.S. Rawail who would often say, '*Tumhari awaaz mein dum nahin hai. Tum* hero *nahin ban sakte.* Your voice lacks the right timbre and gravity. You can never become a leading man.'

But then Rajinder became famous after the super-duper hit *Mother India* and that same man Rawail came and begged him to act in *Mere Mehboob*, a film that was a delight, with its nuanced, poetic dialogue and lyrics and its beautifully composed songs. In fact, I sound so much like my brother that I could actually have dubbed for him.

I was too young to remember the pre-Partition days, but Rajinder had told me that during his college days in Lahore, he had stayed in a hostel and that actor Manmohan Krishnan was his professor at that time.

I lived in Delhi with my parents and brothers, but Mom brought us to Bombay. Later, while living with my brother in his new Carter Road bungalow, I joined National College. I remember Shukla Bhabi [his sister-in-law] calling eleven pundits from south India to perform a puja, an extensive purification ritual, before they moved into the new house.

Later, I would produce four films. Screenplays were my passion and I knew how to appreciate a good script. Writer

Salim Khan used to live on the ground floor of a garage next to [actor] Sanjeev Kumar's home on Turner Road. I often visited Sanjeev and Salim would also drop in. He would say, 'No one is ready to listen to our story.'

I said, 'I will.'

So he took me to his home where I met his wife, Salma, who was busy cooking.

Salim related a brilliant story. I liked it.

He said, 'You pay us ₹25,000 for the script. Take Rajinderji in the police inspector's role and it will be a superhit.'

I did go to RK, but then I couldn't make *Zanjeer*. I cannot disclose the reasons for that.

Rajinder's decline began with *Aman* and other such films and that's when Naresh, our brother, stepped in and made six to seven films with him. In that way, Rajendra Kumar got through eight more years of his career.

Yes, he did betray a bit of his frustration and depression [over his waning career], especially in the mid-1970s, but nothing that could be a cause for worry. That was also the time when he began calling me over to his place more often. Three people would call me every day: one was my brother Rajinderji, the others, my brother Naresh and O.P. Ralhan.

Thereafter, I would turn up at Dimple every day. I saw that my brother seemed to be in a bit of a dilemma and had started smoking more heavily than he ever had. I felt that he was a man with a golden heart, but tended to get easily swayed by glib talkers.

But then he launched Bunty.

'Just wait and watch – *Love Story* will run for twelve weeks,' he'd declared to me.

'Ten weeks max!' I'd retorted.

But the film surpassed all our expectations. If I had foreseen that *Love Story* would become such a big hit, I'd have bought rights in it too. But no one can predict success. My nephew then became so famous that people were falling over each other to sign him [up for their films].

Everybody was calling me up and saying, 'You sign Kumar Gaurav and we will finance your film instantly.'

So I called Bunty and announced, 'I want to make an action film with you.'

My superstar nephew Gaurav didn't hesitate for a second. He replied, '*Chachaji*, I will work in your film, but I will not take a single paisa [as payment] from you.'

I was moved to tears. I [felt as if I] had become a king. Hero *bhi mil gaya aur paise bhi nahin lega!* I had got my leading man and that too for free!

Kumar Gaurav is the finest human being ever. Such a man I've yet to see in our family.

[With no dearth of sponsors] the film sold immediately and shooting began. My film *Albela* was turning out to be one of the most promising films Bunty had ever worked in. But then fate dealt us an unexpected blow. Before the film could be completed, *Star* [featuring Kumar Gaurav and Rati Agnihotri] released and flopped. It was followed by another flop film – RK's *Lovers* [starring Kumar Gaurav and Padmini Kolhapure]. And my distributors then started running away. Anyway, I managed to complete the film and thought that once it releases, I will, at least, break even and maybe make some money. But it didn't release, because during that time every film of Bunty's was flopping, until *Naam* hit the theatres. Only then did I breathe easy. But then, in *Naam*, all credit went to Sanjay Dutt.

My film never did release. I had creditors chasing me and had to pay the interest on the loans I had taken from them. I was exhausted; I had even sold my wife's jewellery. What Kumar Gaurav did for me, even God hasn't done. But then, he could neither change my fate nor his own.

Life today is rife with hypocrisy and ruled by the power of money.

'Till there is fruit [on the trees], people will come,' I had said to my brother on one of his low days. 'We are trees laden with fruit, but once the fruits have gone, no one will look at us.' I saw this in the lives of [actors] Manoj Kumar and Dharmendra too.

## Vikram Tuli

In a phone conversation with writer-director Vikram Tuli, I learned that Vikram was Dimple's favourite cousin. Vikram is the writer of the Amazon series *Breathe* and is currently working on its second season. He is married and has a daughter.

My grandma told me that she knew only one Hindi song after they left their palatial home in Sialkot [following Partition]. It was '*Chal udd ja re, panchi, ke ab yeh des hua begana* (Fly away, little bird. This land is now an alien one)'. My grandfather, one of the richest men in his town, was familiar with only one business – cloth trading. Therefore, when he faced poverty and hunger after Partition, he began to sell cloth on the streets of Delhi and continued to do so even after his son had become an actor.

Rajinder Chacha would be furious with him. 'Put an end to this roadside business!' he would say.

It also upset him that his father, along with his younger brother Naresh, indulged in drinking and smoking. Naresh was described as the 'bad boy [black sheep]' of the family in those days.

Later, my father would come down to Bombay to work with a friend as a photographer, taking pictures, especially of VIPs arriving on flights that landed at the city's airport. But Rajinder Chacha asked him to quit the job and join H.S. Rawail as an assistant director. Soon after, Naresh Kumar started producing films.

When my father began enjoying success in the 1970s, Rajinder Kumar's career was already on the downswing. My father then felt it was his moral duty to cast his older brother in his films and they did many successful films together.

The production house was called Dimple Films, because after [his cousin] Dimple was born wealth had poured in. I have very fond memories of my uncle's home Dimple, especially the concrete-lined pond which would be filled with coloured water every Holi.

When we were kids, Bunty used to have a toy rifle. I remember we were scared of chameleons and he would shoot them with his airgun. He was our saviour. But I also remember how ticklish he used to be.

We attended lots of parties at Dimple. We were usually ten or twelve kids – all between the ages of eight and ten. The ayah Mary would make us queue up and lead us to the kitchens. Here, we ate our dinner, after which we were dumped in Dimple's room.

Everyone felt secure in the presence of Rajinder Chacha. He was a real-life hero for the family. As a child I believed that Dimple Papa (that's what we called him) could do anything. He could fight off villains too.

That's why, whenever he entered the room, we felt Superman had walked in. We kids would wish him namaste and quickly slip out.

## Manoj Kumar

It was after much coaxing that the legendary film actor Manoj Kumar agreed to meet Dimple Kumar Patel and me for an interview. Although he was confined to his bed because of a bad back, Manoj Kumar's mind seemed intensely active. While his robust wife, Shashi, served us tea and sandwiches, the actor's eyes and voice became animated as he regaled us with stories of the times he had spent with Rajendra Kumar.

I first noticed Rajinder Kumar in *Jogan*. He was such a good-looking man! He was from Sialkot and I from Lahore. We had much in common and a rapport developed. He started encouraging me [in furthering Manoj Kumar's career in films].

Rajinder Kumar was such a homebody. He would return home from the shoot, have a bath and sit down for dinner right away.

He never rode fame nor let it ride him. He had kept a room aside for me in his house and every evening we'd go home from work to the superb food Shukla had prepared for us. After dinner, all he had was a paan and a cigarette.

He had no other filmi habits. So simple; a family man. I felt that he found Vyjayanthi [film star and classical dancer Vyjayanthimala] too moody for his liking, and also because it was alleged that after [her dalliance with] Dilip [Kumar] she had started an affair with Raj [Kapoor].

Rajendra Kumar was also very practical, especially where finances were concerned. When [Vijay] Bhatt Saab called me for a film, Rajinder said, 'Bhatt Saab is superb, but if he offers a two-film contract, sign only one.'

And, sure enough, Bhatt did offer me two films. I turned him down. He asked for the reason.

I said, 'My brother has advised me not to.'

And RK was right.

Earlier, when I had signed *Hum Sab Ek Hain* and, like Rajinder, I too received ₹1,000, I went straight over to him and handed him the money. He called for sweets, added ₹100 more to the amount and put it in my pocket, rounding it off to the lucky number 1,100.

At the time that his sister Manorama was getting married to [O.P.] Ralhan, I had very high fever from septic tonsillitis. I was sleeping all day in my room at Dimple. Dr Sinhal had given me medicines, as that very night I had to board the 2 a.m. train to Pune and then go to Mahabaleshwar to shoot for *Banarsi Thug*.

Rajinderji refused to let me go, but I said, 'I have to.'

Dr Sinhal was summoned again and he gave me an injection. And Rajinder had me driven to the location in his own car.

When talks were on for my marriage to Shashi, Rajinder encouraged me to go ahead and get married.

Then I signed a new film and he said, 'Why don't you buy a car?'

I replied, 'No money yet.'

He said, 'How silly you are!' and called up Baljeet Singh, a car dealer.

'Bring a Fiat,' he instructed him.

The new Fiat cost ₹11,000. Rajinderji paid for it and, later, I paid him back in instalments. Little did we know that the car he'd bought for me would soon come to his rescue.

It so happened that when I, along with my mother and my *chachi*, were driving down to Shirdi in the same car, someone flagged us down midway. It was Rajinder. They had met with a minor accident and one of his car tyres was punctured, but all [the occupants of the car] were safe. The surprising thing was that in the pitch darkness of the hills, he had got out of the car, opened the dickey and changed the tyre himself.

I cannot describe my relationship with Rajinder Kumar: was it a father–son one, one shared between brothers or friends or a soul connection? He was my pillar of strength and our journey together was amazing.

The first film in which I worked with him was *Mera Naam Joker*. I had written the first half of the film. At two in the night, he called me and said, 'Pandit, *kamaal likha tu ne!* You've done a superb job!' He was proud of me.

When Rajinder Kumar's success began to fade, two men whose filmmaking careers would not have taken off without his help, whom he had helped establish from scratch and who would once come over to his house, sit on his carpet and say, '*Haan ji, paaji. Haan ji, paaji.* Yes, sir, yes, sir, whatever you say,' now began addressing him with an '*Arre,* Rajinder! Hey, Rajinder!'

I was enraged at their insolence and even refused to work in a film.

Rajinder Kumar was not naturally inclined towards production. He did it for his son. And he faced his decline bravely.

He loved travel and adventure. When Mohammad Ali, the famous Pakistani actor, invited him to Pakistan as the honorary guest of [then President of Pakistan] Muhammad Zia-ul-Haq and he went back to Sialkot, the full mohalla gathered to greet him. In Egypt, Iran and Beirut too, he had a huge fan following.

Later, as we grew older, we would go out for a walk together. Sometimes he'd come over to my place and sometimes I'd go over to his home. He was the golden man of the golden era. From Ashok to Akshay – there have been so many Kumars; but there was, is and will be only one Jubilee Kumar – Rajendra Kumar!

## Asha Parekh

Film actor Asha Parekh was busy ordering flowerpots for her plants, when the maid ushered me into her living room. Seated on a low couch, the jubilee girl of yesteryears seemed to have aged gracefully. Yet, the sparkle in her eyes and the liveliness in her sharp voice instantly transported me back in time; I could quite clearly visualize the impish young girl she had played in popular movies of the era, like *Dil Deke Dekho, Ziddi, Caravan, Mera Gaon Mera Desh* and *Teesri Manzil*, among others. Friendly and hospitable, the Asha Parekh I was meeting turned out to be a delight to talk to. Someone else seemed to share my opinion as well – an old fan of hers whose calls interrupted our conversation twice. Ashaji took the gentleman's calls quite sportingly and spoke to him with a mischievous gleam in her eyes.

Rajendra Kumar was so handsome! I saw him for the first time at Asha Studios in Chembur, where he was shooting for *Goonj Uthi Shehnai*. I hadn't signed any film until then, but was being considered for the lead role in *Goonj Uthi Shehnai*. Rajendra too was pretty new at that time. I saw him and said to myself: *Wow, such a good-looking man he is!* And then [Vijay] Bhatt Saab signed me on for *Goonj Uthi Shehnai* with Rajendra Kumar, I was thrilled. We then did a photo shoot for the film and Kanu Desai, the art director, showed the pictures to V. Shantaram, who said, 'I want to sign this girl.'

The photos were beautiful. But I couldn't sign Shantaram's film, as I had agreed not to take up any film until *Goonj* was released. Unfortunately, after two days of shooting with [actor-director] I.S. Johar, who played a pesky village postman in *Goonj*, I was unceremoniously thrown out of the film. I would learn, early on, that it was a male-dominated film industry, but there was no obvious discrimination. At that time, luckily, S. [Shashadhar] Mukherjee saw me and offered me *Dil Deke Dekho*, which became a big hit.

The following year – 1960 – I got my second chance to work with Rajendra, in *Gharana*. We met once more, before *Gharana* took off, at Rawailji's home in Bandra. The occasion was the wedding celebration of actor Jagdish Raj [actor Anita Raj's father] to Bholi. *Pehle din sangeet tha.* On the first day, the *sangeet* ceremony was being celebrated. Rajendra came up to me and said, 'You are my heroine. We must dance.' And he pulled me up to dance. That's where I also met his family and got to know Shuklaji well. At the *Gharana* outdoors in Mysore, his entire family had come with him. Since Rajendra Kumar and [Tamil and Telugu film actor] Devika had all the drama [dramatically charged scenes] in the film, whereas I was to play a happy-go-lucky girl, I had a lot of fun with Shuklaji and their children.

During the shoot, I don't know why, but Rajendra suddenly started calling me Mickey Mouse. 'Mickey Mouse, how are you? Mickey Mouse, come here.' It was funny, and maybe because I was a little mischievous, he had named me that. After *Gharana*, I didn't work with him for many years.

[Film actor] Sadhana was very close to him. He had his favourite heroines and he would select them [as his leading ladies]. I was very hurt when he got me kicked out from one of his movies. Later, I too turned down a film with him, because I was still angry.

Just as he was nicknamed 'Jubilee Kumar', I too became the 'Jubilee Girl'. In the later years of our careers, we did some mother–father roles. We did *Badla aur Balidan* and *Rani aur Lalpari. Insaaf ka Khoon* was our last film together. It had an interesting theme, but I don't know if it released or not. That was also the last time I saw him. Sometimes, he would invite me home for a cup of tea.

We all know that one cannot play the hero or the heroine after a certain age. And not many scripts for Hindi films are written with older people in mind. You have to step down.

## Salim Khan

Father of superstar Salman Khan, and an actor, producer and famous screenplay writer in his own right, Salim Khan invited me, along with Dimple, into his simple home in Bandra's famous Galaxy Apartments. What the flat lacked in symbols of luxury, it more than made up for with the warmth of the Khan hospitality. Salim Saab's stories were peppered with wit and humour, as he went down memory lane and began with an account of his first meeting with Rajendra Kumar. Every few minutes, he would remind me that I must write about the wonderful, charismatic and sensible person that Rajendra Kumar had been, both as a star and as a family man.

I believe intelligence is overrated. What is important is sensibility, like the sense of choosing [what is] right. Intelligent people are hardly ever happy. Before Rajendra Kumar, many heroes had suffered [when their careers went into a decline], but he was sensible and made sound investments, bought property and established a studio and a theatre too.

He also supported his brothers and others in the film industry. When [veteran actor] Premnathji was in trouble and his payment was withheld by a producer, Rajendraji *ne unke paise dilaaye*. He arranged for his dues to be paid. RK took a stand in support of Premnath and said, 'I will not shoot till you pay him his dues.'

'Only one thing I regret,' he'd say, '[is] selling my home to Rajesh Khanna.'

He didn't need the money, as at that time he was the highest paid actor, but people coerced him and brainwashed him and he sold it. It was prime property.

We had started meeting from the time he lived in Ashirwad [it was named Dimple earlier, after Rajendra Kumar's daughter]. At that time, we'd offered him *Seeta aur Geeta*. He was a big star then. So he turned it down, as it was a female-oriented film. I was writing *Zanjeer* too and that's when I met his brother Virender and I even did a small film with him.

After that, Rajendraji would meet me often and say, 'Our industry needs good writers like you, who are well read and good conversationalists.'

He was such a big star, but his persona was so unassuming. RK was a person who didn't play games and he was incapable of manipulation. He was a fair man.

During [the making of] *Naam*, I had suggested, 'Let me keep the south Indian language rights.'

He said, 'I normally don't give away the rights, but let's do fifty-fifty.'

I said, 'Only if your film is a superhit is there a chance of the language rights being sold. That can take months, sometimes years. So let me keep the rights. I will get only two-odd lakhs. It will be like a bonus for me as a writer.'

He agreed.

We made *Naam* with lots of creative debates, discussions and arguments, but we always came to an agreement. The thing I loved about Rajendra Kumar was that he would give his all to ensure that no stone was left unturned for the betterment of a film. And he was always on set.

After *Naam*, we didn't work together much, but we did maintain our friendship.

We'd have drinks every evening. Sometimes, Waheedaji would drop by and we'd chat about old times, friends and family. He loved his children very much and was a caring and devoted father.

RK was a very practical man, but he was also very sensitive. He would let small things upset him, especially when friends he had helped [in the past] let him down. And many people did let him down. He would feel disheartened and confide in me, at times. But 'God bless him' was his *takiya kalam*, his pet phrase.

His illness came as a shock to him, because he'd always been so health-conscious. It caused him a lot of stress, as did the full blood transfusion. It was very painful. I met him last when he was very ill. It troubled me [to see him in that condition]. That was the last time I saw Rajendra Kumar. I stopped visiting Dilip Kumar too, after he lost his memory and failed to recognize me.

## Randhir Kapoor

I met the cheerful and boisterous Randhir Kapoor in his office at the famous R.K. Studio in Chembur. Like most people, I knew of him as an actor, but primarily as the late Raj Kapoor's eldest son, husband of former actor Babita and the proud father of actors Karisma Kapoor and Kareena Kapoor Khan.

The first observation Randhir made about Rajendra Kumar's life was that it was very inspiring and should have been documented much earlier. He also enquired about my background and was happy to inform me that he'd met my father quite often at the studios. Tea was served and the interview finally took off.

Rajinder Kumar was my father's closest friend. I have never seen my father as affectionate with anyone as he was with

Rajinderji. If anyone said anything [unflattering] about him, Raj Kapoor would thrash the hell out of him.

I first saw Rajinder Kumar when he had dropped in at our place to see my father during the *Sangam* days, but we were kids then and not involved in films. In the mid-1960s, however, I was the second AD for *Jhuk Gaya Aasman* and there I learnt what a fantastic person he was. Rajinder Kumar was especially nice to me, obviously because of his relationship with my father, but he was also fond of me. He liked my work in *Kal Aaj aur Kal* and also got me *Jawani Diwani*, which was presented by him and made by Ramesh Behl. I will always be very grateful to Rajinderji for this connection, because after *Jawani Diwani*, I went on to do lots of films with Ramesh Behl.

Rajinderji had a keen ear for music. Also, as an actor, he was accepted and loved, because in those days *Devdas*-type men – brooding heroes who shed tears and drowned their sorrows in drink – were considered romantic. Sadhana hero *se takra ti hai*, the books she is carrying fall from her hands, '*Mere mehboob*' *gaate hain… Aur aaj tak hamari filmon mein,* leading man *chahe teen-teen bachchon ka baap ho, phir bhi* 'young hero' *kehlata hain aur suhaag raat mana rahein hai*. In the film *Mere Mehboob*, the heroine played by actress Sadhana collides with Rajendra Kumar in the role of the hero, the books she is carrying fall from her hands, he sings '*Mere mehboob*'… Till date, leading men who are already married and have fathered three or four kids, no less, are being referred to as 'young heroes' and playing college students. They are celebrating their wedding night onscreen. The audience couldn't digest this for too long, especially after Raj Kapoor released *Bobby* [a teen romance starring young actors]. Overnight, the older generation of heroes was deemed *buddhas*, old fogeys. Audiences had got their taste of youth for the first time.

Besides, show business is fickle. Actors, artistes are all emotional people. We live from one Friday to the next [when a new film is released and its fate is decided by the audience]. We have no permanent work, no assured income. No guarantees...

As for [his younger sister] Rima and Bunty's relationship – *nahin bani toh nahin bani,* yaar! If it didn't work out, it didn't. So what? We harboured no ill feelings towards Rajinderji, because we don't let others affect our friendships.

My father, for his part, was hardly bothered with what we kids were up to, so much so that he didn't even know which films Chintu [Randhir's younger brother, actor Rishi Kapoor] and I were doing. Also, he never stopped the women in our family from working in films. It [the assumption that the Kapoor women were forbidden from acting in films] was all rubbish talk. And even I feel the same way. I only had reservations [about the Kapoor women acting in films] because there is a lot of heartbreak in this profession. Everybody doesn't make it. You have to be constantly at it. *Yeh bahut lagan ka kaam hai.* You have to be deeply committed.

See Kumar Gaurav. Such a good actor, so good-looking, a meteoric rise, but sheer bad luck! It happened with [Randhir's youngest brother, Rajiv] Chimpu too. After *Ram Teri Ganga Maili*, he got no films. If it's not written in their kismet, no one can do anything.

It's all nonsense that if you ask people for work, you will get it. Only working hard, keeping at it and acceptance [of whatever comes] help one survive. But then it's ninety per cent luck.

## David Dhawan

On an August morning in 2018, Dimple and I met the noted film producer-director David Dhawan in his office. As he sat behind a large desk, my overwhelming impression of him was one of humility. Happy and eager to speak about his namesake [the director's formal name is Rajinder] and mentor Rajendra Kumar, Dhawan shed light on a different aspect of the jubilee star's magnanimity. Soon, his wife, Laali, had joined us and the conversation explored many areas of interest, covering both light-hearted moments and intense ones.

Rajendra Kumar was a strong influence in my life. I learnt from him the way children learn, merely by observing him. He was a very expressive actor, with a special ability to emote. He lived a simple but good life. And if he saw a spark [of talent] in someone, he not only acknowledged it, but even gave that person work.

In 1976, I was with the Film and Television Institute of India (FTII), specializing in editing. I was working on [producer and director Saawan Kumar Tak's] Saawanji's film *Saajan Bina Suhagan*. I knew Saawan Kumar through my brother Anil Dhawan, who had worked with him in *Hawas*. That's where I met Rajendraji. He took a liking to my work and called me to work on *Love Story*. I used to live as a paying guest in Dharm Jyot, a building in Pali Hill which was right next door to Dimple Theatre, located on the grounds of the actor's home. I became a regular at Dimple Studios. Rajendraji would come down and join me. We shared a good rapport.

'*Sham ko kya kar raha hai?* What are you doing this evening? Come over,' he'd say.

And even if I had some work, I'd prefer spending time with him. It was then a routine practice for me to go to his room in the Tulis' bungalow and have dinner with him. He didn't like to have his meals alone. He always had his food served to him on a steel thali. At home, he was a man of simple needs – no shampoo, no shower while bathing. All he ever used was a steel balti [bucket] and a lota [mug].

*Love Story* was such a big film. Bunty became a star overnight. What RK had wanted for his son happened. Rajendraji gave full credit to [director] Rahul [Rawail].

Rajendraji never tired of talking about his best friend, Raj Kapoor. He told me that during the *Sangam* days, when he was living in his Carter Road bungalow, Raj Kapoor had come over to his home one night, unannounced, and said, 'Let's have a drink.'

Raj Kapoor was shocked when he learnt that Rajendra Kumar didn't stock alcohol in any form at home. Rajendraji then called for Scotch. Thereafter, the bottle would find a permanent place in the Tuli home.

Another amusing incident of which Rajendraji had spoken to me was when both he and Raj Kapoor boarded an early morning flight.

Soon after take-off, Rajji surreptitiously put his hand in his jacket pocket and pulled out two boiled eggs. 'One for Pajendra (that's what Raj Kapoor called Rajendra Kumar) and one for me,' he announced, handing one of the eggs to his amused friend.

Theirs was a great friendship.

When Rajji died in Delhi, Rajendraji and I were working together on the film *Jurrat*. At 5 a.m., Rajendraji came over to my house and took me along to Raj Kapoor's home, with the advice '*Tu bhi darshan kar le.* You too should pay your last respects'.

I touched Raj Kapoor's feet. Where would I have got a chance like this? I was fortunate to get his blessings.

Rajendra Kumar was always ready to help; he stood by people, good or bad. In fact, he spoke on my behalf to my future father-in-law [and recommended Dhawan as a worthy match for his daughter] and came all the way to Delhi to attend my wedding. I also met lots of people through him and forged professional connections with them.

We discussed scripts as well, as he loved to write and contributed a lot to a film. He was extremely passionate about films and filmmaking. He recounted how, while shooting *Mother India*, Mehboob Khan would sit with a cane in hand and, for days on end, they had to wait for the perfect shot.

One day, Rajendraji said to me, 'David, you know that I was such a big star, that there would be producers, especially from the south, queueing up to sign me for their films. I had to turn down so many of them, but I would say, "I can't do the film, but please take so and so. That actor will be perfect for the role."'

In fact, Saawan Kumar Tak relied on him to rope in the other actors for his films. Once Rajendraji's suggestion was carried out, he would go beyond the call of duty and even get the leading lady on board, often paying the signing amounts himself and collecting them later from the producer. Even though he was so busy, he'd go to all this trouble for the producer.

Rajendraji understood the pulse of a story. He always played the good son, the good friend, the good brother, the good husband and, in that way, maintained a clean image. I advise Varun [Dhawan's older son] to do the same today.

Rajendra Kumar was very close to Sadhanaji. Their film *Mere Mehboob* was a colossal hit.

Rajendraji was a spontaneous person and it came through in his performances.

He had a comfortable lifestyle and maintained his stardom. Property-wise, he had the best address in town.

'When you want to buy property, buy the best,' he would advise me. '*Thodi takleef hogi, par paise ban jaayenge.* You may have to put up with some hardships initially, but you will profit in the long run.'

The sad thing was, he sold his first home to Rajesh Khanna. Being an emotional man, Rajendraji gave away his bungalow to the upcoming actor for a pittance.

As for depression, Rajendra Kumar managed to come to terms with his situation by turning producer [when the number of opportunities he was being offered as an actor dwindled] and his career got a new lease of life. But even when he was down, career-wise, he was particular about not accepting just any and every film that came his way.

When he fell ill, my wife, Lalli, had called me. 'Let's go and visit him,' she had suggested.

But when I did go to meet him, I was shocked by his condition and could barely hold back my tears. He had been put on steroids.

'*Beta, kaisa chal raha hai?* How are things, son?' he'd asked me.

But when I responded, I couldn't meet his gaze.

Then, one day, when I was shooting in Hyderabad, I received the news of his passing and came back for the cremation.

Rajendra Kumar made me realize my true potential. We shared a special connection. In fact, Bunty would tell him, 'David's your son.'

Just talking about him gives me great pleasure. After all, my name too is Rajinder. David is actually my pet name, but at FTII, they made it my official name.

# Filmography

## Actor

*Patanga*, 1949
*Jogan*, 1950
*Vachan*, 1955
*Toofan aur Deeya*, 1956
*Aawaz*, 1956
*Mother India*, 1957
*Duniya Rang Rangili*, 1957
*Ek Jhalak*, 1957
*Devar Bhabhi*, 1957
*Ghar Sansar*, 1958
*Talaaq*, 1958
*Khazanchi*, 1958
*Santan*, 1959
*Do Behnen*, 1959
*Goonj Uthi Shehnai*, 1959
*Dhool ka Phool*, 1959
*Chirag Kahan Roshni Kahan*, 1959
*Mehndi Rang Lagyo*, 1960
*Kanoon*, 1960
*Patang*, 1960
*Maa Baap*, 1960

*Aas ka Panchhi*, 1961
*Dharmputra*, 1961
*Zindagi aur Khwab*, 1961
*Pyaar ka Saagar*, 1961
*Amar Rahe Yeh Pyar*, 1961
*Sasural*, 1961
*Gharana*, 1961
*Sanjog*, 1961
*Akeli Mat Jaiyo*, 1963
*Mere Mehboob*, 1963
*Dil Ek Mandir*, 1963
*Hamrahi*, 1963
*Gehra Daag*, 1963
*Zindagi*, 1964
*Sangam*, 1964
*Ayee Milan Ki Bela*, 1964
*Arzoo*, 1965
*Suraj*, 1966
*Aman*, 1967
*Jhuk Gaya Aasman*, 1967
*Palki*, 1967
*Saathi*, 1968
*Talash*, 1969
*Shatranj*, 1969
*Anjaana*, 1969
*Geet*, 1970
*Dharti*, 1970
*Ganwaar*, 1970
*Mera Naam Joker*, 1970
*Aap Aye Bahaar Ayee*, 1971
*Gora aur Kala*, 1972
*Tangewala*, 1972
*Gaon Hamara Shaher Tumhara*, 1972
*Aan Baan*, 1972

*Lalkar*, 1972
*Dukh Bhanjan Tere Naam*, 1974
*Do Sher*, 1974
*Do Jasoos*, 1975
*Rani aur Lalpari*, 1975
*Sunehra Sansar*, 1975
*Teri Meri Ik Jindari*, 1975
*Majdoor Zindabad*, 1976
*Shirdi ke Sai Baba*, 1977
*Do Sholay*, 1977
*Daku aur Mahatma*, 1977
*Aahuti*, 1978
*Saajan Bina Suhagan*, 1978
*Sone ka Dil Lohe ke Haath*, 1978
*Bin Phere Hum Tere*, 1979
*Gunehgar*, 1980
*Badla aur Balidan*, 1980
*Dhan Daulat*, 1980
*Oh Bewafa*, 1980
*Yeh Rishta Na Toote*, 1981
*Saajan ki Saheli*, 1981
*Love Story*, 1981
*Rustom*, 1981
*Lovers*, 1983
*Main Tere Liye*, 1983
*Clerk*, 1989
*Insaaf ka Khoon*, 1991
*Phool*, 1993

## Presenter

*Phool aur Patthar*, 1966
*Talash*, 1969
*The Train*, 1970
*Ganwaar*, 1970

## Producer

*Love Story*, 1981
*Lovers*, 1983
*Naam*, 1986
*Jurrat*, 1989
*Phool*, 1993
*The Jungle Book*, 1994 (co-producer)

## Television

*Andaz*, 1995
*Vansh*, 1995